D1576608

BRISTOL LIBRARIES
WITHDRAWN
SOLD AS SEEN

ol Libraries

1805331331

WOUNDING
THE WORLD

———————

Also by Joanna Bourke

FEAR: A CULTURAL HISTORY

RAPE

WHAT IT MEANS TO BE HUMAN

THE STORY OF PAIN

WOUNDING THE WORLD

How Military Violence and
War-Play Invade our Lives

JOANNA BOURKE

virago

VIRAGO

First published in Great Britain in 2014 by Virago Press

Copyright © Joanna Bourke 2014

The moral right of the author has been asserted.

All rights reserved.
No part of this publication may be reproduced, stored in a
retrieval system, or transmitted in any form or by any means, without
the prior permission in writing of the publisher, nor be otherwise circulated
in any form of binding or cover other than that in which it is published
and without a similar condition including this condition being
imposed on the subsequent purchaser.

A CIP catalogue record for this book
is available from the British Library.

ISBN 978-0-349-00432-7

Typeset in Perpetua by M Rules
Printed and bound in Great Britain by
Clays Ltd, St Ives plc

Papers used by Virago are from well-managed forests
and other responsible sources.

MIX
Paper from
responsible sources
FSC® C104740

Virago Press
An imprint of
Little, Brown Book Group
100 Victoria Embankment
London EC4Y 0DY

An Hachette UK Company
www.hachette.co.uk

www.virago.co.uk

For Costas

Contents

PART ONE

War Without End

Introduction

We are a warring people.

Military practices, technologies and symbols have invaded our everyday lives. We rarely even notice it. We enthusiastically commemorate wars. We engage in current ones. Our garrisons are maintained throughout the world and yet the military campaigns we wage abroad seem as real to most of us as the metaphorical wars on drugs or obesity. It is not uncommon to hear people waxing lyrical about the sanctity of life – including that of the two-cell embryo – while revering the troops on Remembrance Day. Militarist incursions into our ways of thinking, talking and enjoying ourselves are barely acknowledged. The blurring of entertainment and war, the infiltration of 'violence-as-fun' into the popular imagination ('militainment') and the advent of warbots – a generic term for drones, robotic weapons, unmanned vehicles, and suchlike – have led many of us to take for granted that war is without end and without borders. Unwittingly, we have effectively been turned into citizen-soldiers.

We have inherited a toxic genealogy. Its names are legion but its purpose is singular: violence. It is precisely its everyday nature – the way it creeps up on us by stealth – that makes it so powerful. But we are not merely passive observers, in thrall to a set of amorphous, militaristic ideologies or corrupting institutions. We are involved in the production of violence: it constitutes who we are and might be and, as such, can be resisted.

Despite what many wish to suggest, this is a British phenomenon, not simply an American one. In Britain, where I live, there is a quaint assumption that the British are a peaceable people, engaging in war half-heartedly and only when threatened by aggressors. Our own role as perpetrators is overlooked. There is still considerable reluctance to admit the vast range of atrocities committed during our imperial conquests and colonial invasions.

During the commemorations around the centenary of the First World War, history books, television and radio programmes, newspapers and museums showcased grandfathers, great uncles and other 'ordinary people' who were physically or psychologically wounded during that war. We heard a great deal about suffering, but what about those British and American soldiers, airmen and sailors who bayoneted, bombed and torpedoed other women's sons? Were they not our grandfathers or great-uncles too?

And what about grandmothers and great-aunts? While writing this book, friends often asked me if my analysis was 'gender-blind'. Isn't the militarization of life really a 'male thing', they suggested. Aren't women either innately or culturally more peaceable? Although the proportion of women in the armed forces is rising, don't surveys consistently show that women are more opposed to militarist ideologies and practices than men?

They are partly right, of course. It remains the case that boys and men are much more likely than girls or women to be entranced by weapons and other things martial. Feminists of both sexes look on with dismay as their seven-year-old sons (not daughters) race around brandishing plastic Kalashnikovs; very few adult women delight in firing replica M16 assault rifles at imaginary enemies, causing 'fantastic splatters of blood' (as one male friend described the thrills of paintballing). In the debates about the commemoration of war, female scholars are much more likely to be heard reminding people of the human, rather than technological or strategic, dimensions of warring. They regard the wounding potential of those big guns as important, not their iron and steel specifications.

But we can't let women off the hook. Weapons possess a social life that includes women as well as men. Wars are routinely justified 'in our name', from the First World War recruitment poster depicting a vicious beast carrying away a half-naked, terrified white woman, to the more recent claim during the war on Afghanistan that it was being fought to save Afghan women from the Taliban.[1] Militarist values and practices co-opt women as well as men, permeating our language, invading our dream-space and entertaining us at the movies or in front of games consoles. Our taxes pay for war machines. Our loved ones are maimed and killed in military encounters. People we care about slaughter strangers we might have learnt from, laughed with, loved.

I believe that knowing the extent to which the military and war-play invade our lives is an essential step in the task of creating better and more equitable worlds. Vast financial resources are poured into militarist projects. There are more productive ways to invest this wealth. In the armed conflicts waged by British and American troops today, 90 per cent of victims are civilians. We need to know how to counter tendencies that objectify the so-called enemy, setting him or her outside the human. It is helpful to be reminded about the invidious languages and analogies that are used when weapons are discussed. Those of us who do not seek war-orientated forms of entertainment should know why they are so enticing, and what role the armed forces have played in their promotion. At a time when the two world wars are being fervently commemorated, it is important to think hard about what it is we are doing. Celebrating war? Honouring those lives that were destroyed? Or telling half-truths? It is essential we know

what forces have brought us to this point in the history of
violence.

Wounding the World explores the cultural, political and military
factors that make imagining, designing, playing with and using
weapons so enticing. Given our warring history and the dire
human consequences of the advancement of weapon technology,
I ask why the military and war-play are so pervasive. How does
the militarization of society normalize and morally neutralize the
effects of violence? What is the relationship between everyday
violence (both imaginary and real) and weapon research?

Why should we be concerned with these matters? Because we
are wounding – and potentially destroying – our world.

Weapons and war have long enchanted British and American culture. Military history is one of the most popular non-fiction
genres; we are mesmerized by war cinema; the release of the
latest first-person shooter computer games make headlines in
even the most respectable newspapers.

We are also nations of guns. In the UK, firearms have been
more prevalent in imperial invasions than domestic contexts, but
even today a sizeable number of guns circulate within our society.
There are nearly eight privately owned firearms for every 100
people in the UK. These figures pale in comparison with the US,
where there are 310 million firearms, or more than 101 per 100
people.[2] Thirty thousand people in the US are killed every year by
guns.[3] In the last half-century, American households possessing at
least one gun went from one third to one half.[4]

Gun ownership excites periodic panics, typically in the aftermath of school shootings. The names Columbine High School
(1999), Virginia Tech (2007) and Sandy Hook Elementary School
(2012) are seared into everyone's consciousness and, at the time,
elicited political promises of gun reform. Unfortunately, such
panics have made little difference.

These panics have enabled critics to avoid confronting much more pervasive forms of militarization. These include not only the most direct and brutal mechanisms of military power (as seen in times of war), but also the processes by which soldierly values and martial organizations wield progressively more power within civilian society. It may even become difficult to distinguish military from non-military conventions, ideologies and institutions.

Britain became a highly militarized power during the two world wars. Outside wartime, though, the militarization of civilian society accelerated from the mid-twentieth century. By the 1950s, the so-called military–industrial complex was firmly entrenched. Today, there are 171,000 people, not including tens of thousands of volunteer reserves, serving in the British forces.[5] The UK has the fourth-highest military expenditure in the world, at £60.8 billion.[6] This is money raised by taxes and invested in projects that many of us abhor.

In the US, the figures are even more striking. At the end of the 1950s, nearly 10 per cent of Americans in employment were working either directly or indirectly for the Department of Defense and the US armed forces, and their firms consumed more than 85 to 90 per cent of all goods and services purchased by the federal government.[7] By the mid-1960s, the US had major military bases in 375 regions and a further three thousand minor military facilities.[8] As a consequence of the Second World War and the post-war draft, 45 per cent of the adult male population in the US were veterans in 1969.[9]

Around 1.4 million Americans are currently on active duty.[10] Civilian contractors are also a growing component of military life, providing base security, interrogating prisoners, escorting convoys, piloting reconnaissance vehicles, constructing bases, and ensuring that basic services (such as food and accommodation) are maintained. In fact, there were almost as many civilian contractors in Iraq as US troops there, and this represents a tenfold increase in civilian contractors since the Gulf War of 1990–1.[11] The US has an annual military expenditure of $682 billion.

If militarization only referred to money spent on military goods and services and the numbers of people actively attached in some way to the armed forces, it would be relatively insignificant. The circle of influence is exponentially wider than this and, ironically, as citizens become reluctant to fight wars, there may be *greater* militarization as the armed forces seek to expand their influence. Millions of civilian jobs depend on the arms industry. In Britain alone, more than £12.3 billion of arms were exported to countries that the Foreign Office admits engage in serious human rights abuses. They include Israel and the Occupied Territories, Iran, China, Sri Lanka, Russia, Belarus, Zimbabwe and Syria.[12] The American export figure is $66.3 billion of weapons, or more than three-quarters of the global arms market.[13] Most Britons and Americans are nonetheless oblivious to the fact that we live in a war economy.

It is hard not to echo the concerns of Michael Hardt and Antonio Negri in *Multitude* (2004), where they warned that the role of the military in our societies is not merely a matter of 'brute force', but the 'production of social life in its entirety'. War is no longer merely 'politics by other means' (as von Clausewitz famously asserted); nor is it a practice that government reluctantly perpetrate as a last resort. Instead, a militarized civilian society is the 'foundation of politics, the basis for discipline and control'.[14]

Being an academic as well as a historian of violence, I hope I can be excused for being especially appalled by the degree to which our schools and universities have been sucked into the military vortex. In Britain today, sixteen-year-olds may not legally drink alcohol, drive cars or vote, but they can join the armed forces. Britain is the only country in Europe that recruits boys and girls under the age of eighteen; one in every five recruits is a child.[15] Let me put a price on this: every year around £94 million of taxpayers' money is invested in enlisting children.[16] If you go to the army website, you will even see a special section (entitled 'Camouflage') devoted to children aged fourteen to sixteen years. When I clicked on 'Camouflage' in March 2013, it featured the 'Bonecrusher', a heavily armoured vehicle 'fresh from the *Transformers* film set'; it provided detailed information on how to sign up and what to expect during military training, and it promised 'sport and adventure'.[17] It is no wonder that one soldier who had enlisted at seventeen complained that the recruiting officers had been deceptive: he bitterly recalled that they had shown him photographs of recruits abseiling and skiing rather than images of 'someone with their head blown off'.[18] Good evidence suggests that young recruits experience significantly high levels of PTSD, alcoholism, depression and suicide. Whatever happened to any duty of care?[19]

It is not surprising that the situation in the US is no better. Even though the Senate ratified the Optional Protocol on the Involvement of Children in Armed Conflicts, which set the minimum age for voluntary recruitment at seventeen years, all branches of the armed forces recruit heavily below this age. In a large proportion of American schools, the Junior Reserve Officers Training Corps is mandatory for children as young as fourteen.[20] In the US Army's *School Recruiting Program Handbook*, which is distributed to more than 10,600 recruiters nationwide, recruiters are advised to

> Remember, first to contact, first to contract . . . That doesn't just mean seniors or grads . . . If you wait until they're seniors, it's probably too late.[21]

One in five children reported that military recruiters had spoken to them in class time and more than a third said that recruiters were present in classrooms and hallways.[22] As in the UK, recruiters routinely used deception and false promises: they did not fully inform prospective recruits of what military service actually entailed, denied that the US was at war and claimed that recruits could be discharged whenever they wanted.[23] The military was simply great fun. As one zealous recruiter told a schoolchild, in the armed forces 'you get paid to jump out of airplanes, shoot cool guns, blow stuff up, and travel seeing all kinds of different countries'.[24]

Nor are universities peaceable towers, free from military interference. This surprised me. Obviously, I had been naive. After all, as early as the 1960s the Democratic senator J. William Fulbright, creator of the international exchange programme that bears his name, warned about the increasing militarization of universities, reminding scholars that 'in lending itself too much to the purposes of government, a university fails its higher purpose'.[25] At the time, military contracts were so extensive at places like the Massachusetts Institute of Technology that the distinguished physicist Alvin Weinberg quipped that it was difficult to know if MIT was a 'university with many government research laboratories appended to it or a cluster of government research laboratories with a very good educational institution attached to it'.[26]

The military's influence has continued apace despite Fulbright's and Weinberg's criticisms. In 2010 it was reported that every year the Pentagon gives around $4 billion to universities for research support. If departments refuse to allow the armed forces to recruit on their premises, the Department of Defense simply threatens to withdraw funding from the entire university. To put this in context: it would mean taking away $400 million from Harvard and £350 million from Yale.[27] As the Dean of the Law School at Yale admitted,

> We would never put at risk the overwhelmingly large financial interests of the University in federal funding. We have a point of

> principle to defend, but we will not defend this – at the expense
> of programs vital to the University and the world at large.[28]

This is not simply an American problem. In Britain too the military involvement in scholarly research and university budgets is substantial. Between 2001 and 2006 there were at least 1900 military projects conducted in twenty-six UK universities and valued at approximately £725 million. The chief beneficiaries were Cambridge, Loughborough, Oxford, Southampton and University College London. In fact, the UK is the second-highest funder of military R&D in the world.[29] In effect, the military is 'subcontracting research to universities, which have world-class, publicly funded staff and facilities'.[30] In this way, the armed forces significantly lower their overheads, while also ensuring that military companies maximize their returns. In other words, our taxes are paying for research that facilitates war and inflates profits for armament manufacturers and investors.

Clearly, catering to all things military is big business. Scientists, engineers and physicists have discovered that applying their talents to weapon research can win them grants, sophisticated laboratory facilities and intellectual prestige. Armament industries, militaries, police forces, manufacturers, engineers, hunting organizations and gun lobbies have significant stakes in the task of inventing more effective technologies for warmongering. They also have an interest in developing new and increasingly violent games that allow people to engage imaginatively in scenarios of terror, maiming and murder.

It is too easy to shrug off the impact of militarization. Engagement with the armed forces is often dismissed as nothing more or less than a matter of choice. In other words, we are told that we can choose not to accept a job in the army, conduct ballistics research, buy a gun for domestic protection or play violent games.

It's just not that simple. The military–industrial–entertainment complex is immensely powerful. War and peace are no longer highly differentiated zones in British and American societies. War has entered, uninvited, into our homes and taken up residence. Domestic spaces as well as outer space (satellite surveillance and missile defence systems) have been militarized. War remnants are present in our everyday lives: global positioning systems that guide our cars, the design of SUVs, the popularity of fitness boot camps and the cut and pattern of fashionable clothing. We can't open our mouths without talking about war. There are wars on terror, women, drugs, obesity. While I was writing this introduction, the *New York Times* reported that the New York State Department of Environmental Conservation has declared a 'war on mute swans'.[31]

That is perhaps just semantics, but, more worryingly, military ideologies and practices are integral to political debate and to international relations. The mother of all fundamentalisms is the belief that a powerful military presence will promote our security. This claim needs careful and rigorous assessment. I believe that knowing the history, science and ethics of weaponry can help us better assess governmental claims to be fighting 'good' wars. In the twentieth century, hundreds of millions of lives were destroyed in war, yet instead of creating a safer world governments, militaries and scientists have developed increasingly sophisticated weaponry to kill and maim more efficiently. And, chillingly, this is being done in the name of humanity.

I have been both dismayed and heartened while writing this book. Although I focus exclusively on the militarist practices of people in Britain and America (simply because they are the countries I know best), the issues I address concern every global citizen. Some of the solutions for the current crisis come from outside the Anglo-American context. When disappointed with the relative acquiescence of British voters to calls to increase military spending and that of American voters to the presence of guns in nearly half of all homes, signs elsewhere in the world that resistance is not only possible but also effective galvanize me. So, that is where I end this book. What can be done? There are real answers.

PART TWO

The Social Life of Weapons

CHAPTER ONE

It's Only Words

Words wound.

They do so by turning what is ugly into something beautiful, by converting a person's gut-wrenching pain into an abstract formula, by wilfully perverting unpleasant realities, and by making the inanimate into something animate. Words are never neutral: they determine what we think about the world and how we experience it. They tell us what to feel and how to act. As George Orwell wrote, 'if thought corrupts language, language can also corrupt thought'.[1] Words are always political.

And what interests me about violence is how words can make it all seem okay. Pleasurable, even.

Killing is a formidable taboo in human society and it almost always leads to self-hatred, shame and guilt – and yet people are constantly inventing ways to aestheticize it and make it enjoyable. Revulsion and elation coexist. If we are to understand the powerful hold that war has on our imaginations, we need to come to terms with the over-blown, breathless, vivid and carnivalesque language associated with violence.

When war is declared, men who had, for example, been perfectly content working on the factory floor or behind the shop counter went to war and began killing other factory workers and retailers. Time and again, British and American men who were in combat during the First and Second World Wars describe their experiences of killing in positive terms. It was an unexpected high. This is often ignored in commemorations of the war, a dirty secret that threatens to minimize the honour of 'our' men.

However, for a secret it is remarkably common, finding expression in countless diaries, letters and memoirs. For example, combatants during the First World War admitted feeling 'joy unspeakable' or 'ecstatic' when killing.[2] It was 'beautiful work' and 'gorgeously satisfying'.[3] Killing incited 'a strange thrill . . . nothing in peace-time could make a man feel like that'.[4] In a letter dated 22 August 1917, a young infantryman described 'popping off those grenades' as 'most awfully good fun'.[5] In the words of another soldier, writing in his diary in 1918, attacking the enemy was 'beautiful and thrilling – one of the most memorable moments of my life'.[6] These were not extraordinary men. Just ordinary soldiers.

Members of the air forces were especially prone to translate their experiences of violence into excitable babble. Flying Corps pilot Wesley Archer admitted in his diary that he revelled in picking off German 'nests' and found it 'Fascinating to watch them topple over'. He described killing from the air as 'Delightfully impersonal'.[7] Night pilot Roderick Chrisholm destroyed two enemy aircraft in 1914, describing the experience as something that could 'never be equalled'. He recalled that

For the rest of that night it was impossible to sleep; there was nothing else I could talk about for days after; there was nothing else I could think about for weeks after . . . it was sweet and very intoxicating.[8]

Similarly, Kenneth Hemingway dive-bombed Japanese soldiers on the ground: 'Oh, boy . . . Boooyy!' he yelled, describing his 'exhilaration' as similar to the joy of drinking champagne on a sunny spring morning. He felt 'ruthlessly happy – quite an atavistic orgy!'[9] A group of pilots during the Second World War admitted that they 'all felt much better' and there would be 'a good deal of smacking on the back and screaming of delight' after killing the enemy.[10] Killing caused a 'jolt of delight'.[11] William Nagle confessed that after killing German paratroopers in Crete he, 'wanted to go on and on . . . I could have kissed the Bren with sheer delight but it was too damned hot to touch'.[12] Or, as someone we just know as 'Bob' confessed after improving his 'score', 'Life wasn't too bad after all'.[13] His own life, that is.

Bob's use of the word 'score' was not coincidental. With almost monotonous regularity, combatants talked about their aggressive acts in sporting terms. This could take a humorous form, as in a First World War trench poem that men would recite in the evening:

> Come my Hun-eey, come my Hun-ey,
> I am waiting here for you,
> Come and hug me, I won't half plug you
> Come you ratter, do.
> Do stop singing, you are bringing
> Down the blooming rain,
> Tommy's waiting while you're hating
> Come and play a fighting game.[14]

Battles were described as a 'good sport', or 'rounds' between two contestants.[15] According to the author of *Winged Warfare. Hunting Huns in the Air* (1918), the enemy were 'like so many rats', running for cover from the machine-gun bullets.[16] Gunners admitted that they 'felt no antagonism'. 'I felt as a boxer or duellist might feel, pitting his skill against that of his opponent', noted one.[17] Hunting or poaching analogies dominated over all others.[18] Typically, rifleman McBride claimed that his chief emotion in combat was not hatred but the 'keen satisfaction and excitement of the same kind that the hunter always knows'.[19] Going to war was the equivalent of being 'blooded'.[20] The enemy were 'specimens' to be 'bagged'.[21] Shooting a man was 'as easy as shooting a fox'.[22] Gunnery was described as similar to stalking deer, with the exception that when stalking animals the 'head of heads' might be just outside of the range of one's gun while, in war, Huns were 'always in season' and a 'glorious target' might only be a few hundred yards away.[23] Enemy soldiers were dismissed as not being fully human: they were merely 'clever animals with certain human characteristics, but by no means the full range'.[24] A 1919 article entitled 'Sniping' began by emphasizing the need for eagerness when hunting other human beings. It 'goes without saying that a sniper must be keen on his job', the author reminded his readers, because

> Anyone can sit in a post and sleep away the hours instead of watching, but a really keen shot will lie in wait for a victim just as a cat watches for a mouse. One's chance of a kill may not come for days, but when it does, and the pointer at the telescopic sight rests squarely on the head or chest of some beast in blue-grey uniform, the hours of patient watching are forgotten as one's finger gently squeezes the trigger.[25]

Arms and the Man, the official journal of the National Rifle Association, contended that sportsmen would never dream of using the 'cruel' shotgun when hunting non-human animals. They would 'rather go forever with an empty bag than to shoot a bird sitting, bring down a squirrel with anything but a rifle, or transgress any of the unwritten laws of clean hunting', but they would 'make use of any device to exterminate vermin'. And 'vermin' was an accurate description of Germans, they insisted. True American soldiers would always prefer to kill with the rifle but once they realized that they could 'kill more Germans with the sawn-off shotgun and its exterminating load of buck-shot', nothing would deter them from using the 'highly efficient, Hun-exterminating sawn-off military shotgun'.[26]

Senior officers deliberately fostered such attitudes in order to stimulate the 'offensive spirit' in their men. Thus, General Sit Thomas Blamey encouraged is men with the following words:

> You are fighting a shrewd, cruel, merciless enemy, who knows how to kill and who knows how to die. Beneath the thin veneer of a few generations of civilization he is a sub-human beast who has brought warfare back to the primeval, who fights by the jungle rule of tooth and claw, who must be beaten by the jungle rule of tooth and claw. Kill him or he will kill you.[27]

Wartime killing was sport with no holds barred.

Such analogies effectively dehumanize the enemy as nothing more than beasts who deserved to be slain. These languages were particularly prominent during imperial conquests. 'Savages' were said to possess 'excessive . . . vitality'; they didn't seem to feel physical pain as Europeans did.[28] Army surgeon Frederick George Engelbach, writing from the Hague Peace Conference in 1899, was unabashed in defending dum-dum bullets, which caused 'explosive' wounds. It was one thing for the French, Italians, Russians and Germans to criticize the use of the bullets, he announced. Soldiers in these armies generally fought their battles against Europeans or 'soft' indigenous people, who were more easily rendered *hors de combat*. Engelbach claimed that 'a European when struck in a vital part collapses utterly or else crawls from the fray with all his lust for fighting gone. Even the Abyssinian or the Shilock knows when he has had enough.' In contrast, British soldiers were pitted against more formidable foes. The 'Afridis, the bhang drunk Ghazi, and the howling dervish or Bagqara love to meet their deaths in action', he maintained. For these foe, death 'opens Paradise, rendering doubly glorious of they achieve before they die the death of the Feringho'. It was pointless to shoot such enemy with the nickel-coated bullet of the .303 Lee-Enfield magazine rifle since that bullet

> drives with a velocity of 2000 ft per second through four or five of them. Mortally hurt, yet they still gamely struggle on to strike one blow before they die. What can be done with a gallant fanatic who actually wriggles up the lance of his enemy to slay before his exhausted muscles give out?

British soldiers would not gain any 'satisfaction' in facing

> a shrieking fanatic with a rifle which will enable them to per-forate their enemy and to kill him – in half an hour? By that time the combatants are lying dead one a-top of the other.

This was grossly unfair to British manhood. Engelbach thundered against what he saw as 'humanity' only being 'exercised on the part of the ill-used savage, while the soldier is to take his chance'.[29] The Director-General of the Indian Medical Service put it more evocatively: a 'fanatical Ghazi', he judged, 'was not checked by the modern bullet, which went through him like a knitting needle through a pot of butter'.[30]

Popular journals dedicated to weapons and war also waxed lyrical over the thrill of bloodshed. Like the first-person accounts, jour-nalists also loved to characterize combat as sport. In July 1919 the magazine Health and Efficiency reported that, before the war, there was 'an enormous mass of men who talked sport, read sport, looked on life through sport spectacles . . . but – practised no form of sport themselves'. This all changed from 1914, when the average man (whom they designated 'John Jones') was

> jerked out of an office or mill into the Army . . . John Jones went through trying times for a few weeks. He literally endured the pangs of a new birth. 'Physical jerks', drills, fatigues, marches, gradually sweated the beef off him and sweated the muscles on, reddened his pale blood and gave his walk a spring. John cursed and went through it all. He was a Briton and a sportsman. He was training for the Great Game, and when at last with a clear eye and a cool hand he crossed the sea, we saw how he played it.[31]

John Jones 'played it' with panache. He invented cute words for bullets in order to minimize as well as aestheticize their destructive properties. As a writer in *Arms and the Man* noted in 1916, projectiles were called 'will-o'-the-wisps', 'humming birds', 'sighing Sarahs' and 'porridge pots'; shells that 'burst in puffs of white, woolly smoke' were 'woolly Marias'; the slang for bullets in general was 'haricot beans', while shrapnel was known as 'sprinkling cans'.[32] *Arms and the Man* enthusiastically celebrated violence, evoking the .45 Colt automatic as the best gun for an American hero to use when 'slinging hot lead in bone-smashing, man-stopping doses'.[33]

The aesthetics of sound obsessed many writers. They insisted that Death announced itself in distinctive ways. The author of 'The Sharpshooter's Rifle and the Telescopic Sight' (1917), for instance, contrasted the 'staccato chatter of machine-gun fire', which 'plants the death-rattle in hundreds of human throats', with the sniper's discreet '*pr-a-ak!*' when his 'steel-jacketed bullet cleav[es] its way through the air'.[34] A year earlier, the author of 'Noises that Bullets Make' boasted an even more exceptional aural sensitivity to weapons. When a bullet travels at over 1500 feet per second, he advised, soldiers would hear a 'sharp crash' as the bullet passes, 'caused by the air closing rapidly in behind the bullet base'. Under certain conditions, they might also hear a hissing sound and, if fired at a very long range and if the bullet was tumbling end over end, this might be replaced with a humming sound. At 100 yards, a revolver bullet 'snarl[ed]' as it passed close by while a bullet from a revolver or low-powered rifle made a sound like 'pl-lke!' or 'a sharp crack, with a touch of whine or shriek in it'. Contrast that with the noise made by a projectile from a large gun firing over water: that was 'like the sudden roar of a distant train passing over a short bridge. It is a peculiar whirring sound, almost like a roar.' Other noises include the 'pack-burr' followed by 'the sound of a long blacksnake whip very violently cracked' when the Springfield rifle was fired.[35] This was the aural pornography of violence.

When aerial bombardment of heavily populated cities was intro-duced, its proponents claimed both that it was 'at once terrible and awe-inspiring'. In the words of Brigadier-General the Lord Thomson, writing in 1925, with its 'horror goes a splendour of achievement' that 'kindles the dullest imagination'. Lyrically, he conjured up an image of squadrons flying at night who

> will reach the upper air above their target at such a height that the roar of their engines will sound to those below no louder than a droning hum; they will then sweep to rain death and destruction; their asphyxiating and incendiary bombs will in a few short moments make of a prosperous city a smoking char-nel house.

He forecast that on many occasions the planes would be intercepted in the air. The antagonists in this aerial battle would comprise

the flower of the male youth in each contending state, manipulating marvellous machines, the latest products of invention
in the conquest of the air. The pilots of these engines of
destruction must be young . . . They must be intelligent above
the average, and possess a rare poise of hand and brain and
eye, enabling them to combine subconsciously their different
functions . . . Each crowded moment may be their last; in
these aerial duels, one surely dies. And when the crisis comes,
these gallant youths will each go out to kill another man,
young, skilful, splendid, like himself.[36]

When he wrote these words, Thomson was fifty years old, which
makes his ovation even more obscene. It was also a eulogy to the
glories of technology, both 'appalling' and 'splendid'. The dismembered bodies of young men were a regretful waste, but their
gesture was grandiose in its symbolism, harking back to the duels
of a long-past chivalric world.

Again, this propensity to aestheticize deadly weapons can be
seen in all military conflicts, even those as atrocious as Vietnam.
In that war, cluster bombs (which cause appalling wounds) were
nicknamed 'pineapples' and 'guavas',[37] and the violence of the
M-79 grenade launcher, which was standard equipment, was
reduced by comparing it to 'brass knuckles in a barroom brawl'.[38]
White phosphorous was colloquially known as 'Willie Peter'[39] –
an innocent name for a chemical that burns incredibly slowly
inside wounds. As one physician observed, 'this slow combustion
lasts up to fifteen days. At night can be seen the greenish light produced by the material that continues burning the flesh and
bones.'[40] 'Willie Peter' doesn't really sum it up.

Even today, positive and sporting images are conjured
up when describing killing. As a twenty-first-century navigator
of the Predator drone bragged, 'I was a patient, silent hunter.
I was armed.'[41] Weapons and weapon systems are given

comforting names – including ones from nature: the Falcon, Hummingbird Warrior, Panda and Walrus are all military programmes or vehicles. When we hear someone talking of 'Bouncing Betties' or 'Rock 'n' Roll', we might not immediately guess that they are referring to explosives that propel upwards before detonating at four feet, or the act of putting a M16 rifle on full automatic fire.[42]

It is important to observe that senior military men also routinely aestheticized weapons as objects of beauty. Textbooks on small arms lauded the 'charm and beauty of well-made weapons'.[43] Others took 'delight in the esoterica of small arms and rifle ballistics'.[44] In the words of the manufacturer of the L2A2 or Sterling machine gun, 'That little lightweight gun of outstanding mechanical beauty gave me an enormous sense of power, especially when shooting from the hip in the full automatic mode.'[45] Missiles could also be flaunted as epitomizing the technical magnificence of civilisation. For instance, dum-dum bullets have a thin nickel shield and a 'soft point', so that, on striking human targets, they 'mushroom' inside the body, shattering bone and tissue with explosive force. For proponents, the dum-dum's ability to cause some of the most devastating wounds ever seen in modern warfare was a cause of celebration. Winston Churchill was a fan, commending this 'wonderful and, from the technical point of view . . . beautiful machine' in *The Story of the Malakand Field Force*. 'On striking a bone', he observed, the bullet would '"set up" or, spread out, and it then tears and splinters everything before it, causing wounds which, in the body, must generally be mortal, and in any limb necessitates amputation.'[46] For Churchill, these were grounds for delight not despair. Figure 1.1 (opposite) shows some of the wounds created by different types of weapons. At the time this photograph was taken, dum-dum bullets were poetically described as 'collapsing like a concertina' inside the victim's body, while another missile was said to assume 'the shape of a lady's sun bonnet or an antiquated top hat'.[47]

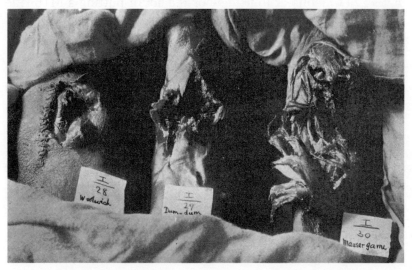

Figure 1.1. From Alex. Ogston's 'The Peace Conference and the Dum-Dum Bullet' (1899). The original caption reads: 'Exit wound (arm)'. The wounds are labelled from left to right, Woolwich, Dum-dum and Mauser game bullet.[48]

One way of talking that weapons experts routinely used is particularly interesting: that is, analogies associated with water. In 1962 some of the most distinguished ballistic experts asked: how can we explain the 'interest and admiration' aroused by photographs of 'rifle bullets in rapid fire'? Surely it was due to their 'resemblance to moving ships with prominent bow and stern waves and a turbulent wake', they mused. They even evoked water when describing the 'blasting out' of soft tissues caused by a bullet: it had a similar effect to a 'stream of water from a fire hose'.[49] Upon hitting human tissue, there is a '"splashing" effect which is analogous to the upward splash when a pebble is dropped into water', explained another commentator in an article in the *Annals of the Royal College of Surgeons of England* in 1981.[50]

Water analogies remain extremely popular in the ballistics literature. The violence of high-velocity bullets led to an impressive 'tail splash'. Or, as one ballistic scientist noted in 1995, the temporary cavity caused by the explosion of a bullet into flesh

can be compared to a diver entering water. If the water is entered aerodynamically and nearly perpendicular, there is little or no splash, and a minimal amount of water is displaced. This correlates to a low-velocity, nondeforming, nonfragmenting missile that does not deviate from its longitudinal axis.

However,

If the same diver deviates from his perpendicular longitudinal axis, even slightly, he will create a bigger splash. The amount of water displaced is proportional to the degree of deviation from the perpendicular.[51]

In case readers had not grasped the full implications, he laboured the point. The diver who assumes the shape of a 'cannonball' (with 'his arms and legs flexed close to the body to create a larger diameter') will create a 'larger splash', 'similar to a missile that assumed a larger diameter ("mushrooms") when coming into contact with tissue'.[52]

The authors of a 2005 article in the journal *Injury* used a similar comparison. They blandly noted that some divers enter the water in a 'clean' fashion, creating little 'turbulence and splash'; others did a 'bellywhopper', in which 'the splash is maximum'.[53] As other ballistic experts freely admitted, this was the destruction and dismemberment of human beings 'treated as a branch of underwater ballistics'.[54]

A related analogy was snow. As physiologist E. Newton Harvey explained in 1948, in order to understand what happens when a low-velocity bullet hits human tissue, simply 'thrust a pointed rod into snow. The ice crystals are pushed ahead and move gently to one side leaving a track, perhaps somewhat larger than the rod, but with no effects at a distance.' This was not the case with bullets travelling at higher velocities. On hitting a person, such a missile

> not only imparts momentum to material in front but also to material at the side, so that a great cavity is formed. This cavity would be a permanent one in snow, but in water or tissue it would be temporary. The effect can be described as explosive.[55]

Why is such language important? After all, water and snow are incongruous stand-ins for crushed, torn and splintered tissue and bone. Clearly, such ways of talking about wounding people perform an important function: they exchange the messy, sticky, bloodiness of actual wounding (not to mention the screaming victim) for a clean, even gentle, image of tissue that will 'move gently to one side' when hit. Given that these commentators were engaged in researching or producing weapons designed to tear living people apart, being able to talk about it using such analogies must have been profoundly soothing.

Weapon scientists and others involved in the military industry indulged in lyrical depictions of the wounding and lethal effect of weapons. But they also possessed two other, very different languages for talking about acts of violence: euphemism and mathematical abstraction. Euphemisms are a prominent means of erasing violence. The neologism 'warfighter' is one example. Although the word had been used sporadically by the defence industry for decades, it only appeared in the public media in an article in the *New York Times* in 2003.[56] Its increasing prominence is interesting. After all, in the mid-twentieth century, military commentators had sought to emphasis the *defensive* rather than *offensive* functions of the armed forces: in 1947, the US Department of *War* was replaced by the Department of *Defense*, and the UK government established the Ministry of Defence, which replaced the War Office, in 1963. In recent years, however, the opposite has been the case. Soldiers, sailors, marines, airmen and airwomen have become 'warfighters' or 'warriors'.[57] These terms perform a powerful rhetorical function, especially because they are frequently juxtaposed against 'insurgents': 'warfighters' conjures up technologically sophisticated, almost god-like capacities of service personnel, in comparison with the primitive-sounding 'insurgents', waging war with improvised tools and weapons.

Other misleading ways of speaking about violence involve a strange kind of distancing. For instance, while discussing ways to bomb populated cities, ballistic experts might use the phrase 'delivery may . . . be achieved', as though they were referring to flowers.[58] Fusion bombs (a thermonuclear weapon) are called 'clean bombs', even though they are seven hundred times more powerful than the fission (or atomic) bomb that was dropped on Hiroshima.[59] The MX missile, which carries ten warheads, each of which contains 250 to 400 times the explosive power of the Hiroshima bomb, is called a 'damage-limitation weapon'.[60]

Understatement similarly encourages this kind of cognitive forgetfulness. An enemy combatant will be described as having 'received' a bullet.[61] The enemy is not 'killed', but was 'had', 'disposed' or 'exterminated' like a bug.[62] Ballistic experts talk about the 'production of the wound'[63] or 'producing the casualty',[64] as though mortal combat is some kind of assembly line. Making a kill is 'good shot placement'.[65] When R. J. Gatling invented the ten-barrel revolving rifle ('machine gun') in 1861, he described it as a 'labour-saving device for warfare', almost the equivalent of the rotary washing machine that had been patented three years earlier.[66] Hollow-pointed bullets were presented as simply being allowed to '"set up" on impact', that is, 'expand, and thus inflict a greater shock'.[67] When such bullets hit a person, they 'burr' before opening backwards.[68] Other projectiles 'jawed' and 'tumbled' inside bodies.[69] The explosive effects of high-velocity missiles were merely 'disruptive'.[70] A particular kind of wound was described as 'cookie-cutter' damage.[71] During the Second World War, Air Chief Marshall Arthur 'Bomber' Harris kept a 'blue book' at his headquarters, with maps of more than ninety industrial towns and cities in Germany that he had 'marked for "emasculation"'. As these areas were bombed, they were 'blued out'.[72] In the 1960s and 1970s, US aeroplanes 'seeded' anti-personnel mines (they were called 'bomblets', but we should not be fooled by the diminutive) over Vietnam, Laos and Cambodia. Once 'seeded', these mines were for ever primed to kill. The main victims were children, attracted by the shape or colour of what seemed to be playthings.[73] Napalm was called a 'flak suppression weapon'.[74] Cluster bombs that would detonate in such a way that fragments would kill or wound people within an area of 300 by 900 metres (to give a perspective, the average UK Premiership football pitch is 104 by 68 metres) were 'area denial' weapons;[75] such bombs, 'succeed in silencing the weapons' (that is, the people holding the weapons and every living person within a wide radius).[76] The Predator drone was 'a big bee . . . with one hell of a sting'.[77]

Mathematic abstraction is a much more austere language used by weapons experts, but that should not blind us to the satisfaction it offers. Precision, reproducibility and exclusivity are highly valued traits amongst scientists, whether specializing in weaponry or not. The ability to convert multiple observations into abstract formulae brings esteem. Standardized behaviour and activities, as well as knowledge of acronyms, are symbols that give clear proof that a scientist belongs to an elite club.

For ballistic scientists, statistics 'stand in' for suffering. Instead of talking about the number of people maimed and killed, these scientists exchange data about SCRs and SKRs – standardized casualty and killing rates. These rates are based on a population density of one person per thousand square feet (or 92.9 square metres) in the area at risk. For example, in Hiroshima the 'vulnerable area for the killed was 2.85 square miles, and for all casualties 9.36 square miles'. This gave 'a SKR of 79,450 and an SCR of 260,900 . . . About 6,500 times as great as for a High Explosive bomb in Britain.'[78] When seeking to discover how 'the desired wounding effect could be achieved',[79] ballistic experts tell us that it is helpful to know the 'index of wounding capacity', or the 'level of energy absorption at a tissue depth of 15 cm . . . as this is the depth at which most vital structures lie'.[80] In the words of Eric Prokosch in *The Technology of Killing* (1995),

> A weapons designer is not, first and foremost, a murderer; he is a statistician, a metallurgist, or an engineer. He is trained for his profession and he thinks in its terms. When presented with a problem, he seeks solutions which are 'elegant' and 'rigorous' (as a mathematician would say). A neat solution satisfies his scientific bent and earns praise from his colleagues.

Prokosch observes that when scientists speak about 'sensitivity studies' and 'compatibility tests' they are not referring to 'a form of marriage counselling, but a procedure for making sure than a given bomb can be used with a given airplane'.[81] Theirs is the language of mathematics and engineering employed in the art of killing.

This is language to render violence beautiful, fun and exciting. But language can also erase violence. One way it does this is by omitting the most salient features of an activity. At its most basic, weapon research, development and manufacture fails to acknowledge that the primary goal is to maim and kill other human beings. This is what Velma Maxson was doing when she spoke about her job working in Raytheon's missile factory in Tucson, Arizona. She admitted that

> I don't want to go to war . . . I understand we make missiles.
> I know they're going to be used on something [sic]. I prefer to think they're going to be used for testing.

She followed up this hope with the statement that, however they were used, 'they need them to work perfectly'.[82]

Examples proliferate and, as with the other languages, can be found throughout twentieth-century conflicts. For instance, in 1930 the author of an article entitled 'Ballistics as Applied to Police Science' claimed that the science of ballistics was composed of two elements, interior and exterior ballistics, or what happens inside the weapon and then when the missile leaves the weapon. He omitted the crucial third element, terminal or wound ballistics – or what happens when the missile hits.[83]

That could have been an oversight. A more shameless sleight of hand involves presenting weapons research as analogous to life-*saving* endeavours. For instance, in 1953 one scientist brazenly claimed that military operational research (that is, research into improving decision-making – 'effectiveness' – in the use of weapons) was equivalent to 'seeking a cure for cancer'. In cancer-treatment endeavours, he rightly noted, the 'exact processes that will lead to this achievement' is unclear. But he then drew a parallel with a very different enterprise. He asserted that the same was the case with weapons research: the fulfilment of the goals of weapons researchers was made more difficult because much previous research was classified.[84]

An extreme version of this kind of cognitive error occurs when service personnel are portrayed as peacekeepers and weapons are said to save lives. After the atomic bomb was dropped on Hiroshima and Nagasaki, exterminating more than two hundred thousand people (most of whom were unarmed civilians), a Methodist minister was quoted as telling his congregation that they should 'thank God for the work of the scientists which had shortened the war and saved thousands of lives'.[85] 'Peace is our Profession' is the motto of the Strategic Air Command, which was established in 1946 to command and control America's land-based strategic bomber aircraft and intercontinental ballistic missiles.[86] This was the slogan that General Curtis LeMay (who, as I discuss at the beginning of Chapter Three, was responsible for more civilian deaths than any other person in the history of war) returned to time and again in his memoirs.[87] While I was writing this chapter – in January 2013 – the British army introduced a new combat sidearm, the Glock 17, which replaced the long-standing (1954+) Browning Hi-Power pistol. Without any sense of irony, soldiers informed reporters that these new sidearms were 'lifesavers'.[88] The people intended to be maimed and killed by Glock 17s did not truly possess 'lives'.

Euphemism and military abstraction had an anesthetizing effect on participants of war and other militarist enterprises. They provided a substitute language, a numbing techno-speak. In 1945, a sociologist exploring the way civilians 'adjusted' to militarism observed how men engaged in 'keen discussions' about the 'rival merits of particular weapons'. They became so engrossed with 'physics and ballistics' that they forgot that the chief function of these weapons was to kill fellow human beings. He drily noted that

> A discussion on the most efficient ways of killing the enemy is not pleasant; however, a technological debate on the range and characteristics of a certain caliber rifle can be challenging and impersonal.[89]

The hypnotic fascination with statistics and specifications enabled these men to disconnect their actions (care of weapons) from their consequences (corpses). They were just 'screwing fuses into sockets', as one bomb technician put it.[90]

An example of this process comes from the war in Vietnam. In his memoir, journalist Jacques Leslie recalled the day when Nick Ut took the famous photograph of three children running down a road after being hit by napalm dropped by a South Vietnamese plane. The image of nine-year-old Phan Thi Kim Phuc in particular has been seared into our memory of that war. A fellow journalist called Alex had been present when the incident happened. Leslie noted that Alex

> saw the canister explode, saw the girl tear off her burning clothes, saw the children scream as they ran down the road. The only problem was that the scene didn't interest him.

That afternoon, Alex had sent his report to the *Newsweek* office, telling them 'all about the fighting, as usual emphasizing its tactical dimension'. He wrote up his story 'full of references to battalions and flanking movements' and 'mentioned the napalm only in passing'. The controller, however, wanted Alex to include the human dimension. But Alex was unable to do so. As Leslie commented,

I could imagine Alex's frustration as he sat at his typewriter, yearning to think like a general while being asked to write about children. Alex wanted to breathe the rarefied air of military abstraction, for it was safe from children, safe from emotion, nearly safe from life itself.[91]

Faced with violence, is that what we all actually want? To be spared the other person's suffering?

The final distortion involves giving agency to inanimate weapons. It is as if they possess lives independent of their human creators and users. Weapons move in time and space. They have a trajectory. They are creative, forging cavities that collapse perilously ('temporary cavities') or for ever leave a trail ('permanent cavities'). They literally explode inside living bodies.

In other words, weapons are spoken about as if they are autonomous agents. The social existence of weapons starts with their birth — a male nativity scene. The atom bomb was Oppenheimer's 'baby', according to one of the scientists at Los Alamos; they hoped that it was a boy, not a girl (or dud).[92] As General Leslie Groves, who directed the Manhattan Project, cabled the Secretary of War Henry Stimson after the first atomic test,

> Doctor has just returned most enthusiastic and confident that the little boy is as husky as is big brother. The light in his eyes discernable from here to Highhold and I could have heard his screams from here to my farm.[93]

Like babies, weapons are given names. Often, these are highly ironic. The Colt .45 calibre single action six-shooter was known as the 'Peacemaker', for example, while President Ronald Regan dubbed the MX missile, with its intercontinental nuclear warheads, 'The Peacekeeper'. The scheme to send huge pilotless planes to bomb Germany during the Second World War was christened 'Project Aphrodite', after the goddess of love. Other names attempted to link modern war with courtly tales: Britain's first ballistic rocket was called the 'Black Knight', for instance.[94]

Weapons experts routinely speak as though the missile, rather than the person wielding the gun, is responsible for the destruction. Indeed, the term 'terminal ballistics' is frequently described as the 'behaviour of the missile in tissue', as though a missile is capable of 'behaving' one way or another.[95] Ballistic science is defined as a kind of 'bullet-body interaction' in which there is a 'transfer of energy from the projectile to the medium'.[96] Lieutenant-Colonel W. C. Moffat's article 'Influence of Missile Type and Velocity' (1977) provides a subtler example of this process of giving agency to a missile. He writes:

> Flight stability in air flight, necessary for accuracy and range, is achieved by *imparting to* a bullet a carefully calculated amount of spin by firing from a rifled barrel. Although by this means the bullet *can be made to* maintain stable nose-on flight in air, it will rapidly become unstable in the gelatine target or in human tissue, and because of this loss of stability within such a target the missile *is induced to* yaw. Its presenting area, that is its *attitude*, is thus changed and *it is forced to* exchange its energy at a faster rate. The faster the *energy is exchanged* between the missile and the tissue the greater will be the damage.[97]

In other words, weapon designers are described as 'imparting' to a bullet certain intentions (it is 'made to maintain' accuracy and range and is 'induced' to 'yaw' or inflict extensive tissue destruction). The bullet is even said to possess an 'attitude'. In such ways, the victim's flesh is a partner in the interactive wounding process: her body participates in 'exchanging' energy with the missile.

Weapons not only have agency – choosing to behave or interact with targets – they also possess emotions. Bullets spring 'blithe-fully [sic] through a set of distorted German features', according to an article in *Arms and the Man* in 1919.[98] Machine guns were commended because they were always calm, boasted Hiram Maxim, its inventor. Previously, Maxim observed with dismay, even experienced gunners when 'confronted by a dangerous enemy' would 'work the handle faster than the cartridges would drop into their places', leading to the gun jamming. In contrast, he observed, with his automatic system 'the recoil energy has no nerves, it never gets excited and can always be depended upon to work the gun with mathematical precision'.[99] Or, jumping to the twenty-first century, the missile called 'Special K' (which blasts out razor-sharp shrapnel to 'slice and dice anyone within a twenty-foot radius') does not allow anyone, even at fifty feet, to 'escape its wrath' entirely.[100]

It is important to point out, however, that while weapons are portrayed as deeply enmeshed in social relations they are curi-ously abstracted from wider, *political* relations. They exist independently of the military and political apparatus behind them. They are the legendary fetishized object.

These four ways of talking about violence – aestheticizing it, con-verting it into an abstract formula, ignoring pertinent aspects and giving weapons agency – overlap. Logically, they are confused and they often work at odds with one another (for example, the lurid languages of exquisiteness and ecstasy are a world apart from austere mathematical formulae). But converting violence against others into something attractive, abstract or absent makes it easier to bear. They share a commitment to violence as some-thing that can be represented in language in ways that blind us to the other person's pain.

CHAPTER TWO

───────────

The Circulation of Violence

Vera Brittain had no liking for guns. During the First World War she had volunteered to work as nurse in military hospitals in England, Malta and France. For almost four years, war's horrors invaded Brittain's life. In her autobiography *Testament of Youth*, she wrote about witnessing, reaching out to touch and seeking to comfort 'men without faces, without eyes, without limbs, men almost disembowelled, men with hideous truncated stumps of bodies'. She recalled

> standing alone in a newly created circle of hell . . . and gazing, half hypnotized, at the disheveled beds, the stretchers on the floor, the scattered boots and piles of muddy khaki, the brown blankets turned back from smashed limbs bound to splints by filthy blood-stained bandages. Beneath each stinking wad of sodden wool and gauze an obscene horror waited for me.

It was a 'butcher's-shop' in which 'dying men, reeking with mud and foul green-stained bandages' lay 'shrieking and writhing in a grotesque travesty of manhood'.

This was not the life she had envisaged. Brittain had been born into an upper-middle-class family and educated at boarding school

before studying English at Somerville College, Oxford. The declaration of war in 1914 stalled her narrow and comfortable life.

Naively, at the start of the war she had lamented that 'Women
get all the dreariness of war, and none of its exhilaration,' but then
her fiancé Roland Leighton, two close male friends (Victor
Richardson and Geoffrey Thurlow) and her beloved brother
Edward were catapulted into the front lines. By the end of the
war, they had all been killed.

Left stunned and alone at the end of the war, Brittain realized
that her life had been permanently changed. While ministering to
the wounded, she mused, nurses possessed a 'kind of psychological shutter which we firmly closed down upon our recollection of
the daily agony, whenever there was time to think'. But she confessed that 'We never dreamed that in the years of renewed
sensitiveness after the War, the convenient shutter would simply
refuse to operate'. She was haunted by agonizing memories of
what she had seen, and chilling suspicions about what had been
kept from her about the deaths of her loved ones.

What were the survivors to do now that the men they had
laughed with, talked to and held were gone? They discovered the
meaning of suffering. Children woke to find that their fathers had
left for distant battlefields while they slept. In Britain, three hundred thousand never saw their fathers again; 160,000 wives
received the dreaded telegram informing them that their husbands
had been killed. Countless others like Brittain lost lovers and close
friends. They got on with their lives, as they had to, fretting end-
lessly about whether they were inadvertently dishonouring the
dead. In 1925, when Brittain contemplated getting married, she
was consumed by fear lest developing new emotional relationships
'destroyed yet again the men who had once uncomplainingly died'.

Violence had a macabre way of circulating back home, long
after people imagined that it had been banished. For Brittain and
millions like her, trauma was not only due to having witnessed the

atrociousness of war but also surviving it. This was the second, ever-present wound. 'Why couldn't I have died in the War with the others?', Brittain lamented. Instead, she was fated to live the rest of her life 'without confidence or security'. War has a capacity to wound everyone: or, as Brittain put it, war is 'a human event, not a happening which affected one age or sex rather than another'.[1] Once tasting its bitter fruits, there is no end to it.

Brittain's fiancé, friends and brother were the immediate and intended casualties of wartime violence. Millions of young, fit men and women volunteered or were conscripted during the two world wars of the twentieth century. Mothers and fathers, sisters and brothers, friends and neighbours waved them goodbye. Hundreds of thousands of them were killed. Millions more were physically or psychologically wounded. Many were harmed by their own comrades. In a remarkable official report on American participation during the Second World War, we read that 18 per cent of American casualties during the New Georgia and Burma campaigns were caused by 'friendly fire'; the proportion was a scarcely less reassuring 12 per cent in Bougainville.[2] They were collateral damage.

But there are also casualties like Brittain, who were indirect and unintended targets. They are also the collaterals of war. The reason no one can afford to ignore the effect of weapon research, development, manufacture, stockpiling and use is because they affect all of our lives. Put in other words: even those of us who are civilians inevitably and irrevocably become casualties of our own armed forces. Our violence rebounds on us. Violence circulates from soldiers to civilians, from friends to enemies and from foreign nations to the heart of our homelands. It poisons our local and our global environments.

The first circulation of violence flows from soldiers to civilians. In conflict and post-conflict worlds, the traffic in weapons works in two directions: out from munitions factories to the sites of conflict, and then back in again after the signing of the armistice. Rifles, bullets, hand grenades and bombs are brought from the theatres of war into our homes and streets. After the two world wars, British and American governments were forced to institute major disarmament campaigns to encourage the handing over of illegal weapons.[3] As one pathologist warned in aftermath of the Second World War, it had been a 'short-sighted' government policy to allow 'repatriated soldiers to retain as "trophies" any kind of foreign small arms they might have, prohibiting only those with machine-gun mechanisms'.[4] He warned readers not to forget that young men who had been taught to hold 'a loaded gun in their hands' and 'to kill other men with firearms' were hoarding these trophies.[5]

After each war, panicky predictions about the effects of combat on returning men were bandied about. In 1921, Stephen Graham argued that the war had been 'a Bacchanalia for the animal in man'. The hearts of soldiers

> hardened. They told themselves they wanted nothing and cared nothing. Their minds fell victims to a dull passivity or false boisterousness. They banished the bright ego and took up with a Cerberus, yowled the dog-language of the army ... Coarse hair grew apace, brows grew lower, hands that had any cunning in them grew to mere claws and clutches, eyes dullened, and the ear-gate stood ajar for the sound of animal noises and animal confessions.[6]

What would happen to all this repressed aggression when they returned home? In The Remaking of a Mind (1920), social theorist Henri de Man issued dire predictions. He warned that

Should conditions arise in the life of these masses that either make it in their interest to murder, or else create a common feeling in favour of class terrorism, they [ex-servicemen] might remember how easy it is to take another man's life, and what a delight there is in doing it.[7]

Was it any wonder, mused psychoanalyst Therese Benedek in her analysis of the psychological effects of the Second World War, that men whose aggressive impulses had been nurtured within the military murdered their wives and girlfriends when these women refused to 'comply with their demands', or that they had fewer (if any) inhibitions against aggressive outbursts?[8] Would there be a regression to more primitive forms of life?

If these fears were strong after the two world wars of the twentieth century, they were greatly exacerbated in the context of the brutal conflicts fought in Indo-China. As Jerome Johns, an army instructor at Phan Rang, anxiously admitted, 'Whenever I see something about a killing in the paper, I look to see if it was done by a Vietnam veteran ... You remember how we had to motivate those kids to kill; we programmed them to kill, man ... Well, nobody's unprogramming them'.[9] As distinguished psychiatrists Mardi J. Horowitz and George F. Solomon asked in 1975, wasn't there a risk that the 'conditioned inhibitions to destructive behavior' would have been diminished by exposure to military indoctrination and combat, making it 'difficult to reimpose' once the men returned home?[10] Interestingly, some commentators wondered whether the experience of war might brutalize civilians as much or even more as it did combat veterans. This was the conclusion of sociologists Dane Archer and Rosemary Gartner in their huge statistical survey in the 1980s. They found that war

involves homicide legitimated by the highest auspices of the state. During many wars, the killing of enemy soldiers has been treated not merely as regrettable and expedient measure but as praiseworthy and heroic ... This legitimation is directed at both the nation's soldiers and the home front; but it may be more credible to civilians than to combat soldiers with direct experience of the realities of war.[11]

In other words, civilians might become more inured to violence than men and women who actually saw active service.

Violence also circulates from friends to enemies, increasing the likelihood that we will become casualties of our own military technologies and practices. Research on how best to control, maim, and kill foreigners has a disturbing tendency to ricochet back on ourselves. Our enemies eventually acquire the technologies we developed to fight them, and use them in their own battles against us. Like the other arguments made here, this threat is present whatever the technology employed or strategy implemented, and can therefore be seen in military contexts throughout the centuries.

For instance, at the beginning of the twentieth century this was the argument of those who opposed the use of dum-dum bullets and other cruel weapons. For many commentators, the development of particularly nasty weapons should be halted, not for reasons of morality or compassion but because they would eventually be deployed by the enemy. As the author of 'Bullets – Expansive, Explosive, and Poisoned' (1902) warned, it was important not to forget that 'we might not remain the sole possessors of this "beautiful machine". The Afridis captured some of our rifles and dum-dum ammunition, and turned them against us with great effect.'[12] Our enemies might even invent more destructive strategies for using these technologies and knowledges. In the twentieth century, such risks attained global proportions in relation to nuclear weapons (North Korea and Pakistan) and chemical and biological weapons (Syria).

Similarly, with the advent of drone warfare in the twenty-first century, two questions became paramount. The first was whether targeting individuals for assassination by drones reduces or increases our risk of terrorist violence. There is a great deal of evidence suggesting that killing leaders of terrorist organisations pushed those groups into becoming more aggressive, in part by fuelling fury about the power of Western nations such as the US.[13] The second question was: if *we* can violate national jurisdictions by carrying out planned assassinations, why can't *they*? In 2010 it was estimated that at least fifty-six nations were developing robotic weapons, including drones for targeted assassinations.[14] Extrajudiciary assassinations may soon come to our shores. In fact, American civilians have already been targeted for assassination abroad: take the CIA-initiated drone strike of 30 September 2011 that killed American citizen Anwar al-Awlaki without judicial or due process.[15] Philip Alston, the UN's Special Rapporteur on Extrajudicial, Summary or Arbitrary Executions, warns that US drones are 'being operated in a framework which may well violate international humanitarian law and international human rights law'.[16] As a consequence, we should be anxious about the undermining of Just War precepts and their replacement by realist power politics, with its emphasis on shows of military might.

Finally, violence circulates from overseas territories to our government back home. In other words, it is not only our enemies who learn from our destructive inventions: our politicians and security forces also learn from the destructive technologies and practices adopted by our armed forces. When peace breaks out, industries devoted to the invention and development of weapon technologies prove to be very useful in policing and punishing those of us at home. I will explore this point in more detail by using four examples: nuclear technologies, drone warfare, gas attacks and the use of so-called non-lethal projectiles.

The most dangerous threat to British and American societies is not terrorism but nuclear accidents. And this fear is not a product of the apocalyptic imaginations of science-fiction writers: there have been near disasters in the past. In *Command and Control. Nuclear Weapons, the Damascus Accident, and the Illusion of Safety* (2013), investigative journalist Eric Schlosser catalogues a series of near misses, when our own nuclear warheads almost exploded above or on British and American soil. Even the Pentagon's *official* list admits to thirty-two occasions when 'mishaps with nuclear weapons' might have harmed the American public. This number is a gross underestimate. In 1970, a study by a leading nuclear weapons laboratory noted that at least 1200 weapons were involved in accidents between 1950 and 1968 alone.[17]

As examples of both the trivial nature of the accidents and the enormity of the potential consequences, Schlosser gives two examples. In Grand Forks, North Dakota, on 15 September 1980, a B-52 bomber loaded with four hydrogen bombs and eight short-range missiles with nuclear warheads caught fire. It burned for two hours, and if it were not for gale force winds blowing in the right direction, and the intrepid feats of a fireman who managed to shut off the aircraft's power, there might have been a detonation. Just three days later another catastrophe was narrowly averted near Damascus, Arkansas. A carelessly dropped tool inside the silo of a Titan II intercontinental ballistic missile, carrying the most powerful nuclear warhead ever built in the US, made a hole in the side of the missile, causing a fuel leak. The Titan exploded but – luckily – the warhead did not detonate. In both of these cases, entire states could have been destroyed.[18]

The British record is not reassuring either. Sir Ronald Oxburgh, chief scientific adviser at the Ministry of Defence from 1988 to 1993, catalogued nineteen accidents involving British weapons between 1960 and 1991. However, Eric Schlosser was able to identify other accidents that had not been mentioned. On 27 July 1956, for instance, an American B-47 bomber at RAF Lakenheath in Suffolk crashed into a storage igloo containing Mark Six atomic bombs. It was 'a miracle that one Mark Six with exposed detonators sheared didn't go', claimed an officer in a classified telegraph. If the bomber had hit another igloo, a large cloud of plutonium would have been released. As Schlosser observed, 'Plutonium dust can be lethal when inhaled. Once dispersed, it is extremely difficult to clean up, and it remains dangerous for about 24,000 years.'[19] On 16 January 1961 a US F-100D fighter plane caught fire, engulfing a Mark 28 hydrogen bomb. Fire-fighters were able to extinguish the blaze before any explosion occurred. On other occasions, two retrorockets on a Thor missile carrying warheads sixty times more powerful than the bomb that destroyed Hiroshima suddenly fired while undergoing a routine check (17 August 1962), and RAF trucks carrying hydrogen bombs skidded off an icy road in Wiltshire (7 January 1987).[20] When anti-nuclear campaigners complain about the risk to (our) human lives caused by stockpiling nuclear weapons, they are not exaggerating.

Drones are another example of a technology that was originally developed to stake out and slay enemy subjects. They were, however, swiftly adopted by homeland security to monitor criminals and borderlands. Are illegal immigrants crossing the Arizona–Mexican border, for instance?[21] Are people dumping rubbish or speeding? Are they living in garages without planning permission? Are they protesting against munitions proliferation? Drones can be used to identify the culprits.[22]

Drones have been used domestically in the US since at least 2004. Their numbers are not insubstantial. In February 2012 Congress effectively approved more than thirty thousand drones for domestic use, thus giving drones a role in 'controlling domestic populations on US soil'.[23] As social critic Naomi Wolf warns, the Pentagon can now send a domestic drone to hover outside your apartment window, collecting footage of you and your family, if the Secretary of Defense approves it. Or it may track you and your friends and pick up audio of your conversations, on your way, say, to protest or vote or talk to your representative, if you are not 'specifically identified', a determination that is so vague as to be meaningless. What happens to those images, that audio? 'Distribution of domestic imagery' can go to various other government agencies without your consent, and that imagery can, in that case, be distributed to various government agencies; it may also include your most private moments and most personal activities.[24]

So-called 'interested' organisations include the Department of Defense, Department of Homeland Security, Federal Bureau of Investigation, the US Secret Service, Environmental Protection Agency, Immigration and Customs Enforcement, state police departments and private security companies.

I want to devote more space to the third military technology that has come back to haunt us: chemical and biological weapons. This threat comes in four ways: 'rogue' attacks, injuries to employees in these industries, harm to experimental subjects caught up in weapon development and the pacification of political and other dissenters at home.

The first threat is that chemical or biological agents will be used by a home-based terrorist or a by a 'lone wolf' from within the biological defence programmes. Indeed, this has already happened: in 2001 Bruce Ivins, a senior scientist at the US Army Medical Research Institute of Infectious Diseases, sent weapons-grade virulent anthrax to various individuals and institutions in the US. Seventeen people were infected; five died.[25]

Equally damaging, chemical and biological agents have a devastating effect on employees in the weapons industries. Here I am not referring to highly remunerated scientists, but to the lowly labourers who carry out the most dangerous jobs within those industries. Since the mid-1990s, the destruction of chemical weapons in the US has involved the labour of an astonishing number of contract workers who are responsible for manually transporting munitions from storage bunkers and disposing of them. This 'dirty work' involves handling unstable and lethal weapons; it is extremely dangerous.[26]

The third threat is the ethical harm to experimental subjects caught up in weapon development. Often, people did not realize that their bodies were being used for such research. Between 1995 and 2001, for instance, the Salisbury Health Care Trust sold surplus skin from plastic surgery patients to the Defence Evaluation and Research Agency at Porton Down without the patients' knowledge. The Trust had been receiving around seventeen thousand pounds a year for this skin.[27]

Human guinea pigs are also collateral damage. Chemical warfare experiments on human subjects were widely carried out in both British and American laboratories. A particularly revealing account was given in 1946 by Harry Cullumbine, head of the Physiological Section at the Chemical Defence Experimental Station at Porton Down. He claimed that 'all the subjects were volunteers'. They were recruited from the staff of Porton or the three armed services. These volunteers were exposed to two types of chemicals, lacrimators (weeping agents) and sternutators (sneezing agents), both of which were euphemistically labelled 'harassing' chemicals. These chemicals were tested on people placed inside gas chambers as well as in more 'realistic' conditions on assault courses. Cullumbine also oversaw trials of 'vesicant' (blistering) compounds, such as mustard gas. Not surprisingly, he concluded that the warm, damp skin of the genitals were most sensitive and produced the worst blisters.[28]

Informed consent to these experiments was rarely given. This was admitted by the chemist George Box, who worked as a lab assistant at the Chemical Defence Experimental Station at Porton Down during the Second World War. In his autobiography, Box recalled that

> The army decided that every army unit should be issued a small sample of liquid mustard gas so that volunteers could have a drop put on their skin and see how a painful blister appeared. In army operation orders, you always had to sign off on a line that said 'All informed', but I'm afraid this protocol was not followed with mustard gas samples. Cullumbine, who was the expert on the treatment of mustard gas casualties, was kept very busy by the misuse of these samples.[29]

An independent ethics committee was only established at Porton Down in 1988.[30]

In addition, military technologies may have been developed with far-away places in mind – pacifying men and women in the empire, for instance, or deployed against wartime enemies – but they are too valued not to be used closer to home. Chemical and biological weapons have proved useful in domestic riot control and for keeping dissidents and minorities – including workers, socialists, African-Americans, and the mentally ill – in their place. Despite the proliferation of international treaties forbidding the use of gas in warfare in inter-state conflicts, certain toxic gases are considered lawful for domestic use. Indeed, the 1997 Chemical Weapons Convention classifies gases like SK, CN and CS as riot-control agents rather than chemical weapons.

Their use has been varied. In 1997 a London ophthalmologist protested about the utilization of CS gas by police attempting to restrain mentally ill persons in the cells. He complained that the police were spraying the gas directly into the face and, given the

fact that the person had probably already been sedated and therefore had 'impair[ed] natural defence mechanisms, such as blinking
or coughing', the result could be serious. He reminded the police
that 'CS gas is not a restraining agent but [a] harassing one . . .
People so exposed become highly motivated to escape from the
environment contaminated with the agent'.[31]

More commonly, gases have been used to quell protestors. In
America, CN (known commercially as Mace) was used extensively by the police from the 1920s, although it was gradually
superseded by CS gas, which had been developed at Porton Down
and was quicker acting. Noxious gases were deployed in the UK
from 1969, when the Troubles flared up in Northern Ireland.
The first use of CS gas against UK rioters was in Bogside,
Londonderry, in August of that year. The British government
clarified their position in 1970, stating that CS and similar gases
were 'outside the scope of the Geneva Protocol' so could be used
domestically.[32] Since 1973, the British government has authorized
an even stronger toxin – CR, or dibenzoxazepine, a severely inca-
pacitating, lachrymatory agent – for use in certain circumstances.[33]
The differences between these irritants are considerable. Judged
on the basis of the concentration of irritant found to be intolerable by 50 per cent of people within one minute of exposure, a
20.50 concentration of CN was intolerable to half of people
within that time, compared with only a 3.6 concentrate of CS and
a 0.7 concentrate of CR. In other words, each new sensory irritant was significantly more toxic than the previous one.[34]

When the British government first began using gas in a military
context – during the British invasion of Mesopotamia (now Iraq)
in 1914 – Winston Churchill declared that he was 'strongly in
favour of using poisonous gas against uncivilised tribes' because
the weapon would 'cause great inconvenience and would spread
a lively terror and yet would leave no serious permanent effects
on most of those affected'.[35] The benign long-term effects of gas

was repeated more than half a century later when a Porton Down spokesman reassured journalists that CS was 'no more toxic than bonfire smoke'.[36] However, this was not the experience of protestors, many of whom faced longer-term damage such as bronchitis, asthma, lung damage, eye damage, allergies and prolonged diarrhoea as a result of exposure.[37] Indeed, this should not have surprised the military authorities, since tests carried out by the US army in June 1966 showed that CS gas could cause severe skin blistering, requiring hospitalisation.[38]

Gases did not only affect protestors. The gentlest of breezes would cause the poison to waft into built-up areas around protests, affecting neighbouring people, sometimes for days. This was what incensed Raymond McClean, who treated more than two hundred people affected by CS gas during the Londonderry disturbances of August 1969. He was anxious about the effect of CS on the densely populated area of Bogside and, in the longer term, the 'toxicological effects of the hundreds of empty gas canisters left lying on the streets'. Children were at greatest risk, he warned. McClean disparaged the scientific experiments undertaken at Porton Down that purported to show that the gases had only temporary effects (on animals at least), arguing that they would not show the effect of the chemicals on 'previously diseased lung tissue' due to bronchitis or asthma, for instance. In addition, he noted that the worst affected people would not go to hospital because of 'fear of recrimination'. He accused the British government of human experimentation. As he put it,

The human 'clinical trials' in the Bogside would support the theory of a high reluctance to be subjected to a second dosage [of CS gas]. However, I can assure you, it did not deter young men and boys who believed, rightly or wrongly, that they were fighting to preserve their homes and families. These

young men and boys were subjected to several acute expo-
sures, even to such an extent that many of them claimed that
they were 'becoming used to the gas'.[39]

In fact, there is some evidence that the Troubles helped to
rescue a section of the British ballistics industry from its post-
Cold War hiatus. Prior to the late 1960s, wound ballistic research
at Porton Down had been in steep decline. They were haemor-
rhaging staff and funding. Domestic woes changed their fortunes.
According to a confidential document entitled 'A Review of
Wound Ballistics Studies at CDE Porton' (1971), Major W. G.
Johnston confided that, by the 1960s, wound ballistics was fading
'into obscurity, due apparently to a lack of ... problems presented for study'. But

> suddenly, in 1969, with the Ulster crisis, came a continuous
> flow of problems from various departments concerning the
> lethality and wounding capability of a variety of weapons.
> With the production of answers to these problems the capa-
> bility of this Establishment to cope with this field of work
> apparently became more widely known, and with this a fur-
> ther increase in the problems presented.[40]

In other words, as the value of the work done by scientists at
Porton Down became more widely appreciated, they were given
responsibility for solving still other 'problems'. It was a change
celebrated by Robert Scott in a letter to Professor T. K. Marshall
of the Department of Forensic Pathology at Queen's University
Belfast on 19 September 1974. He noted that recent research at
Porton Down

> has gone forward at varying levels of activity and in varying
> emphasis. Partly due to the situation in Northern Ireland and

partly due to police interest in small arms ammunition effects, we carried out a number of programmes of weapon assessment last year and this year.

He was honest enough to admit that 'the results of much of this are not of direct medical interest'.[41] It was the militarization of domestic policing.

Gas was not the only 'non-lethal' weapon used against dissident and minority civilians in the US and UK. Bullets that were intended to wound but not kill people were first developed for use in Hong Kong. Originally, the missile was made of wood and was a mechanical variation on the wooden baton (this is why some commentators still speak of firing 'baton rounds'); when used in Northern Ireland, hard rubber was substituted for wood. Ironically designated 'Ulster's principal gift to mankind's arsenal',[42] these bullets are fifteen centimetres long (that is, as large as a hand) and 3.8 centimetres in diameter; they have a muzzle velocity of around 73 metres per second.[43] They are designed to be fired at 25 to 30 yards, and to bounce off the ground and hit at knee height. They are intended to administer a 'painful slap' from a range of over fifty metres.[44]

Like gas technologies, there was an escalation in state violence due to gradual increases in the amounts of explosives used to propel the rubber bullets (thus leading to an increase in the kinetic energy released upon impact with a person).[45] In 1976, the army in Northern Ireland stopped using the rubber bullet as it had proven inaccurate and too unstable in flight. Starting in 1973, it was gradually replaced with a bullet made of polyvinyl chloride (PVC). This plastic bullet was similar to its predecessor, but instead of having a pointed end had a blunt one; and it had a muzzle velocity of 71 metres per second.[46] The plastic bullet was a little lighter than the rubber version, but this was 'offset by greater hardness and the fact that it was designed to be fired directly at targets and not ricochet off the ground'.[47]

These new bullets were more lethal, in part because they 'seem to hit more victims head on', as doctors at the Royal Victoria Hospital in Belfast observed.[48] The fatality rate for rubber bullets was one death for every 18,000 bullets fired; for plastic bullets it was one for every 4300 fired.[49] Jack Kerman, a chief constable in the Royal Ulster Constabulary, defended the use of the plastic bullet on the grounds that it was only used against 'rioters who are themselves determined to kill or wound or cause destruction'. He 'asked critics of the plastic bullets if they were prepared to demand a ban on petrol bombs, or an enquiry into the nail bombs or rockets used by the Provisional IRA and their supporters'. In the early 1970s, he reminded people, the army had actually been allowed to *shoot* petrol bombers.[50] It was a line echoed by Lieutenant Sid Heal of the Los Angeles Sheriff's Department: 'If using a standard bullet was the alternative, what would've happened?'[51]

However, as already mentioned, non-lethal bullets could still cause serious wounds and fatalities. Based on an analysis of ninety patients who had come to the Royal Victoria Hospital between 1970 and 1972 after being hit by rubber bullets, it was reported that nearly half suffered significant injuries, including fractures, ruptured eye globes (all resulting in blindness), brain damage and injuries to lungs, spleen, liver and intestines.[52] The Royal Victoria physicians and surgeons observed that while the bullets had been designed to be fired at distances over twenty-five metres, half of their patients had been shot at distances of less than fifteen metres and one third at less than five metres.[53] In one case they documented, a woman was hit between the eyes with a rubber bullet as she sat in front of an open window in her home. They reported that both eyes had 'burst' and she suffered severe fractures in her face. An account of her injuries published in the *British Journal of Surgery* coolly informed readers that she 'remained fully conscious' during and after her wounding. Treatment involved having her face repaired using 'fine stainless steel wires'. She had to have both eye globes 'enucleated'. In everyday language, that means removed.[54]

Gas, rubber bullets and PVC missiles are just three examples of 'non-lethal' weapons. Others include water cannons, stun guns, tranquillisers and extreme light or sound. For many commentators, the development of such equipment may have lowered the bar to attacking civilians. At the very least, these weapons simply add to rather than replace lethal weapons, and they represent a significant militarization of civilian society.

It is telling to note that, when designed, great attention was paid to ensuring that these weapons presented a benign appearance. Bruising was legitimate; blood not. This was explicitly stated by US military scientists working for the civilian Law Enforcement Assistance Administration. In their words, 'It is preferred that onlookers not get the impression that the police are using excessive force or that the weapon has an especially injurious effect on the target individuals.' Because of this, 'a flow of blood and similar dramatic effects are to be avoided'.[55]

It is not only the case that violence circulates from soldiers to civilians, from friends to enemies, and from foreign nations to the heart of our homelands. In some cases, weapons that had been designed to injure and kill foreigners in military contexts could actually be banned by international law but endorsed for domestic use. Nowhere is this more striking than in the debates about whether police forces should use dum-dum or soft-nosed bullets to enforce the law.

Dum-dum bullets had been rendered illegal in international affrays since the First Peace Conference at The Hague in 1899.

This prohibition of semi-jacketed bullets was based on their devastating impact when hitting the bodies of human and non-human animals. One series of experiments compared the wounding effect of normal .38 Special bullets, Super Vel hollow-point bullets and Super Vel soft-point bullets. Fired into bucks at a distance of ten feet, the entrance wounds created by all three types of bullets were identical. However, when the skin was pulled back, the 'entrance wounds caused by the Super Vel bullets were at least two to three times the size of those caused by the standard bullet'. Furthermore, hollow-point bullets 'mush-roomed' when they penetrated tissue and this made larger and more irregular entry and exit wounds than soft-point ones.[56] In other words, the hollow-point bullets released two and a half times greater kinetic energy into the tissues and thus created more severe wounds.[57] The semi-jacketed bullets created signifi-cantly larger permanent and temporary cavities; they caused hydrodynamic shock; and tissues, blood vessels and vital organs were seriously mashed.[58] Yet, many people argued that these bul-lets – which had not been banned for domestic use – should be used 'at home' to 'stop' criminals.

Whether or not policemen were permitted to use soft-point, hollow-nosed or semi-jacketed bullets became especially power-ful in the 1970s and 1980s, when heightened political anxieties about a wave of violent crime sweeping through American cities led to a political commitment to show 'toughness'. The Governor of Connecticut put the issue robustly. In 1974 he defended sup-plying police with the new .357 Magnum pistol and hollow-nosed ammunition with the words: 'those who would use lollipops on gunmen will have to go elsewhere'.[59]

Officer morale was also important, according to some propo-nents. As one ballistic expert admitted, 'using a dum-dum bullet makes cops think they have an edge . . . It's now becoming a trendy thing, like owning a Porsche'.[60] Highly sensitive issues about the reform of the police force became enmeshed in the debates. For instance, the police chief in one unnamed Midwestern city chose to issue hollow-point bullets to law enforcement officers at least in part because it would 'demonstrate his support for the rank and file' who were becoming increasingly concerned about changes in promotion policy and affirmative-action initiatives among ethnic minorities. The city's mayor shared the police chief's concerns. He also did not want to be seen to oppose the new ammunition (despite community disapproval after a robbery suspect was killed) because banning the hollow point would 'earn him the animosity of many police officers' and jeopardize plans to reform the force. In other words, 'if the police do not win on this issue, a general demoralization will ensue which will result in increased opposition' to affirmative-action programmes.[61]

Bizarrely, some advocates of the missile queried whether wounding a person causes unnecessary or disproportionate suffering. As in the debates about the use of dum-dum bullets in wartime, proponents of soft-point bullets in civilian contexts sought to demonstrate that the weapons was not simply vicious. Thus, a report by an FBI agent in the 1970s bluntly stated that 'there is no humane way of shooting an individual without causing pain and suffering', before going on to conclude that shooting him with a soft-point bullet might not be the most painful method. In this agent's words,

> Perhaps it could be considered that greater suffering is caused to the subject by hitting him five or six times with standard ammunition without stopping him than is caused by striking him with a single bullet which does stop him.[62]

The superior 'knock-down power' of these weapons trumped any concern about cruel and unnecessary suffering of civilians.[63]

In the late twentieth and early twenty-first centuries, these debates took another twist. In large part this is because military forces are increasingly being called upon to deal with domestic riot control and law enforcement in 'failed states'. If soldiers are sent to deal with domestic riots, are they barred from using semi-jacketed bullets even though policemen can use the ammunition? In the case of terrorism, who is allowed to use semi-jacketed bullets? In 2001, in his keynote address to the Third International Workshop on Wound Ballistics, Christopher Greenwood (who is currently a Judge of the International Court of Justice) argued that there were

> circumstances, particularly in street warfare and in counter terrorists operations where it may be necessary to make a trade, in effect, between the principle of 'unnecessary suffering' to combatants ... One cannot regard suffering as unnecessary if it is inflicted for the purpose of protecting the civilian population. In other words, if the civilian population's protection is enhanced by the use of a particular weapon, then the adverse effects of that weapon on combatants cannot properly be regarded as unnecessary.[64]

In other words, in protecting civilian lives using expanding bullets is legitimate.

This was also the point Kenneth Watkins made in 'Chemical Agents and "Expanding" Bullets' (2006). He was interested in reigniting debates about the legitimacy (or otherwise) of using hollow-point ammunition and poisonous gas in the contexts of domestic riot control and 'three-block wars' ('that is, wars in which, within a three-block radius, soldiers are expected to fight insurgents, control riots, and spread peace'). Although he refused to state categorically that bans of certain weapons ought to be removed, he warned that the 'underlying rationale for these prohibitions, created more than half a century ago' needed to be critically analysed. 'Given the continuing complexity of 21st-century conflict', he pointed out, 'the need to be flexible and to search out humane approaches to applying force remains an important goal'. Terrorism presented people with a 'new challenge to the rule of law', forcing analysts to re-interrogate bans on the use of chemical agents and explosive bullets 'in order to ensure the protection for uninvolved civilians and other non-combatants is not unduly handcuffed by rules designed for large scale inter-state conflict'.[65] It was a carefully worded statement, but the presumption is for a relaxation, if not overturning, of the prohibition. Implicit in such arguments is that the 'new challenge to the rule of law' comes not only from the terrorist but also from international law experts like himself.

Finally, any discussion about the way militarist violence circulates back to harm those of us at home has to take account of its effects on our environment. The military complex is responsible for the most ecologically destructive behaviour in the world. In times of war, of course, eco-destruction is deliberate: defoliation and the release of chemical toxins transforms landscapes beyond recognition. They have made some battlefields too dangerous even to assess.

However, injury to the environment is not only inflicted in times of armed conflict. The military services occupy and pollute the world's land, sea and skies. In Britain, military training even takes place in national parks (such as Dartmoor) and holidaymakers are advised to consult the 'Firing Times' schedule before visiting.[66] In 2009 the US Department of Defense's audit of their 'real property portfolio' reported the presence of 539,000 military faculties located in more than 5570 sites; 716 of these sites were outside the US.[67] Military bases poison local environments with chemicals, fuels, high explosives and radioactivity. When environmental historian John Robert McNeill and international historian David S. Painter claim that 'US military bases generated massive amounts of hazardous wastes as part of normal operations', they are not exaggerating. They point out that

> The routine maintenance of the vast numbers of ships, aircraft, combat and support 2004 vehicles, and weaponry produced such pollutants as used oil and solvents, polychlorinated biphenyls (PCBs), battery and other acids, paint sludge, heavy metals, asbestos, cyanide, and plating residues. Sometimes the size of small cities, US bases also produced large amounts of ordinary garbage, medical wastes, photographic chemicals, and sewage. Often these wastes, toxic and nontoxic alike, were disposed of casually.[68]

These pollutants paled alongside those caused by atomic and nuclear testing. The UK has conducted nuclear tests in locations such as Malden Island, Christmas Island and in Australia. Between 1945 and 1992 the US conducted 1149 nuclear detonations, which have devastated many areas of the globe, including the Marshal Islands (Bikini and Enewetak Atolls), Christmas Island and Johnston Atoll, as well as lands populated by Native Americans, such as the Shoshone Indians in Nevada.[69] When I discuss the way in which the military is destroying our world, I mean it literally.

Vera Brittain's *Testament of Youth*, with which I started this chapter, sounded a death knell for her youth, her innocence. Her book is a heartfelt reminder that we are all responsible for war, and we all end up immersed and drowning in the tsunami of military conflict. This belief led Brittain to work passionately to establish 'a higher order of human relationships in which war is no more, the exploitation of man by man unknown, and the subjection of women a cruelty of the past'.[70]

Brittain was all too aware that violence circulates in the lifeblood of any society, whether in times of war or so-called peace. Of course, unlike Brittain, we may choose to focus only on our 'peaceful' worlds. We may ignore the people we wound and kill in distant places. We may believe in the intrinsic value of military–scientific research, lamenting only when it is put to 'bad' use. We may decide to protest noisily against women who abort their foetuses but silently acquiesce when men drop bomblets for five-year-old Arab children to pick up. But if our teenage children were at risk of being conscripted or drafted to war would we be so gung-ho? Either our loved ones or ourselves risk becoming collateral damage in our own wars.

PART THREE

Incitement to Murder

CHAPTER THREE

Kind-Hearted Gunmen

Curtis Emerson LeMay (aka 'The Cigar', 'Iron Ass' and the 'Caveman in a Jet Bomber') was the cigar-chomping, ass-kicking, US Pacific Air Commander during the Second World War.[1] He rarely smiled or spoke; he was surly and tactless; he was (as even an adoring biographer had to admit) 'the prototype of the brutal, inhuman militarist'.[2] There is a reason for this harsh judgement: LeMay had been responsible for the 1945 incendiary bombing campaign against Japan that killed over one million civilians and totally destroyed sixty-three cities.[3] In the words of General Thomas Sarsfield Power, who directed the firebombing of Tokyo and had been the Deputy Chief of Operations during the atomic attacks, the incendiary attacks were

> the greatest single military disaster incurred by any enemy in military history. It was greater than the combined damage of Hiroshima and Nagasaki. There were more casualties than in any other military action in the history of the world.[4]

At the beginning of LeMay's autobiography (ghostwritten by the journalist and novelist MacKinlay Kantor), he shrugged off legal prohibitions to wartime killing of civilians, sneering that he had 'tried to stay away from hospitals, prison camps, orphan asylums, nunneries and dog kennels'.[5] Well, he failed.

LeMay was not a 'kind-hearted gunman'. However, he was fond of telling a story about a 'stupid man who was not basically cruel', but would 'cut off the dog's tail an inch at a time so that it wouldn't hurt so much'. The moral of the story? LeMay was blunt:

> To worry about the *morality* of what we were doing – Nuts. A soldier has to fight. We fought.[6]

For LeMay, it was more 'humanitarian' and more smart to slaughter the enemy outright – and the enemy's grandparents and children and grandchildren and so on. Laws that sought to restrict violence were hogwash. 'Nuts.' His unapologetic revelling in mass murder appalled many people. Indeed, he was the model for the unhinged General Jack D. Ripper in Stanley Kubrick's *Dr Strangelove or: How I learned to Stop Worrying and Love the Bomb*. In the film, General Ripper destroyed the world; General LeMay only tried.

In contrast to LeMay, most of us believe that certain moral principles should be adhered to, even in wartime. We take it for granted that humanitarian principles are a good thing and that international prohibitions, which include laws and conventions relating to war, are there to safeguard innocent people from terror and atrocities. For some, humanitarianism is such a good thing that they seek to spread it to other nations at the point of the bayonet.

But we should not be overly confident in the goodness of law. No one is suggesting that declaring and conducting war should become a free-for-all, without constraints and prohibitions. *Jus ad bellum* (rules concerning the legitimacy of declaring war) and *jus*

in bello (what is allowable once war is under way) remain powerful concepts with applied as well as theoretical authority. Treaties
and conventions have succeeded in outlawing chemical and biological weapons; the manufacture, stockpiling and use of
antipersonnel landmines have been severely curtailed. Since 1945
there has not been another world war – although this is probably
due more to political and economic interdependency than any
scruples about adhering to *ad bellum* principles – and the Cold
War is over.

However, we would be like LeMay's 'stupid man' if we became
complacent. A major tension characterizes the legal regulation of
war and the development and adoption of humanitarian principles: both are part and parcel of the act of declaring and then
waging war. Affluent Western governments routinely appeal to
humanitarianism to justify military assaults on other nations.
Indeed, humanitarian wars have become the norm in modern
times. In 1998 legal scholar Michael N. Schmitt coined a term for
this new form of warfare: '*Bellum Americanum*', or conflicts initiated by high-tech military–industrial complexes and legitimized
using the languages of human rights and opposition to terrorism.[7] It is difficult to find a single example of armed intervention
carried out by the Americans, Europeans and their allies in the
past century that has not been justified on benevolent grounds.
The idea that humanitarian causes are, by definition, 'just' is
deeply engrained in modern political discourse. Kind-hearted
gunmen routinely boast that their hearts beat strongly with sym-
pathy for those they seek to maim and kill.[8]

There is another way to make this argument: law is a blessing
to militarists everywhere. Not only does it provide the symbols,
ideological justifications and rationale for violence, it also confers
international validation. As Chris af Jochnick and Roger Normand
of Harvard University remind us, the laws of war 'have facilitated
rather than restrained wartime violence. Through law, war has

been legitimated'.[9] But international law does more than merely shield perpetrators of violence from scrutiny: it actually bestows honour and esteem upon certain categories of perpetrators. Crucial to the ethos of international law is an underlying assumption that 'legal' or 'humanitarian' wars are somehow more humane. This is despite the fact that bullets and bombs launched by armed philanthropists cause as much pain and suffering as those wielded by the most vicious tyrant.

Even before Hugo Grotius' influential *De jure belli ac pacis* (*On the Laws of War and Peace*) was published in 1625, wars were conducted within legal constraints. There is a huge literature on its history, which I cannot summarize here. Others have done this much better than I could.[10]

Briefly, however, in the modern period the first codification of the law of war was the Lieber Code, which President Abraham Lincoln signed on behalf of the Union Army in April 1863. Rather crudely, Francis Lieber described his Code as 'short but pregnant', and 'weighing like some stumpy Dutch woman when in the family way with coming twins'.[11] Nevertheless, this 'stumpy' code did seek to curb a range of wartime practices. Less than a year later several European nations signed the First Geneva Convention, which was primarily concerned with protecting *hors de combat* (those no longer engaged in battle, such as the wounded) as well as military and religious personnel and civilians.

In 1868, international delegates at the St Petersburg Convention declared that 'civilized nations' had a duty to alleviate 'as much as possible the calamities of war'. As a consequence, 'the only legitimate object which States should endeavour to accomplish during war is to weaken the military forces of the enemy', and 'this object would be exceeded by the employment of arms which uselessly aggravate the sufferings of disabled men, or render their death inevitable'. Among other things, this

Convention banned explosive projectiles under 400 grams in weight. Britain signed the declaration (America had not been invited to attend because it was not considered a great nation at that time), thereby promising not to 'uselessly aggravate the sufferings' of men at war.

It took another twenty years for the next initiative. In May 1899, Tsar Nicholas II convened the First Peace Conference at The Hague with the aim of 'seeking the most effective means of ensuring to all peoples the benefits of a real and lasting peace, and, above all, of limiting the progressive development of existing armaments'. Twenty-six nations were represented, and agreement was reached on 29 July 1899, with the Convention coming into force on 4 September 1900. Along with prohibiting the use of asphyxiating, poisonous gases and the 'discharge of projectiles and explosives from balloons and other new analogous methods', the delegates sought to prohibit bullets that 'can easily expand their form inside the human body such as bullets with a hard covering which does not completely cover the core, or contain indentations'. They were referring to dum-dum bullets.

All these international treaties and conventions have severe limitations. The first set of problems associated with the laws of war are pragmatic: prohibitions are defined by state powers driven by political rather than humanitarian objectives, they are formulated in ambiguous ways and are often unthreatening to the armed services because they are obsolete from the moment they are imposed.

Obviously, the laws of war are a creation of powerful elites and they reflect the limitations that these elites are willing to accept. They privilege the military necessity of the great powers. For example, the Lieber Code did seek to curb certain atrocious practices but, in so doing, *explicitly* condoned other acts. These included starving civilians as well as bombarding towns, villages

and buildings without warning. Given that the Union Army practised these acts of violence, it is no wonder that James Seddon (the
Confederate Secretary of War) attacked the Code as actually legitimizing 'a barbarous system of warfare under the pretext of a
military necessity'. He claimed that it was

> in this code of military necessity that the acts of atrocity and
> violence which have been committed by the officers of the
> United States and have shocked the moral sense of civilized
> nations are to find an apology and defence.[12]

Similarly, the Hague Peace Conference was tainted by partisanship, and many of its decisions flouted in practice, because it was
believed that Tsar Nicholas II had called it largely with Russian
interests in mind (he was anxious about Russia's comparative military weakness in Europe). Count Munster, the head of the
German delegation, called the conference 'a political trick – the
most detestable ever practiced'.[13] So why did so many nations
even bother to send delegates? The answer was simple: it was
politically expedient to be seen to support peace. Delegates had
in any case been carefully schooled by their governments not to
accept any meaningful restrictions on their use of weapons.[14]

The starkest illustration of the partisan nature of international
laws of war emerged in the aftermath of the Second World War.
At the war crimes trials, the Allies were careful to ensure that
unrestrained submarine warfare and aerial bombardment were
not prosecuted as war crimes. Even the atrocious incendiary
bombing of Japan that had been carried out by LeMay's men and
the world-shattering atomic bombs that fell on Hiroshima and
Nagasaki were deemed lawful acts of war. They were 'militarily
necessary', a concept I will be interrogating further in the next
chapter. When Winston Churchill heard the news about the death
sentences passed on the Nazi leaders at Nuremberg he turned to

General Sir Hastings Ismay, his chief military assistant, and commented: 'Nuremberg shows that its supremely important to win. You and I would be in a pretty pickle if we had not.'[15]

This partisanship continues to vex debates. Whether at major international conferences or between representatives of individual states, debates about the legitimacy of certain weapons have always appealed to local interests and priorities. This is why it was so easy with the declaration of war in 1939 for all states to ignore Article 25 of the 1907 Hague Regulations, which prohibited the 'attack or bombardment, by whatever means, of towns, villages, dwellings, or buildings which are undefended' and to violate the 1938 League of Nations' resolution on aerial bombardment. It was simply in their interests to do so. It is hard to disagree with the author of *Aerial Bombardment and the International Regulation of Warfare* (1928) when he concluded that 'a weapon will be restricted in inverse proportion . . . to its effectiveness . . . the more efficient a weapon or method of warfare, the less likely there is of its being restricted in action by rules of war'.[16] And, notwithstanding panics about terrorists wielding bolt-cutters or hiding explosives inside shoes, the most 'effective' weapons are those wielded by nations with powerful military arsenals.

Not surprisingly, states that cannot afford the technological wizardry available to more advanced nations are rather sceptical about initiatives to regulate the use of particular weapons. From their point of view, the vast chasm between what high-tech states can use to cause mayhem and what the technological 'have-nots' can employ is asymmetrical. Humanitarian law is very kind to sophisticated, Western military forces: it comes down hard and unremittingly on 'murder by machete' yet turns a benign face to mass murder by atomic bomb or targeted assassinations by drones. On those occasions when some restraint in the use of weapons can be agreed — against the use of antipersonnel landmines, for instance — it turns out that they represent relatively cheap technologies which hamper less technologically advanced militaries much more than those operating at a high-tech level. This is why international conventions such as the 1980 United Nations Convention on Prohibitions or Restrictions on the Use of Certain Conventional Weapons and the 1997 Convention of the Prohibition of Anti-Personnel Mines have been accused of being 'low-cost laws' for states that have access to high-tech weaponry. As one international relations expert observed, 'contemporary laws of war *are* humanitarian at the low-tech end, and have been crucial in condemning atrocities . . . associated with ethnic and other civil conflicts'. He went on to warn, however, that 'if high-tech violence is shielded from prosecution, this may sap the moral force of the law'.[17]

Legal irrelevance is another pragmatic technique for shrouding violence in a mantle of legitimacy. Prohibitions against particular weapons always lag behind technological developments, making it foolish to take too seriously. According to the author of *Constraints on the Waging of War* (1987), there is no evidence of any state abandoning a weapon because of the 1868 St Petersburg ban on causing 'unnecessary suffering'.[18] When the St Petersburg Declaration prohibited explosive bullets weighing less than 400 grams (a weight decided upon for practical rather than public-spirited reasons), these weapons were already obsolete and unpopular. Similarly, the 1899 Hague Convention restricted the use of asphyxiating shells, although such shells had never been used in war, and balloon-launched munitions (which had proved useless in combat and were about to be superseded by motorized aircraft anyway). Even the Convention's ban on dum-dum or semi-jacketed bullets was redundant, since it prohibited a very specific bullet that was already being replaced by a 'superior' one. This was the round-nose, hollow-point bullet or .202 Mark III, modified as the Mark VII in 1910, just in time for the First

World War. In other words, in 1907, when Britain very reluctantly agreed to adhere to the Hague Declaration, the country was developing new projectiles as devastating as the dum-dum but which stuck to the 'letter but not the spirit' of the law. The Mark VII seemed to be fully jacketed but, in reality, its front third was filled with aluminium and wood pulp, which meant that it still 'tumbled' inside the body. Another reason made the prohibition on dum-dum bullets rapidly redundant: between 1899 and 1914 the velocity of bullets increased from 2000 feet per second to 4000. While the so-called 'explosive' effects of missiles were uncommon at velocities of less than 2000 feet per second, they were extremely common at muzzle velocities above 2500 feet per second. The injuries such weapons inflicted were terrifying. There was no need for dum-dums.

The author of 'The Text-Book for Military Small Arms and Ammunition' (1899) linked arguments about weapon redundancy with those about moral repugnance. He maintained that *all* weapons were viewed as morally repugnant when they were first utilized. Even stone-throwing must have been regarded as an innovation when it was introduced in mortal combat, he noted, and using crossbows against Christian foe had originally been sternly condemned. Most new weapons were 'denounced as cowardly, brutal, and inhuman' until the 'advantages became recognized and its science was practised'.[19] The same was true of the dum-dum bullet, projectiles under 400 grams in weight and so on. By signing these protocols, states could claim to be restricting their use of abhorrent weapons while actually carrying on as normal.

The historical specificity of weapon technology was crucial to these arguments: armies possess much worse weapons than those that had been banned, so appealing to prohibitions was foolhardy. In the words of a 1977 report,

No one has paid much attention to the dum-dum ammunition issue in recent years when the use of claymore mines, fragmentation grenades, antipersonnel bombs, flame-throwers, and many other far more devastating warfare weapons than expanding bullets have been in common use.[20]

As one FBI agent scoffed, the fact that submarines and firing from balloons were prohibited in 1899 and 1907 'would be a shallow justification for dismantling our air and submarine forces on whose might the safety of the free world has relied since World War Two'.[21]

Imprecision of the law of war is the third pragmatic way in which they undercut their own moral authority. A British officer laconically observed when commenting on the widespread killing of wounded Japanese: 'There are many grey areas around the Geneva Convention, I suppose.'[22]

Restrictions were so vaguely or broadly defined that almost any military practice could be deemed lawful. For instance, Articles 22 and 23 of the 1907 Convention ruled that 'the right of belligerents to adopt means of injuring the enemy are not unlimited' and militaries must not use 'arms, projectiles, or material of a nature to cause superfluous injury'. However, neither 'unlimited means' nor 'superfluous injury' was defined. The rules were innately ineffective; governments and militaries unaccountable. 'Military necessity' was allowed to trump all legal constraints. Because 'necessity' was never defined, its meaning was completely at the discretion of military strategists or commanders. And, from their point of view, everything was necessary for victory.

Finally, and before I turn to more fundamental problems with the laws of war, it is interesting to note that these three pragmatic problems – the fact that they are biased, redundant and ill- or un-defined – are accepted by both militarists and anti-militarists. Proponents and opponents of the laws of war share these critiques, but they draw different conclusions. The pro-war faction criticize the law to claim that in military affairs 'anything goes'. They echo LeMay's contention that 'To worry about the *morality* of what we were doing – Nuts.'[23] For humanitarian commentators, practical problems associated with the laws of war signal an urgent need for reform: we need more and better rules.

This leads to the second way in which legal regulation and wartime violence are symbiotic: the codification of the laws of war has created the category of 'humanitarian' war, or legal war, which legitimates and facilitates violence.

This has two aspects. The first, and most basic, is that the laws of war provide a language to authorize violence against civilians. This was what General Norman Schwarzkopf was appealing to during the Gulf War when he said,

> I think that the very actions [of] the Iraqis themselves demonstrate that they know damn well that we're not attacking civilian targets . . . Since right now they've dispersed their airplanes into residential areas, they've moved their headquarters into schools . . . They've put guns and things like that on top of high-rise apartment buildings. Under the Geneva Conventions, that gives us a perfect right to go after those things if we want to.[24]

It is a subtle legitimation of wartime killing. The laws of war authorize killing the enemy, even if to do so kills schoolchildren. Their deaths are the fault of the 'insurgents', not us.

Military commanders are not the only people recognizing the usefulness of the law. Weapons researchers also routinely appeal to humanitarian laws when making their case for increased resources. This was exactly what ballistic experts at Porton Down were encouraged to argue in 1975. During a press briefing, they were asked how they would respond if a journalist wanted to know how they would 'justify spending money on a new facility [for weapons research] in these times of acute financial stringency in the defence field'. The correct answer included their 'obligation to look at the effects of weapons under development to enable effective participation in ICRC [International Committee of the Red Cross] activities'.[25] In other words, arguments for boosting resources to develop offensive weapons were predicated on the need to adhere to humanitarian precepts. The slip from offensive to defensive was seamless.

The rhetoric associated with the laws of war does more than simply provide a way to justify bombing civilians and conducting weapons research. It encourages the incorporation of new technologies and techniques of inflicting pain and suffering. For example, when international delegates met at the Second Peace Conference at The Hague in 1907, they were aware that developments in aircraft design meant that future military commanders would inevitably authorize aerial bombardment. They could have chosen to bring air warfare under the existing (1899) ban on balloon-launched munitions. Instead, the delegates subsumed it under Article 25, which applied to attacks by land and sea. In this way, aerial bombardment was '"legalized" without being restrained'.[26] This decision was important because Article 25 only prohibited attacks on 'towns, villages, dwellings or buildings which are *undefended*'. Any town, village or dwelling that was 'defended' — often merely by the presence of a military objective — became fair game.

The incorporation, rather than resistance, of violence was also at the heart of attempts made in 1899 by British and American representatives to foil international calls to outlaw dum-dum bullets on the grounds of their obvious cruelty. It was 'false humanity to allow our own men to be killed rather than take means to effectually [sic] prevent this by disabling the enemy', noted the Director-General of the Indian Medical Service. Bizarrely, British spokesmen contended that using dum-dum bullets was actually a humanitarian act. This was the view of Surgeon-Major-General J. B. Hamilton. He explained that

> If the Dum-dum bullet be used, it, as a rule, will injure but one man, as when 'set up', its power of penetration rapidly ceases; if, on the other hand, a projectile entirely covered with nickel be employed, it will possibly pass through two or three men, and gradually 'setting up', inflict greater injuries on a fourth.[27]

Anyway, weren't there worse ways to kill people? Hamilton observed that an admiral in command of a fleet would never 'hesitate to "ram" a battleship or blow her up with a torpedo, destroying perhaps 800 men in the operation'. Indeed, such an admiral would 'gain renown for the action; but if our War Office uses a projectile calculated to "stop" individuals, it is condemned as "inhumane"!' 'War cannot be made with rose-water,' he cried.[28]

Hamilton engaged in a popular pastime among militarists: the calibration of pain. Were the wounds inflicted by dum-dum bullets actually more agonizing than those caused by the Snide or Martini-Henry?[29] Was it more terrible to be burnt alive by napalm than by conventional fire? Was drowning worse than dismemberment? Indeed, everyone from ballistics experts to popular journalists routinely engage in these 'comparative cruelty' debates. The arguments generally follow the logic of a man writing to the official journal of the National Rifle Association in 1922. If flamethrowers and poisonous gases are 'dirty and devilish inventions of obscene minds,' he asked, does this mean that

rifles are 'a goodly weapon'?[30] Similarly, in 1963 the *Daily Mail*
admitted that flechettes (darts the diameter of a pencil and just
over an inch long) caused 'gaping wounds as big as [the] dum-dum
bullets outlawed by the Geneva Convention'. Nevertheless, it
reassured readers that, 'however deadly', they were 'no more
horrible than napalm, a flame thrower or any of the nuclear
weapons'.[31] It was certainly setting the bar high if a weapon had
to be rated as worse than a nuclear bomb to be classed as
abhorrent.

Such reasoning enabled commentators on the laws of war to
repeat LeMay's mantra: a short, 'vigorous' war is a 'humanitarian' one. Not surprisingly, this was LeMay's view about the
atomic bombs that devastated Hiroshima and Nagasaki. He lam-
basted those 'moon-calves' and 'beatniks' who 'would have you
convinced that a big bang is far wickeder than a little bang. I suppose they believe also that a machine gun is a hundred times
wickeder than a bow and arrow'. On the contrary, he argued that
'There was no transgression, no venturing into a field illicit and
immoral' and reminded his readers that 'soldiers were ordered
to do a job. They did it.' Men like LeMay were 'in the bombardment business' and 'just weren't bothered about the morality of
the question'.[32]

It was a refrain heard throughout the centuries. In fact, it was
also the view of Francis Lieber, who insisted that 'the more vig-
orously wars are pursued, the better it is for humanity. Sharp
wars are best'.[33] Elbridge Colby (a prolific commentator on the
laws of war) agreed. In 1925, he argued that an effective officer
should steep himself in military history in order to

> guard . . . against excessive humanitarian notions. It will teach
> him that certain severities are indispensible for war, nay more,
> that the only true humanity lies in a ruthless application of
> them.[34]

Such comments are based on a narrow, legalistic definition of what constitutes 'humane' – a definition embedded in international law and abstracted from the suffering of real human beings.

Finally, by delineating categories of 'illegitimate violence', the rules and regulations of war implicitly and explicitly construct what is legitimate violence. I have already alluded to this in the context of the St Petersburg Declaration of 1868 which, by creating the category of 'unnecessary suffering', allowed for 'necessary suffering' in the name of 'military necessity'. It was also at the centre of arguments by leading lawyers such as W. Hays Parks, Special Assistant for Law of War Matters at the Office of the Judge Advocate General, US Army, when he sought to justify the use of shotguns in war. He was addressing accusations that the bullets used in shotguns expanded or flattened easily when hitting a person and thus were in violation of the 1899 Hague Declaration Concerning Expanding Bullets. Parks defended shotguns in his usual serene, sanguine style. Did the lead-and-antimony buckshot deform on hitting a person? Yes, but not to worry: the

> prohibition in the 1899 Hague Declaration on projectiles that 'flatten or deform easily' constitutes an acknowledgment of the inevitability of some deformation, and it does not prohibit projectiles that may deform mildly in limited circumstances.[35]

This is casuistry in an extreme form: who is to say when 'easy' is 'too easy'? Despite continued political opposition to America's use of shotguns,[36] they were employed by the US Marines and Special Forces in Iraq and Afghanistan on the grounds that the 'characteristic spray of six to sixty pellets with a single trigger squeeze . . . makes it idea for the narrow confines of a cave'.[37]

The codification of suffering goes much deeper than these debates about specific weapons, however. The ICRC has, for instance, made a principled attempt to formalize the category of 'superfluous injury or unnecessary suffering'. The most active person in this formulation is the indefatigable humanitarian advocate Robin M. Coupland.

Coupland trained as a surgeon in Britain, then between 1987 and 1991 he volunteered to work in Red Cross hospitals on the borders of Afghanistan and Cambodia, dealing with the devastating wounds inflicted by antipersonnel mines. It was a traumatic experience. In his words,

> I simply found myself dreading the radio call announcing that another mine-injured person was on his or her way to hospital. The dread was generated by the knowledge that my team would be faced with a long and difficult operation which entailed excising large amounts of damaged tissue or amputating a limb. This quickly turned into abhorrence for the weapons which caused such injury as a function of their design.

Coupland was familiar with injuries caused by bullets or fragmentation munitions, but mines created wounds that were significantly worse. 'This was the first time I heard of "superfluous injury or unnecessary suffering",' he recalled, adding, 'Nobody could tell me what it was, but I was sure I had seen it caused by antipersonnel mines.'[38] Coupland's epiphany convinced him that he had a duty to use his professional expertise to become an advocate for a ban on mines. His emphasis shifted from treatment to prevention.[39] The first step was to interrogate why some weapons were deemed legitimate, while others were legally objectionable. Previous campaigns seeking to relegate antipersonnel mines to the 'unlawful' category had focused on their indiscriminate nature. Scattered over wide swathes of land, these mines routinely maimed and killed civilians.

There was, however, another way in which people could judge the legality or otherwise of a weapon: what if a weapon was assessed according to whether its 'nature or technology could be proved to be excessive compared to the military advantage gained from its use'?[40] In fact, this had been the rationale behind the prohibition of explosive bullets by delegates at the St Petersburg Commission in 1868, dum-dum bullets at the 1899 Geneva Conference, and poison gas at the Geneva Conference in 1925. What none of these conventions had done, however, was give governments – let alone military or legal advisers – a useable definition of what might constitute 'superfluous injury or unnecessary suffering'. Coupland recognized that war surgeons could translate the terrible wounds they were seeing near battlefields into a codified language that could be applied legally.

Coupland and others set about to devise an 'objective' way of judging injury. The result was the ICRC Wound Classification System, a radical departure because it classified *wounds*, rather than *weapons*. The classification involved measuring the size (in centimetres) of the entry and exit injury, and asking whether there was a visible cavity (judged according to whether the cavity could 'take two fingers before surgery'); whether there was a fracture (the options are: 'no', 'simple' or 'significant comminution'); whether a vital structure was injured; and whether a metallic body was present in an X-ray.[41] This EXCFVM checklist – Entry, eXit, Cavity, Fracture, Vital structure, and Metallic body – allowed for quick and easy numerical scoring. If there were multiple wounds, only the two most serious were scored.

Once the wounds had been scored, the sum was categorized in one of three grades. Coupland explains:

> Grade 1 wounds have laceration only or 'low energy transfer' wounds: they include tangential skin wounds. Grade 2 wounds are those expected from modern assault rifles or 'high energy transfer' missiles. Grade 3 wounds have massive tissue destruction as expected by the use of deforming or frag-menting bullets.[42]

The project was developed further during The Medical Profession and the Effects of Weapons, an ICRC symposium at Montreux, Switzerland, in March 1996. Called the SIrUS (Superfluous Injury or Unnecessary Suffering) Project, it collected data from more than 26,600 victims injured during armed conflicts throughout the world in an attempt to quantify mortality and permanent injury rates from different types of wounds. Relevant criteria included the number of large wounds, operations and blood trans-fusions, as well as how long the patient stayed in hospital and the extent of any permanent disability.[45] To qualify for the dishonour of causing 'superfluous injury or unnecessary suffering', a weapon had to lead to a specific disease or abnormal physiological or psy-chological state, permanent disability or disfigurement, field mortality of more than 25 per cent or hospital mortality of more than 5 per cent, a Grade Three wound as measured by the Wound Classification Scale, or produce effects for which there was no beneficial treatment.[46] Coupland pleaded with individual physi-cians and medical organizations to write to the ICRC in support of SIrUS. Endorsement, he wrote, was 'an attempt at preventive medicine in the domain of weapons'.[47]

Although no one questions the honourable intentions of the creators of the Wound Classification System and SIrUS (and I hold them in very high regard), they have their critics. As already

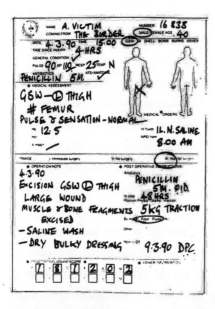

Figure 3.1. The ICRC's Wound Classification Scoring System. Original caption: 'An example of the admission sheet used in International Committee of the Red Cross hospitals. The wound score is at the bottom.' This patient's wound can be seen in Figure 3.2.[43]

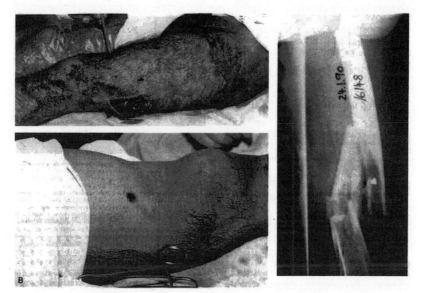

Figure 3.2. The ICRC's Wound Classification Scoring System. Original Caption: 'A. Bullet wound (exit) of the left thigh. The entry is indicated by the pencil. B. The thigh prepared for surgery showing the small entry wound on the anteromedial [in front and middle] aspect. C. Radiograph of the patient's thigh. The fracture and metal fragments are seen. The score for this patient is: E1, X8, C1, F2, V0, M2 (grade 2, type F).'[44]

mentioned, the chief problem is that codification practices serve a political function in their justification of maiming and killing. The classification is explicitly intended to be comparative: it is a means for judging whether a particular weapon should be placed beyond the pale – *or not*. Indeed, proponents of SIrUS argue that conventional weapons would not violate the criteria for 'superfluous injury or unnecessary suffering'. In other words, both the Wound Classification System and SIrUS establish a hierarchy in which certain ways of maiming and killing people are acceptable. They reproduce an ethic willing to minimize certain harms. Like the Red Cross generally, they assume that war is inevitable and that the aim should be to *reduce* rather than *eradicate* violence against people. The first sentence of an article on the Wound Classification System states that the 'use of weapons by human beings to inflict physical harm on each other is an integral part of our heritage, and likely predates the development of speech'.[48] By making certain weapons more abhorrent than others, it legitimates the use of those weapons that, from the victims' point of view, may not be less terrifying and painful. Indeed, fighting a war that adheres to protocols for preventing 'superfluous injury or unnecessary suffering' might even encourage armed conflict by lowering the bar for starting a war in the first place.

This is the most serious problem with the Wound Classification System and the SIrUS Project. There are more. Criteria concerning hospital mortality, for instance, were derived from data sustained in wars over the past fifty years and do not take account of the effects of contemporary technologically sophisticated armaments. It accepts the forms of killing available to militarily advanced nations (with access to 'precision weapons', for instance) as opposed to less heavily endowed ones. Some critics also point out that SIrUS should rule out the use of sniper fire because of its high mortality, yet accurate sniper fire kills a person quickly and relatively painlessly.[49]

In addition, SIrUS says nothing about 'military necessity'. States may inflict 'necessary suffering' on a people out of malice while remaining within SIrUS's bounds.[50] It also implies that once the design of a specific weapon is known, the effect it has on victims can be accurately assessed. This is not the case, since a vast amount of evidence shows that there is not necessarily a connection between the type of wound inflicted and the degree of suffering experienced.[51] In other words, SIrUS and the Wound Classification System may underestimate the emotional and psychological components of suffering.

Finally, Red Cross officials insist that the aim of both evaluative methods is simply to 'provide a rational and science-based reference point for discussions on the legality of weapons and to provide an objective element in the debate'.[52] But is this the appropriate way to look at the suffering body? Aren't all the wounds in these databases superfluous and unnecessary? What actually is being judged? Is a wound 'superfluous or unnecessary' in relation to what? Who is to decide what is 'necessary', and to whom?

I agree with these critiques. I do not, however, accept the strong objections to SIrUS that have been raised by military personnel. Some of these commentators reject *any* attempt by *any* international body to restrict their ability to wage war, a position that can be summarized by looking at an article published in the *Air Force Law Review* in 2001. Written by Major Donna Marie Verchio (a judge advocate with the US Air Force, but at the time she was writing on assignment as a legal adviser at the Information Operations Technology Center of the National Security Agency), it is a furious attack on what she regarded as the anti-American bias of the project. Verchio argues that because the quality of hospital care strongly affects mortality rates, SIrUS has 'perverse implications with regard to a weapon's legality'. In effect, 'the legitimacy of one side's weaponry would be tied to the medical expertise of its enemy'. It 'contemplates legality based on a race between weapon technology and medical technology', but by failing to 'specify a baseline for medical facilities . . . it could be used by one party to seek a perverse advantage'.[53] Furthermore, Verchio writes, the project misunderstands the role and duty of military commanders, which is to win. SIrUS displays 'ignorance, or intentional disregard' of the crucial fact that 'the law of war entitles a military commander to bring maximum power to bear on an enemy force'.

However, her main attack on SIrUS emphasizes the power of governments to wage war in whatever way they choose. 'Governments, not the ICRC bear the responsibility for self-defense and maintaining world order,' she insists, and this means that 'governments, not the ICRC, have the responsibility for determining what weapons are lawful'.[54] I will return to her argument at the end of this chapter: it encapsulates militaristic dogma at its most triumphant.

Robin M. Coupland is aware of the criticisms from anti-militarists and their opponents, but remains committed to his attempt to 'make a difference'. For him, it is 'irresponsible' for physicians and surgeons to enter war zones to treat the wounded and then simply shrug and say, 'Yeah, I've done my job.'[55] He is right.

One of the outcomes of the work of people like Coupland was the Ottawa Treaty of 1998, officially known as the Convention on the Prohibition of the Use, Stockpiling, Production, and Transfer of Anti-Personnel Mines and on their Destruction. This was a major achievement, even though it has not been signed by the United States, Russia, China, Myanmar (Burma), United Arab Emirates, Cuba, Egypt, India, Israel or Iran. Nonetheless, Coupland would agree with me that a great deal of work remains to be done. He argues that 'the effects on human beings of weapons commonly used by armies now are bad enough, and that if possible, anything worse should be prevented'. Nevertheless, his position is not pacifist and he is committed to not being 'antimilitary'.[56] My respect for Coupland and other physicians, surgeons and officials working tirelessly to limit rather than eradicate weapons is immense. But they simply don't go far enough.

It is fair to ask critics of international law whether wartime violence would be worse without the regulations. Some scholars suggest that it wouldn't make much of a difference. After all, international laws have not been effective in protecting civilians or others in times of war. In 2006, three legal scholars – Benjamin Valentino, Paul Huth and Sarah Croco – created a database of all interstate wars between 1900 and 2003. They found that there was 'no evidence that signatories of international treaties on the laws of war are significantly less likely to kill civilians in war than are nonsignatories'. Indeed, they concluded, strategic concerns easily overweighed any perceived need – morally or otherwise – to adhere to law.[57]

Their findings were similar to those of Oona Hathaway in 'Do Human Rights Treaties Make a Difference?' (2002). She amassed a database of 166 nations and explored their record over a forty-year period in terms of human rights laws associated with genocide, torture, fair and public trials, civil liberties and the political representation of women. Her results? 'Treaty ratification is not infrequently associated with worse human rights ratings than otherwise expected.' In the cautious, legal prose common to the *Yale Law Journal*, Hathaway concluded that

Given that I have not found a single treaty for which ratification seems to be reliably associated with better human rights practices and several for which it appears to be associated with worse practices, it would be premature to dismiss the

possibility that human rights treaties may sometimes lead to
poorer human rights practices within the countries that ratify
them.[58]

So why do states even bother to sign treaties and conventions?
Given the huge external pressure to adhere to human rights
norms, the symbolic nature of signing is important. Since the
process of monitoring and enforcing the treaties are minimal
(making the costs of actually putting the agreements into practice
very low), signing gives signatory countries a position and a moral
standing on the world stage. This is not a concern for the US,
which may be one reason why they are one of the world's least
compliant nations. But for less powerful countries – and particularly those with poor humanitarian records – signing helps
appease critics.[59]

Concerns about the function of law during international conflicts should make us aware of the role that lawyers increasingly
play in decisions about whether or not to use military force (*jus
ad bellum*) and about the conduct of armed conflict once underway (*jus in bello*). In this chapter, my interest has been the
second category – *jus in bello*. In this, I am (regrettably) following a trend that has become more pronounced since the end of
the Cold War. With the exception of the recent furore over
alleged weapons of mass destruction, less emphasis has been
placed on the legitimacy of *declaring* war – the US's technological and political power means that they dominate that field –
and more on the *conduct* of armed forces during conflicts. Of
course, the latter has much more serious repercussions for small
states than for large ones. In other words, regulating conduct
within war has become more prominent than the wrongs of
engaging in state-legitimated violence in the first place. This
emphasis should concern us.

At the same time, military lawyers have increasingly claimed a major stake in decisions about the legitimacy (or otherwise) of particular weapons and tactics. Protests over American warmongering in Vietnam – and, in particular, the international outcry over the use of napalm, the atrocity in My Lai in March 1968 and other innumerable acts of exceptional violence and cruelty – delivered a powerful punch to the self-confidence and prestige of the US armed forces. In an attempt to reverse this, some commentators began to ask whether international law could be a constructive, as opposed to constraining, tool in their arsenal of response. In 1971 the Red Cross Experts' Conference mooted an idea for increasing the role of military lawyers, a suggestion that was echoed at the Government Experts' Conference of 1972.[60] In 1983, the US Joint Chiefs of Staff issued a memorandum greatly expanding the role of military lawyers from merely disseminating information to reviewing all operational and contingency plans, as well as rules of engagement. Lawyers were to vet every stage of military operations. In the words of a 1999 Instruction issued by the Joint Chiefs of Staff,

> all operation plans . . . concept plans, rules of engagement, executive orders, deployment orders, policies, and directives are [to be] reviewed by the command legal advisers to ensure compliance with domestic and international law.[61]

Modern Western powers turned war into a legal institution.

There were some dissenting views, most notably Defense Secretary Donald H. Rumsfeld, who claimed that lawyers were 'like beavers – they get in the middle of the stream and dam it up'.[62] Initially at least, lawyers frequently claimed that military commanders were rather disdainful of them. This was what struck W. Hays Parks, General Counsel of the US Department of Defense during the war in Vietnam:

> Frankly, any time I'd tell a group [of officers] that I wanted to
> talk about the Law of War, I'd get a groan . . . The attitude
> was, this is going to be somewhere between a lecture on
> check cashing and one on VD. So I tried changing it. I'd say,
> we're going to talk about law affecting military operations.
> From there, we shortened it to operational law.[63]

Comparing wartime atrocities with cheque fraud and venereal
diseases was not an auspicious beginning. In addition, questions
were raised whether International Law applied *at all* to the preeminent world power. In the words of John Norton Moore in
'Law and National Security' (1973), 'The question is not whether
international law will be controlling, but the more modest one of
whether it will be taken into account'.[64] A lively debate continues
about whether the US President is even subjected to international law (although all other leaders of states are).[65]

Nevertheless, senior military officers increasingly recognized
that law could do much more than merely present an ethically
acceptable face to the international community: it could actually
be a strategic asset. It is characteristic that the role of the Judge
Advocate General's Corps was defined in terms of finding legal
ways to achieve the goals of their 'clients', that is, military commanders and their political masters. As Thomas W. Smith argues
in 'The New Law of War' (2002), the Corps' task 'shifted visibly
from restraining violence to legitimizing it'.[66]

The Gulf War of 1990–1 is often regarded as decisive in this
regard. During that conflict, the US forces employed around 430
lawyers.[67] These advisers were active at every level: they
instructed individual soldiers, sailors and marines on legal issues,
advised commanding officers about targets and weapons use, and
were present and commented on decisions made at the headquarters of the Central Command.[68] As a consequence, the US
Department of Defense was able to boast to Congress that

Coalition forces had 'scrupulously adhered to fundamental law of war proscriptions' and had conducted 'the most discriminate military campaign in history'.[69]

By taking such a prominent role, the laws of war inevitably highlighted tensions between military commanders and civilian advisers, which could only be resolved by more fully integrating lawyers within military systems and by carefully negotiating their exact role and rank. Lawyers were gruffly informed that they were not military ombudsmen.[70] As Captain Matthew E. Winter of the Judge Advocate General's Corps explained in 1990, lawyers needed to 'convince commanders and staff members' that they were 'a force multiplier and can assist in the accomplishment of the mission'.[71] Colonel Wayne Elliott, chief of the International Law Division at the Judge Advocate General's (JAG) School in Charlottesville, Virginia, issued a similar edict. 'Every decision a commander makes can be made legally or illegally,' he noted, 'and it's the lawyer's job to help him make it legally and to give him options, all of which are legal.'[72] Or, as the author of 'Lawyers in the War Room' (1991) admitted more bluntly, Commanding Officers understand that 'as in the relationship of a corporate counsel to CEO, the JAG's role is not to create obstacles, but to find legal ways to achieve his client's goals – even when those goals are to blow things up and kill people'.[73]

The role of lawyers is not simply to legitimize pre-existing decisions about armed violence. They are expected to be proactive in proposing ways of acting violently in war. A 'Memorandum of the Joint Chiefs of Staff' (1983) told them to 'address not only the legal *restrictions* upon operations but also legal *rights* to employ force'.[74] They are encouraged to tell commanders that it is 'okay to do something the commanders had assumed was illegal'.[75] By way of explanation, Colonel Robert Bridges, chief of the International and Operations Law Division of the US Air Force, conjured up a scenario during which commanders assumed that – in order to prevent the deaths of civilians – they would need to order pilots to drop a type of bomb that would require them to fly at a low altitude. Unfortunately (for the pilots, that is, not the people beneath the bombs), 'That would have made pilots unnecessarily vulnerable.' Bridges believed that this was legally unnecessary. 'We had to tell them that they can take a more liberal approach,' he noted, adding:

> Yes, the Law of War requires that you spare the civilian pop-
> ulation as much as possible from suffering, but you can't
> guarantee that no one will be killed.

Such advice, 'probably won some friends [with commanding offi-cers] and saved some lives on our side', he blandly noted.[76]

Embedding lawyers within the military inevitably facilitated the process of cooptation. It certainly encouraged them to adopt the goals and ideology of their taskmasters. Colonel Gerald Draper argued in 'Role of Legal Advisers in Armed Forces' (1978) that military advisers were required to be 'fully conversant in the language and modes of thinking of military planners and with the latest technological developments in weaponry systems, their use and deployment'.[77] The author of 'Lawyers in the War Room' (1991) put it more strongly, pointing out that

> Without an understanding of what soldiers do, operational
> lawyers will tell you, a headful of legal knowledge doesn't
> count for much. In an effort to arrive at that understanding,
> operational lawyers have been known to jump out of air-
> planes, learn to drive tanks, and accompany special operations
> units on dangerous missions.[78]

Occasionally, lawyers might be required to perform the role of speakers of conscience, in order to 'bring a new and forgotten perspective to the decisionmaking process'. However, a senior member of the Judge Advocate General's Corps warned, 'It must be sparingly used . . . and care must be taken to avoid appearing as an unrealistic and out-of-touch obstructionist'.[79]

As with embedded journalists and physicians, lawyers interacting with junior and senior officers rapidly slid from cooperation into cooptation. Rank would have made it difficult to do otherwise. How could a relatively junior, militarily 'green' lawyer do anything except defer to the judgement of a seasoned combat commander?[80] In addition, once a military decision had been made about the legality of an operation or weapon, lawyers were not only *expected*, but also legally *required* to acquiesce. In the words of the author of '"Finding the Law" – The Values, Identity and Function of the International Law Advisor' (1990), 'candor and objectivity are crucial during the decisionmaking process', but for 'foreign policy reasons' it was 'essential that the Legal Adviser support decisions once they are made'. It turns out that 'loyalty becomes the critical factor' for embedded lawyers.[81]

To illustrate the precise role played by the various parties – not only lawyers and senior military officers, but also civilians in the Defense and State Departments – we can turn to the debates around the legality of napalm and cluster bombs during the war in Vietnam. No one questions the fact that both of these weapons are indiscriminate, inflict horrific injuries and cause unimaginable suffering on civilians as well as combatants. Napalm, for instance, sticks to skin and tissue, burning at incredibly high temperatures. It burns 'skin to a crisp . . . like fried potato chips' explained one marine pilot, adding that 'Men begged to be shot. [But] I couldn't.[82] The impact of cluster munitions is scarcely less sickening, as multiple projectiles slice through body parts.

How was it, then, that napalm was (only initially, unfortunately) subjected to restrictions while the use of cluster bombs was rarely even questioned? According to security analyst Michael Krepon, the answer lies in the tug of war between civilians in governmental departments and the Chiefs of Staff. This tension was palpable when it came to the use of napalm. The Pentagon was keen that napalm be authorized for air operations, especially after US forces became 'directly engaged' in Laos and then North Vietnam in 1964 and 1965. In contrast, officials in the State and Defense Departments opposed its use, not on the grounds of its 'inhumanity' but because they feared an international backlash. In his typically understated way, Krepon noted that this 'political argument was extremely frustrating to the Joint Chiefs'. Between 1961 and 1964, therefore, napalm could only be used in certain circumstances, including 'search and rescue operations, for Vietnamese forces flying under American tutelage, and for specified operations in Laos'. It was only after the escalation of the war in March 1965, and strenuous lobbying of the President by the Chiefs of Staff, that these restrictions were lifted.[83]

This battle of wills between civilian and military authorities had a major influence on the response of the Chief of Staffs to the development of the new, highly deadly cluster bomb, the CBU-24. Each of these bombs fling out 665 fist-sized fragmentation bombs with a time-delay function, rendering the area lethal for a period after the attack and therefore impeding the recovery of casualties.[84] Crucially, CBU-24s were able to saturate a significantly wider area than their predecessors. A single CBU-24 could disperse fragments liable to wound and kill at a range of 300 by 900 metres. In the words of Krepon, 'the area coverage remains extraordinary, bearing in mind that the ordnance package for a single F4 Phantom can include eight CBUs or, with special racks, as many as 15 to 20'.[85] 'Given this wide area of use,' Krepon chillingly observed, one can say with assurance that a weapon with a damage radius of several square kilometers must have caused extensive civilian casualties, and in a high ratio to the military damage it unquestionably inflicted on its intended targets.[86]

So why was no political fuss made about the use of CBU-24s? There were two reasons. First, the armed forces chose not to have the weapon formally classified in the first place. If they had done so, civilians would have been involved in the process, inviting 'some discussion of the political consequences of deploying a weapon that was not only far more effective than any previous ones, but also far more likely to cause civilian casualties'.

Second, the Joint Chiefs never made a formal request to any political authority to use the bombs. According to Vice Admiral Lloyd Mustin (Director of Operations for the Joint Chiefs of Staff),

> In our view, they [CBU-24s] were a purely conventional weapon, and we regarded them as available, and the less said, the better. Somebody somewhere would want to raise the argument, 'Well, do we or don't we want to authorize the use of this weapon?' . . . We in J-3 [Directorate for Operations] had ways of exchanging information with our subordinate echelons all the way out to pilots on the line, and we just said, 'As far as we know, that's authorized to you, you've got 'em, use 'em when you want, and keep your mouth shut, or somebody will tell you that you can't.'[87]

In other words, the Pentagon downplayed the use of cluster bombs in order to avoid what they regarded as the unnecessary political interference that had occurred with napalm. As a result, CBUs were 'categorized and explained as a standard weapon' that could be 'taken off the shelf' when needed. As Mustin admitted, the bombs were treated as if they were simply 'conventional iron-mongery'. They were described as another 'flak suppression ordnance, demonstrably effective in protecting the lives of US pilots'. As such, 'how could civilian channels argue against them?'[88] The policy was 'don't ask, don't tell'. The Pentagon and senior military officers didn't volunteer information; political representatives and civil servants never enquired too deeply. Indeed, Krepon observed, 'at least one senior civilian official had the impression that the weapon was merely a more decisive way to use fragmentation – with no idea of the very wide effective range involved'.[89]

By the time the use of CBU-24s was noticed, it was too late – at least from a strictly political standpoint. When questions arose, there were significant numbers of American troops on the ground in Vietnam and the American's tactical operations did not seem to be working. Military imperatives trumped political judgements and, given that cluster bombs were 'cost-effective', financial arguments against their use were easily swatted away. As a consequence, 'civilian input on CBUs related mostly to the question of revealing or not revealing the weapons in question'.[90] By 1973, an estimated 29 per cent of the Air Force's ordnance procurement budge was being spent on various types of cluster bombs.[91] As one senior Pentagon official noted, this terrifying and indiscriminate weapon quickly became 'the darling of the aviators'.[92]

In the twenty-first century, the outstanding technical elasticity of the laws of war is regarded by the armed forces as its chief asset.[93] Before I conclude, however, I will return to Major Donna Marie Verchio's arguments about the role of law in armed conflicts. As discussed earlier, she focuses on the threat (as she sees it) of the SIrUS Project, but her main concern is with any attempt to dictate what is or is not permissible for the US armed forces. She worries that regulations will gain support, particularly among those with the least to lose . . . Nations with long records of failure to implement or respect the law of war treaties . . . could try to prevent a nation such as the United States, with its long record of respect for the law of war, from developing, acquiring, and using illegitimate weapons with which it can fight and win.[94]

The statement is incredible in its audacity, given the US's reluctance to sign most legal conventions, their role in developing the most devastating and cruel weapons (including atomic and nuclear bombs as well as incendiary, cluster, chemical and biological weapons), and their colossal investment in new forms of weaponry. Her statement also reminds us of a point I made earlier: the relentless focus on weaponry – legitimate versus illegitimate – is a distraction from much more fundamental problems associated with the right to unleash war in the first place.

Verchio urged other governments to adopt weapons-review procedures similar to those that had been employed by American forces since 1996, which placed lawyers at the centre of weapon testing, evaluation, acquisition and use. A judge advocate would give legal advice 'balancing . . . the weapon's military necessity against the injury it produces'. In Verchio's words,

> The relevant factors considered and balanced under the military necessity standard include: the degree of injury the weapon may cause, the weapon's intended use, the threat posed by the potential enemy, and the weapon's enhanced utility. In the weapon review, the weapon's intended use is balanced against the military advantage afforded and the injury caused. This factor includes specific findings on the intended use of the weapon, whether it serves as a nonlethal alternative

to other wounding mechanisms, and whether the injury caused by the weapon is incidental or collateral to its intended use.

Verchio also argues that the legal advisers need to judge how the injury sustained 'measures against other weapons that perform similarly' – evidence of similar wounding effects justifies the adoption of a new weapon. She insists that, when balancing 'injury against military necessity' (that is, balancing the suffering *felt* by the victim as against the *gains* of the person inflicting the injury), attention must be paid to the perceived severity of 'the threat posed by the potential enemy'. Under such definitions, it is hard to see what weapon would be excluded, especially in the context of the post-9/11 'war on terror'. The 'military necessity' argument can trump all others – if it is 'militarily necessary' for the US and its allies.

When Verchio concludes her remarks by stating that 'The prohibition on "unnecessary suffering" constitutes the acknowledgment that, in war, there is such a thing as "necessary suffering"', she shows that she has perfectly understood the function of legal prohibitions.[95] They are to facilitate, legitimate and honour the military decisions made by the preeminent military powers. And they generally achieve all three of these aims.

I don't want to sound too negative. International laws and conventions against certain, rather narrowly designated acts of aggression do sometimes act as a brake on the armed forces and government-legitimated violence. At the very least, they can provide a way to express righteous indignation at the violence of war. None of us would want to be at the mercy of Curtis LeMay, with his empty promise of attempting to avoid napalming 'hospitals, prison camps, orphan asylums, nunneries and dog kennels'.[96]

However, in doing research for this chapter, I was struck time and again by the obscenity of talk about maiming, mutilating and murder in 'lawful' or 'legitimate' ways. It still seems macabre that soldiers stationed in France during the First World War were informed that it was against the law to shoot pheasants, yet were encouraged to shoot people.[97] There is something obscene about (mis)using the language of humanitarianism, with its emphasis on benevolence, to justify butchery.

The laws of war legitimate and facilitate violence. Although their authority is derived from their claim to be based on universal principles, they actually undercut such ideals by being blatantly partisan, deliberately vague and redundant at the time of adoption. The codification of the laws of war itself has created a category – 'humanitarian war', or legal war – which facilitates violence. So-called humanitarian wars end up inflicting pain and suffering on other (and sometimes even the same) people. And attempts to constrain acts of violence in wars explicitly create categories of 'legitimate violence'. In fact, law frequently becomes an end in itself: it needed to be protected above and beyond its human victims. This was what the author of an article entitled 'International Humanitarian Law and Combat Casualties' (2006), meant when he warned against 'setting legal standards which are impossibly high'; if we ignore what is 'militarily practicable' we risk bringing 'the law into disrepute'.[98] I imagine that if his family was threatened with becoming 'collateral damage', he might not be quite so worried about bring the 'law into disrepute' by setting high legal standards.

My assumption that law is something that strives at least to be impartial, universal and ethical was obviously foolish. After all, as early as 1946 historian and international relations theorist E. H. Carr observed that people often 'treat law as something independent of, or ethically superior to, politics', but failed to recognize that it is nothing of the sort.[99] Indeed, as I have argued in this chapter, weapons scientists and medical personnel adhere closely to humanitarian precepts and international law precisely in order to circumvent them. By tenaciously interpreting and applying international rules and customs concerning the legitimacy or illegitimacy of particular technologies, they can increase the suffering inflicted on their victims. In fact, customary restraints on declaring war have been undercut by the appeal to law. No one has put this more succinctly than legal philosopher Costas Douzinas in *Human Rights and Empire* (2007): the 'industrial–military complex has been replaced by the humanitarian–military project'.[100] We should all be worried.

CHAPTER FOUR

Wounding the Innocent

In the twentieth century, between forty-three and fifty-four million non-combatants were killed as a result of war.[1]

What happened to the eleven million people we are unsure about? Were they not killed after all? Or did they die in 'skirmishes' or 'campaigns' rather than 'wars'? Were their deaths a result of military strikes on their communities' infrastructure (razing farms, polluting water, demolishing electricity grids and disrupting medical services) rather than exploding munitions? Were they dumped in mass graves and not individually mourned? Or are the militarists among us unsure whether or not they should be considered non-combatants?

Were they not innocent after all?

There is something crushing and cruel about hawks. These majestic birds of prey dive from great heights at speeds as fast 270 kilometres (168 miles) per hour, the shadow of their wings like dark knives on the plain. They are ravenous for flesh but, being birds, it does not make sense to call them pitiless.

The same is not true of human-hawks. Belligerent humans were first called hawks by Thomas Jefferson in a letter to his ally James Madison on 26 April 1798. For Jefferson, 'war hawks' were Federalists who 'talk of septemberizing' (or assassinating) opponents and were prepared to risk war with France. In 1810, the term was used (along with 'war dogs') by the Republican John Randolph against 'war republicans', who were willing to engage in war with England in order to take Florida from Spain and expand into Canada.[2] Today, the term refers to men and women who promote military interventions – that is, people who are casual with (usually) other people's lives.

I don't like human-hawks. They are too careless about the damage and destruction they bring not only to people, but also to environments and non-human animals. Despite having written about war and violence for more than two decades, I still feel nauseous whenever I hear people justifying killing, especially when they do so in lucid, urbane, even beguiling, tones. One of the most insidious concepts they employ is 'collateral damage'.

When I think about this concept, the writings of Colin H. Kahl came to mind. He is a respected political scientist and, according to his website, a regular consultant for the US Department of Defense and the intelligence community. They must have appreciated his advice because, in 2011, he was awarded the Secretary of Defense Medal for Outstanding Public Service.[3] True, I don't know Kahl, so cannot say whether he considers himself a 'hawk' or not, but his 2007 defence of the American war in Iraq strikes me as hawkish.

Kahl believes that the American forces in Iraq have 'done a better job of respecting non-combatant immunity than is commonly thought'. He observes that public dismay about US conduct during the war in Vietnam has made politicians and senior military officers profoundly sensitive to accusations they are reckless with innocent lives. In particular, the atrocity at My Lai on 16 March 1968 in which around five hundred civilians were slaughtered is seared into the American conscience.

Obviously, children, women and old men should never be deliberately targeted by the military.

Kahl argues that contemporary US military culture has internalized this 'norm of non-combatant immunity'. It is committed to 'the use of overwhelming but limited force', or what he terms the 'annihilation–restraint paradox'.[4] Kahl maintains that this 'tension between annihilation and restraint' explains both the high levels of US compliance with non-combatant immunity in Iraq and also the fact that civilian casualties 'have still probably been higher than was militarily necessary or inevitable'. We should note his use of the word 'probably'. One example of American compliance with the 'norm of non-combatant immunity' was the fact that the army is prepared to send in infantry to clear buildings rather than 'simply leveling them with artillery or air strikes'. He insists that civilian casualties have been 'low by historical standards'.[5] After a century characterized by two world wars in which tens of millions of non-combatants were killed by starvation, rifle fire, artillery, aerial bombardment, incendiaries and atomic explosions, that is hardly reassuring.

Where Kahl's analysis becomes particularly interesting, though, is when he seeks to explain why there were civilian casualties *at all*. The usual suspects appear, including the 'fog of war', a term introduced in 1837 by Carl von Clausewitz in *Vom Kriege* (translated into English as *On War* in 1873).[6] Kahl also notes that American troops had been placed in extremely stressful situations, where they had been ambushed, witnessed their comrades being killed and had to handle corpses. In his words, 'like all human beings in war, US forces under attack are vulnerable to confusion, fear, and narrowing of perception'.[7] There had also been 'insufficient preparation' by the military for the period after the initial invasion and battles, which led to a situation in which soldiers 'fresh from major combat, or trained and equipped for major combat' were deployed just as 'the fighting was winding down'. These troops 'had a difficult time transitioning to the types of non-violent behavior – such as manning checkpoints, policing crowds, and conducting searches – required for the "postwar" environment'.[8] It may seem churlish to ask why Iraqi civilians were to be punished for any of these factors.

Finally, Kahl notes that some 'hawkish commentaries argue that the United States' strategic difficulties in Iraq are largely the by-product of being far *too compliant* with the norm of non-combatant immunity'.[9] It seems that some people believe that compliance with 'non-combatant immunity' is something voluntary, which commentators more 'hawkish' than Kahl believe can be overridden in the interests of strategic goals.

Kahl does admit that, despite having 'internatiz[ed] . . . non-combatant immunity', armed members of the US military and its allies did kill civilians. This, for Kahl, is deeply regrettable, but the 'fog of war', the stresses and strains of active service, and inadequate preparation for the aftermath of the invasion meant that a certain number of non-combatant killings were unsurprising. Does that make it slightly more excusable? Kahl was (presumably) writing at some geographical distance from the killing fields of Iraq and Afghanistan. Members of his family were not at risk of becoming collateral damage.

There are two other justifications of extreme violence that appear in analyses like Kahl's. The first is the valorization of emotions. There is an underlying assumption that maintaining a correct *emotional* response to civilian casualties is the correct *ethical* response. For example, in recent commemorations of the First World War it was considered *de rigueur* for even hawkish historians to preface their justifications for armed conflict with sincere regret for the horror meted out to non-combatants. Anti-war poetry seemed to be the most convenient foil for their remorse. In one case, immediately before applauding members of the British navy who enforced the blockade of German cities (resulting in mass starvation of civilians), one scholar recited those terrible lines in Wilfred Owen's 'Dulce et Decorum Est':

> If you could hear, at every jolt, the blood
> Come gargling from the froth-corrupted lungs,
> Obscene as cancer, bitter as the cud
> Of vile, incurable sores on innocent tongues,
> My friend, you would not tell with such high zest
> To children ardent for some desperate glory,
> The old Lie; Dulce et Decorum est
> Pro patria mori.

While it is obviously neither wonderful nor honourable to die for your country, might it be sweet to kill for it?

The recourse to emotion as a factor that mitigates guilt over civilian deaths has been a remarkably common response during all major wars, and not simply during recent commemorations. Indeed, it is at the heart of many religious justifications of killing. For instance, the author of *The Christian Witness in War* (1918) reminded his readers that the 'Christian soldier in friendship wounds the enemy. In friendship he kills the enemy . . . His heart never consigns the enemy to hell. He never hates.'[10] Or, as E. Griffith Jones advised a conference of Wesleyans in 1915, soldiers should be like shepherds – intent on destroying wolves, while avoiding the 'wolf spirit' at all costs.[11] As they plunged their bayonets into human flesh, clergymen encouraged soldiers to murmur, 'This is my body broken for you,' or to whisper prayers of love.[12] At least these commentators were referring primarily to killing other armed men. But it was equally prominent when the victims were civilians. For example, during the Second World War, William Temple (then Archbishop of Canterbury) defended the aerial bombardment of German cities with these words:

A nation should fight effectively if it is to fight at all. To fight
ineffectively only leads to a lengthening of the war and the
increase of misery. Of course what a Christian must at all
costs resist is the temptation to fight in a spirit of hatred or of
gloating over the suffering inflicted; what is so difficult is to
fight effectively in the right spirit.[13]

Or, as another priest advised soldiers during that very different
conflict in Vietnam, it is legitimate to kill 'but not with hatred in
your heart'.[14] Confusing emotional responses with ethical ones is
a glib way to justify killing.

The second response to killing civilians is more common: a
resigned shrug. When British and American armed personnel
violate non-combatant immunity, one of the most frequent reactions by military commentators is a resigned 'shit happens'.
Reflecting on atrocities committed by Australian troops during
the Vietnam War, historian Kenneth Maddock even drew an analogy with traffic infringements. He mused that

the rules of war are like the rules of the road: any honest and
realistic person will expect them to be broken, but some
drivers will commit more frequent and more serious violations than others, and there may be other drivers who very
rarely offend.

He added that 'more than one code can exist even within the
same country's armed forces'. For instance, men who served in
covert programmes like Phoenix, which captured, tortured and
assassinated suspected members of the National Liberation Front
of South Vietnam, were not

'driving' by the same rules as the men of the infantry battalions, and must often have acted criminally by the standards the

latter were required to observe. Judged by their own standards, however, the covert operators were not necessarily
exceeding any 'speed limit'.[15]

Is speeding really an appropriate comparison with torturing and
killing people? Should we simply 'expect' the rules of warfare to
be broken? Who among us really believes that atrocity-prone servicemen (or, for that matter, speeding drivers) ought to be
'judged by their own standards'?

More disturbingly, some commentators belligerently *defend* military personnel who kill civilians. Kahl does not go so far. He
identifies the trauma of Vietnam as one explanation for American
sensitivity to accusations that they kill innocent people. I think he is
correct, but it should not be exaggerated. After all, during the war
(especially in the early years) there was much less ambivalence
about killing Vietnamese civilians. Many Americans gloated over
such aggression. Senior military advisers echoed Kahl's unnamed
hawks who believed that the US forces could be 'far *too compliant*
with the norm of non-combatant immunity'. In 1976 (and in the
context of the war in Vietnam), some senior military commentators
even argued that the laws of war were 'contrary to the conduct of
warfare, an unnecessary, unrealistic restraining device inhibiting
the combat commander in the accomplishment of his mission'.[16]

The celebration of slaughter of non-combatants even infected
debates about the most talked-about atrocity of all; that at My Lai
when Charlie Company, First Battalion, 20th Infantry Brigade,
American Division Combat Air (which was already notorious for
rape) entered My Lai, where three platoons killed around four
hundred civilians. They raped at least twenty girls and women,
killing many of them afterwards. Drill Sergeant Kenneth Hodges,
one of the men who trained Charlie Company for combat,
claimed that he was 'pleased' with their performance that day in
March 1968. He boasted that

They turned out to be very good soldiers. The fact that they were able to go into My Lai and carry out the orders they had been given, I think this is a direct result of the good training they had.[17]

Lieutenant William Calley (the senior officer who had ordered the killings) was convicted of premeditated murder in March 1971, but just a day later was released by presidential order into house arrest. Nearly 60 per cent of Americans did not think he should even have been prosecuted in the first place; many believed that it was 'unfair to send a man to fight in Vietnam and then put him on trial for doing his duty'.[18] Many people did (and do) believe that in wartime there are no innocent civilians on the 'enemy side'.

It is too easy to dismiss accounts of barbarism in Vietnam as aberrant. The name 'Vietnam' has itself become a code for atrocity. 'Vietnam' is now nothing more than a topographic space, a new frontier populated by marauding Americans creating mayhem against nameless and unidentified, yet highly racialized, victims.

But, as I observed in the Introduction, complacency about British atrocities is also rife. This is obviously the case during the period of imperial and colonial expansion, but remains with us today. While I was writing this book, evidence emerged time and again about the killing of civilians by British servicemen in Iraq and Afghanistan (the Coldstream Guards, Royal Marines and the Rifles, in particular, have been singled out as perpetrators).[19] Equally disturbing were some of the responses to the conviction of Sergeant Alexander Wayne Blackman for the murder of an injured fighter in Helmand Province in September 2011. A helmet-mounted camera recorded him shooting the wounded man, with the words, 'There you are. Shuffle off this mortal coil, you cunt. It's nothing you wouldn't do to us.' He

then turned to his comrades and said, 'Obviously this doesn't go
anywhere fellas. I just broke the Geneva Convention.' When
convicted of murder and sentenced to life imprisonment (with
a minimum of ten years before he would be eligible for parole),
there was an uproar among tabloid readers. Typical responses
included: 'Let's hope the courts see sense and remember these
are brave men who have been sent to the Middle East to act out
a sens[e]less war . . . Free him and free him now!!!' and
'Sergeant Blackman is very accustomed to the horrors of
combat, and this may just be the necessary action for him to survive the mental traumas of the conflict'.[20] Lord Ashcroft, the
former Deputy Chairman of the Conservative Party and one of
the richest men in Britain, pledged that, 'If asked I would con-
tribute towards the legal costs of sergeant Blackman's appeal.'
Lance Corporal Matthew Croucher (recipient of the George
Cross for bravery) dubbed him a 'leader of men', and one of the
highest-ranking Royal Marines, Lieutenant-Colonel Simon
Chapman, pledged his 'full support'.[21] Chapman even argued
that 'fundamentally [Blackman] is not a bad man. In fact, in
almost every respect, he is a normal citizen tainted only by
the impact of war.'[22] By July 2014 an e-petition demanding
Blackman's immediate release had been signed by more than
seventy-one thousand people.[23]

One of the main arguments war-hawks use for ignoring non-
combatant immunity is that such prohibitions are redundant in
irregular warfare, such as against non-Europeans or 'savages'.
Historically, such views were forged in innumerable imperial
invasions, from the European conquest of Native American lands
to the formidable expansion of the British Empire in the nineteenth century. By the early twentieth century, a small island off
the coast of continental Europe claimed sovereignty over the sub-
continent of India, as well as sixty other colonies and five

dominions: this empire subsumed around a fifth of the world's population.[24] This was only possible through bloodshed. These empire territories were important laboratories for experimenting with new and ever more deadly military technologies, which would then be exported to other countries and used against other enemies.[25]

In other words, it was no coincidence that the particularly vicious dum-dum bullet was designed and manufactured in the British East India Company's ammunition factory in Dum Dum, a region about fifteen kilometres from the centre of Kolkata, the 'City of Joy'. It was a missile intended to inflicted wounds so horrific that they would instantly stop any 'fanatic'.[26] As the *Daily Mail* reported on 28 June 1898 in relation to the Khartoum Expedition, the dum-dum bullets 'came into use for the purpose of stopping the rush of hordes of fanatics, it having the advantage of spreading out whenever it encountered resistance'.[27] 'Spreading out' is, incidentally, a euphemism for the way these bullets were designed to mushroom inside human bodies, shattering bone and tissue with explosive force.

Aerial bombardment – a particularly formidable way of ensuring that large numbers of civilians are killed – was also initiated in the context of imperial conquests of 'recalcitrant tribes' in Arabia (now Iraq). Just after the First World War, the Royal Air Force patrolled the region from the sky, deliberately creating terror among villagers in order to 'awe tribes into submission'.[28] In 1925, Brigadier-General the Right Honourable Lord Thomson even defended the aerial bombardment on the grounds that, although 'some destruction and loss of life were inevitable', all 'other measures for restoring and maintaining order would have been far slower and therefore less effective, much more expensive, and in the end less humane'.[29] The head of the British colonial administration in Arabia, F. H. Humphrey, made a similar point when, in 1932, he told Sir

John Simon, the Foreign Secretary, that 'the term "civilian population" has a very different meaning in Iraq from what it has
in Europe . . . The whole of its male population are potential
fighters.'[30]

At the heart of these discussions is one assertion: certain dead
people simply don't count. They are not counted. This was what
Sir John Bagot Glubb meant when, in *Arabian Adventures*, his
memoir of his service in the region, he insisted that to the
Bedouin, the 'tragedies, bereavements, widows, and orphans'
were regarded as 'natural and inevitable'; they were a 'normal
way of life'.[31] In 1930, Lord Trenchard, the former Chief of the
Air Staff, made a similar point in the House of Lords when he
claimed that 'these tribes love fighting for fighting's sake . . . They
have no objection to being killed.'[32]

A detailed exploration of this issue can be found in a series of
articles written in the 1920s by Elbridge Colby, an officer in the
US Army and a professor in the Journalism Department at
George Washington University. Colby was at the forefront of a
movement to ensure that warring nations abided by regulations
concerning the conduct of war and that infractions were severely
punished at both individual and sovereign level. Writing in the
Michigan Law Review, he reminded readers that the laws of war had
to be enforced in order to 'insure decent morality, decent respect
for persons and property, and the maintenance of modern standards of humanity and life' even in wartime.[33]

However, just two years later he published an impassioned
defence of combat without rules in the influential *American
Journal of International Law*. It turns out that, for Colby, the need
to ensure 'decent respect for persons' does not include *all*
people – only European and American ones. He titled his article
'How to Fight Savage Tribes', and in it 'savages' were resolutely
excised from the category of 'human'. When fighting 'savages',
he argued, European troops should have no compunction about

legality. He gave many reasons for this verdict, including his belief that 'combatants and non-combatants are practically identical' in 'primitive' societies; 'savage or semi-savage peoples take advantage of' European scruples 'to effect ruses, surprises, and massacres'; and international law was fundamentally a 'Christian doctrine', so could not be applied to 'pagans'. Colby exhorted readers to examine the 'long list of Indian wars in which the troopers of the United States have defended and pushed westward the frontiers of America'. In such conflicts, the 'almost universal brutality of the red-skinned fighters' was indisputable. Colby approvingly cited the comment of a prominent general during those wars that 'red-skins' respect 'no rights and knows no wrongs'.[34] Indeed, the only kind of language such 'savages' understood was that of 'devastation and annihilation'. Anyone who sported 'excessive humanitarian ideas' and acted 'overkind' to the enemy was actually being 'unkind to his own people'. As Colby put it, 'against such [a people] it is not only perfectly proper, it is even necessary, to take rigorous measures'.

Colby felt that it 'is good to use proper discretion. It is good to observe the decencies of international law', but such niceties were wasted on uncivilized people. In case his readers did not quite get the point, he gave a concrete illustration contrasting the effect of certain military acts on civilized Frenchmen with the effect on their uncivilized counterparts:

> To a Frenchman, a shell striking Rheims Cathedral . . . is a lawless act of the enemy which infuriates the temperamental soul and arouses wrath, and gives a fine incident for overseas propaganda. To a fanatical savage, a bomb dropped out of the sky on the sacred temple of his omnipotent God is a sign and a symbol that that God has withdrawn his favor. A shell smashing into a putative inaccessible village stronghold is an

indication of the well-equipped energy and superior skill of
the well-equipped civilized foe. Instead of merely rousing his
wrath, these acts are much more likely to make him raise his
hands in surrender.

In other words, commanders should not be reluctant to kill non-
combatants ('if there be such in native folk of this character'). It
was also possible to argue, Colby noted, that the mass slaughter
involved in dropping a bomb on a village was 'actually humane'
because it would shorten the conflict and thus prevent 'the shed-
ding of more excessive quantities of blood'.[35]

Colby may sound particularly bloodthirsty, but many others
shared his views. In 1923 Professor Jesse S. Reeves of the
University of Michigan also argued that 'international law is not
applicable to uncivilized peoples and could have no influence
upon them. It is merely a body of rules and customs that have
grown up among nations more or less similar for use among
themselves'.[36] Colonel J. F. C. Fuller made a similar point in his
hugely influential *The Reformation of War* (1923), stating that
'uncivilized' societies were 'like the organism of the lower animals'; they were 'controlled by a series of nervous ganglia rather
than centralized brain'. As a consequence,

in small wars against uncivilized nations, the form of warfare
to be adopted must tone with the shade of culture existing in
the land, by which I mean that against peoples possessing a
low civilization, war must be more brutal in type (not necessarily in execution) than against a highly civilized nation;
consequently, physical blows are more likely to prove effective
than nervous shocks.[37]

Even the official British *Manual of Military Law* (1914) ruled
that

It must be emphasized that the rules of International Law Warfare apply only to the warfare between civilized nations, where both parties understand them and are prepared to carry them out. They do not apply in wars with uncivilized States and tribes, where their place is taken by the discretion of the commander and such rules of justice and humanity as recommend themselves in the particular circumstances of the case.[38]

Perhaps not coincidentally, Elbridge Colby's son William went on to become the Director of Central Intelligence between 1973 and 1976. In Vietnam, he served as Chief of Station in Saigon, chief of the CIA's Far East Division, and oversaw the covert Phoenix programme. We are back to Calley and the massacre at My Lai.

What about non-combatants in the heart of 'civilized Europe'? I may have been unfair on Kahl when I criticized him for pointing out that civilian casualties in Iraq were 'low by historical standards'. One of those 'historical standards' serves as a useful illustration of another common defence for the mass killing of non-combatants: the argument that slaughtering them was acceptable because civilians were not deliberately targeted.

There are many examples I could draw upon (including LeMay's firebombing of Japan that I discussed in the last chapter), but I will focus on 13 to 15 February 1945, when nearly eight hundred Allied aircraft assaulted the people living in Dresden, the seventh-largest city in Germany and also, by that time, crowded with refugees fleeing the Soviet advance. 'Tally ho!' called the marker-leader pilot into his radio when, on St Valentine's Day, he started the attack.[39]

The bombers used an unusually high proportion of incendiary bombs. In fact, approximately three-quarters of them were fire-bombs, creating a fiery conflagration that spread over thirteen square kilometres (eight miles).[40] It was a flaming hell that could be seen two hundred kilometres (124 miles) away.[41]

The men, women and children who managed to survive the flames were asphyxiated by carbon monoxide poisoning. Thousands were blown to pieces while rescuing people or while putting out the fires caused by the explosion of delayed-action fuses. In total, 2640 tons of bombs killed between eighteen and thirty-five thousand civilians.[42]

Survivors never forgot this hell on earth. A resident Margaret Freyer recalled running into the street to see a 'witches' cauldron . . . no street, only rubble nearly a metre high, glass, girders, stones, craters'. To her horror, she suddenly saw

> a woman. I can see her to this day and shall never forget it. She carries a bundle in her arms. It is a baby. She runs, she falls, and the child flies in an arc into the fire. It's only my eyes which take this in; I myself feel nothing. The woman remains lying on the ground, completely still. Why? What for? I don't know, I just stumble on.[43]

Arthur Harris, the commander-in-chief of RAF Bomber Command, issued a callous judgement: 'I do not personally regard the whole of the remaining cities of Germany as worth the bones of one British Grenadier,' he famously wrote, adding that 'the feeling . . . over Dresden could easily be explained by any psychiatrist. It is connected with German bands and Dresden shepherdesses.'[44]

This was just one attack on a single city. It was preceded and followed by many other aerial bombardments on primarily civilian targets. In the final reckoning, almost every major city in Germany went up in flames. The RAF dropped 955,000 tons of bombs on Germany; the USAAF dropped nearly 400,000 tons. Almost half of the British bombs and a fifth of the American ones

fell on populated areas. They represented a new phase in the will-
ingness of the Allies to stretch the rules of war to allow the mass
killing of civilians, not as a *consequence* of attacking legitimate military bases but as an end in itself.

In total, around seven hundred thousand civilians were killed.
The majority were women. For every 100 male casualties, there
were 181 female casualties in Darmstadt, 160 in Hamburg, 136 in
Cassel and 114 in Nuremberg. Just under one fifth of those killed
were children under the age of sixteen (that is, 140,000 children) and another fifth were over the age of sixty.[45]

Why should we bother about such statistics? What is the
debate?

No one disputes this statement: aerial bombardment involves
the mass slaughter of civilians. There is disagreement about the
next statement: does it matter? In other words, So what?

It is distressing to realize that the aerial bombardment of
densely populated cities has many defenders, including Christian
ones. As two theologians in the *Clergy Review* explained in 1941,
there was no alternative. They agreed that 'the innocent, that is to
say, the harmless (if, apart from infants, there are any)' should be
'immune from direct attack on their lives'. However, 'in modern
conditions the theologian cannot tell *who* they are, and the attacking airman does not know *where* they are'.[46] Or, as another
chaplain reckoned in the context of the bombing of Dresden, it
was nothing more than the 'extension of two soldiers shooting at
each other'.[47] It seems bizarre to me that anyone would doubt that
many people really are 'harmless', or that dropping incendiary
bombs on them is somewhat different from combatants hurling
missiles at other heavily armed combatants.

Defenders of aerial bombardment find a rationale in the doc-
trine of double effect, first formulated by the theologian Thomas
Aquinas in his *Summa Theologica* (1265–74). According to
Aquinas, 'Nothing hinders one act from having two effects, only

one of which is intended, while the other is beside the intention.'[48] An evil is not morally wrong so long as 'the action in itself is directed immediately to some other result' and 'the evil effect is not willed either in itself or as a means to the other result'. In other words, there is a moral distinction between *intending* harm as an end or a means (to a higher good, for instance) and doing something you *foresee* will cause harm but merely as a side effect (that is, collateral damage). Crucially, even foreseen bad consequences are allowable. Aquinas also insisted that the force used had to be proportionate.

How do defenders apply this doctrine to bombing residential and commercial areas of populated cities? In itself, the bombing could be seen as having a good effect: defeating a pernicious enemy as well as destroying its war industries, communications networks and military installations. Admittedly, this aggression led to something evil – the mutilation and killing of innocent civilians by bullets, shrapnel, fire and asphyxiation – but this appalling effect was not *intentional* in the sense that it was not a means to the good end but simply its 'incidental accompaniment'. Aerial bombardment could also be said to be proportionate in the sense that there were important reasons for destroying the enemy and ending the war, including saving our own soldiers' lives.

There are more colloquial ways of appealing to the doctrine of double effect. The first is to echo a padre writing in the *Church Times* in 1940. He argued that a nation is not inevitably 'degraded' morally, 'even by doing horrible things' like bombing cities. He went on to state that killing civilians was legitimate in a war that was 'morally right in waging', so long as the conduct was done 'utterly against its will, only as others do them against itself, and only if and as long as it seems to be necessary to do them in order to avert serious risk of defeat'.[49] Or, as Father George Zabelka, the chaplain to the bombers on Tinian Island who dropped the 'gimmick bomb' (as they called the bombs that killed 140,000 people in Hiroshima and between sixty and eighty thousand in Nagasaki), exclaimed: 'Gosh, it's horrible, but gosh, it's going to end the war. Finally the boys will get home.'[50]

This was the line taken by 'Iron Ass' LeMay, the commander introduced in the last chapter. LeMay had been responsible for killing more civilians in a six-hour period than any person in the history of humanity. For him, these deaths saved (other people's) lives. Pragmatism was his watchword. He killed these people not because he wanted to, but as an unavoidable consequence of the need to destroy their industries and munitions. As LeMay put it,

> No matter how you slice it, you're going to kill an awful lot of civilians. But, if you don't destroy the Japanese industry, you're going to have to invade Japan. And how many Americans will be killed in an invasion of Japan? . . . Do you want to kill Japanese, or would you rather have Americans killed?[51]

Not everyone agreed. Indeed, even those who dropped the bombs may have harboured doubts. This was certainly the case for one radio operator who had been involved in a mass raid on Hamburg. For him, it was 'a nightmare experience looking down on the flaming city beneath':

> I felt sick as I thought of the women and children down there being mutilated, burned, killed, terror-stricken in that dreadful inferno – and I was partly responsible. Why [. . .] do the Churches not tell us that we are doing an evil job? Why do chaplains persist in telling us that we are performing a noble task in defence of Christian civilization? I believe that Hitler must be defeated; I am prepared to do my bit to that end. But don't let anyone tell us that what we are doing is noble.

He was not convinced by the doctrine of double effect, stating that 'What we are doing is evil, a necessary evil perhaps, but evil all the same.'[52]

I believe this radio operator was alluding to a major problem with the doctrine: that is, its artificial treatment of intention. It is not clear that there actually is a distinction between intended effects and merely foreseeable effects. All the doctrine says is that combatants should *not try* to harm civilians, rather than *try not* to harm them. The doctrine also promotes a view of intention as an interior mental act: so long as a person believes that they do not *intend* an evil, their actions are legitimate. This casuistry remains at the basis of the legal doctrine of collateral damage.

Even when faced with the most extreme depravity of our time, that of Nazism, there could be strident opposition to the doctrine of double effect. One critic was the Jesuit priest John C. Ford who, in 'The Morality of Obliteration Bombing' (1944), pleaded with his readers to have some common sense. When was it possible, 'psychologically and honestly', for a person 'to avoid the direct willing of an evil effect immediately consequent upon one's action', he asked. When

> is an evil effect to be considered only incidental to the main result and not a means made use of implicitly or explicitly to produce it? . . . Can we say that the training and death of hundreds of thousands of innocent persons, which are its immediate result, are not directly intended but merely permitted? Is it possible psychologically and honestly for the leaders who have developed and ordered the employment of this strategy to say they do not intend any harm to innocent civilians?[53]

At the very least, defenders of the doctrine of double effect were playing with words. More probably, they were manipulating them.

The doctrine of proportionality is also problematic. The ultimate good that supposedly comes from the mass slaughter of unprotected civilians was only speculative (would it work or not?) and did not guarantee that the future world would be peaceable. After all, the enemy might retaliate by firebombing British cities, thus further exacerbating the evil effect.[54] As John Ryan pointed out in *Modern War and Basic Ethics* (1940), the evil effect of firebombing cities was 'first, immediate and direct, while any military advantage comes through and after it in a secondary, derivative, and dependent way'.[55]

These debates have led the distinguished scholar Michael Walzer to modify the doctrine of proportionality to include 'double intention'; that is, 'combatants must act with an intention to reduce the risk of harm to civilians'. In *Just and Unjust Wars* (1977), Walzer notes that

> simply not to intend the death of civilians is too easy . . . What we look for in such cases is some sign of a positive commitment to save civilian lives . . . And if saving civilian lives means risking soldiers' lives, the risk must be accepted.[56]

Walzer loses his nerve, however, when he accepts that there are two exceptions to the norm of non-combatant immunity for attack: reprisals and in 'extreme emergency'. These give military hawks far too much leeway for committing atrocities.

Appealing to the doctrine of double effect was not the only way in which aerial bombardment was justified. A more typical response was simply 'blame the victim'. John Herold, a vicar in Faversham, Kent, made this argument in a letter to the *Church Times* after the atomic attacks on Japan. He admitted that 'a weapon used *by* an aggressor is a weapon of aggression', but insisted that this could be contrasted to a weapon used *against* an aggressor, which made it 'a weapon of defence'.[57] He said not a word about how the women, children and unarmed men in the two Japanese cities should be considered aggressors.

An even more pragmatic approach involved the statement that committing atrocity was the only option. In 1939, Prime Minister Neville Chamberlain told the House of Commons that 'His Majesty's Government will never resort to the deliberate attack on women and children and other civilians for the purpose of mere terrorism'.[58] By July 1940, however, Britain was in more desperate straits. France had fallen; the Germans were attacking British cities. Churchill wrote to Lord Beaverbrook, the Minister of Aircraft Production, saying,

> When I look around to see how we can win the war I can see there is only one sure path. We have no Continental army which can defeat German military power . . . But there is one thing that will bring him [Hitler] back and bring him down, and that is an absolutely devastating, exterminating attack by very heavy bombers from this country upon the Nazi home-land. We must be able to overwhelm them by this means, without which I do not see a way through.[59]

It was a line reinforced by Arthur Harris. In a letter to his American counterpart Ira Eaker, Harris observed:

> You destroy a factory and they rebuild it. In six weeks they are in operation again. I kill all the workmen and it takes twenty-one years to provide new ones.[60]

Indeed, military officers have proclaimed time and again that it would have been immoral *not* to kill as many as possible. In is customarily blunt way, LeMay put it like this:

Actually I think it's more immoral to use *less* force than necessary, than it is to use *more*. If you use less force, you kill off
more of humanity in the long run, because you are merely
protracting the struggle.[61]

It was an argument used to justify atrocity throughout the
century.

Other problems have emerged in debates about 'collateral
damage'. I will briefly mention two. The first is to draw attention
to what is left out of these debates: primarily, the assumption that
if civilians are not killed *directly*, there is no collateral damage. In
other words, it is legitimate to bomb their roads, destroy their
clean water supplies and limit access to food and medicine; if
they die of hunger or illness or diarrhoea, we are not responsible.
In the case of Iraq, the public-health disaster that killed so many
civilians was entirely foreseeable, as suggested in the title of Peter
Kandela's *Lancet* article on the Gulf War: 'Iraq: Bomb Now, Die
Later'.[62]

The second problem concerns definitions of precision. When
British and American airmen were bombarding the cities of
Europe and Japan during the Second World War, their missiles
were incredibly imprecise. The American air force's emphasis on
'precision bombing' was, in practice, a charade. In fact, airmen
had very little way of knowing exactly where their weapons would
land. Crews were often given vague target directions, poor
weather hindered visibility and forced bombers to release their
weapons prematurely, and inaccurate radar systems were
endemic. Even the USAAF's official history stated that around '80
per cent of all Eighth Air Force and 70 per cent of Fifteenth Air
Force missions during the last quarter of 1944 were characterized
by some employment of blind-bombing devices'. In the last three
months of 1944, only between 25 and 40 per cent of bombs

dropped by both the Eighth and the Fifteenth Air Forces fell within about three hundred metres (or a thousand feet) of their target.[63]

Some people claim that technological advances in the late twentieth and early twenty-first centuries have overcome this problem. This is not the case. For all the rhetoric about 'surgical strikes' and 'precision bombing' during the Gulf War of 1990–1, for instance, fewer than 8 per cent of the bombs dropped were precision-guided; the rest had an accuracy of between 25 and 50 per cent.[64]

In fact, most weapons of war are highly indiscriminate. Even on clear days, undisturbed by the 'fog of war', human-hawks scatter thousands of sub-munitions hidden inside cluster bombs over vast stretches of land. Between 5 and 10 per cent of these bomblets fail to detonate immediately: they wait for an unsuspecting person – perhaps a child attracted by the bright colours – to step on them or pick them up.[65] I am not talking here about just a few thousand primed sub-munitions. According to *Off Target* (2003), US forces dropped at least 1.8 million sub-munitions in Iraq. Given than (on average) 5 per cent failed to detonate immediately, this leaves about ninety thousand 'duds' lying around.[66] They are, in effect, antipersonnel landmines.

Cluster bombs have rightly attracted international censure. They can make land uninhabitable for decades. Farmers cannot farm their fields. Vast swathes of land become 'out of bounds' to productive activities. Children, the elderly and the sick dare not cross certain roads to go to school or to hospital. Survivors of mine detonations are usually rendered limbless, and live out the rest of their life in poverty and pain.

But what if imprecision could be eliminated? What if the 'bad guys' could be correctly identified and disposed of, allowing the innocent to live in tranquillity?

This is the aspiration of designers of precision weapons and has driven the development and employment of weapons in conflicts involving British and American forces in recent decades. As mentioned above, during the 1991 Persian Gulf conflict, 8 per cent of bombs dropped were designated precision ones. This increased to one third during the 1999 Kosovo War and just over 60 per cent in Afghanistan in 2002. By the time of the invasion of Iraq, two-thirds of all weapons were capable of precise targeting.[67] Many of these were 'delivered to their target' – that is, individually identified combatants – by unmanned aerial vehicles (UAVs, or drones).

There is a problem, however: the designations 'combatant' and 'precision' are very deceptive. For one thing, in the wars in Iraq and Afghanistan the US administration defined a 'combatant' as any male of military age who lived in areas in which the US was conducting military operations ('unless there is explicit intelligence posthumously proving them innocent').[68] This has enabled them to claim that the number of civilians killed has been extremely low.

In addition, bombing usually relies on human intelligence, which is anything but precise. When targeting individuals in Iraq and Afghanistan, US forces and their allies are extraordinarily dependent on intercepts from satellite telephones. But *phones* are tracked, not individuals. It is anyone's guess who might be using a specific telephone at any precise moment, let alone the proximity of people eavesdropping on the person taking the call.[69]

In addition, the most common phones that were tracked – that is, those subscribing to Thuraya Telecommunications Company – have an internal GPS chip that allows tracking within a hundred-metre (328-foot) radius. What this means in terms of targeting is that the caller could be anywhere within a radius of 31,400 square metres radius.[70] How precise is that?

This point can be stated more strongly: the definition of

precision is inherently imprecise. Specifically, the precision of a weapon is expressed in terms of 'circular error probable' (CEP), which is the radius of the circle within which half of a missile's projectiles are expected to fall.[71] In other words, the missile will *not* fall on the target half of the time. As Carl Conetta, director of the US-based Project on Defense Alternatives, explains in 'Disappearing the Dead: Iraq, Afghanistan, and the Idea of a "New Warfare"' (2004), the CEP of guided munitions used in Iraq 'ranged between 3 and 15 meters, with the mean being 8 meters or 25 feet. This is sufficiently *inaccurate* to guarantee that a significant percentage of weapons aimed at the center of a building will land in the street – or on the building next door.'[72]

Of course, the reality is even worse. The CEP of a weapon is calculated in experimental or ideal conditions. What is ignored? Elementary facts such as human slip-ups, informant error or malice, the weather, dust, built-up urban environments and technical malfunctions.[73]

Nevertheless, and irrespective of these facts, the illusion of precision allows American and British authorities to portray collateral damage as the result of inadvertent mistakes rather than as inherent aspects of the targeting process. The CEP formula and the contexts in which weapons are being employed make the slaughter of civilians foreseeable. Maiming and killing civilians becomes militarily acceptable and ethically justified through the language of precision.

Just as worryingly, the emphasis on precision and surgical strikes sets the scene for a war without borders. Lacking spatial limits, drone warfare blurs the clear distinction between military and terrorists operations. State action becomes indistinguishable from terrorist action, since both are committed to stealth, absolute power and a disregard for international law. War does not occur in clearly demarcated spaces but is everywhere. The full-spectrum warrior of video-gaming becomes full-spectrum warring throughout all our worlds.

Proponents of drone warfare bullishly defend their use of this technology to kill identifiable 'enemies' or 'insurgents'. They repeat the mantra that drone warfare reduces the chance of killing innocent people, and because drone pilots often spend significant time tracking individual suspects they actually become *more*, not less, intimate with the people they eventually kill.

With these arguments in mind, I will end this chapter with Matt J. Martin's reflections on collateral damage in relation to drone warfare, from his autobiography, *Predator. The Remote-Control Air War Over Iraq and Afghanistan: A Pilot's Story* (2010), written with Charles W. Sasser. Martin revelled in the technical sophistication of the Predator, a twenty-seven-foot craft with a 48.7-foot wingspan that could reach attitudes of twenty-five thousand feet and stay in the air for twenty-four hours without refuelling. He recalled that when he was a cadet in the ROTC at Purdue University in Indiana, trainees used to run in formation to the cadence of a Vietnam War chant. The chant went:

> Flying down a river bed, one hundred feet high;
> Drop that napalm, watch 'em fry.
> Kids in the schoolhouse trying to learn;
> Drop that napalm, watch 'em burn.

As twenty-first century 'warriors' bombed their enemies in Iraq and Afghanistan from 7500 miles away and from unmanned aircraft high in the heavens, Martin suggested updating the chant to:

> Flying over Baghdad at ten thousand feet;
> Listening to those beeps and squeaks.

Hajji in his house talking on his cell,
Hellfire's coming, sending him straight to hell.

Martin was an experienced navigator, who sincerely believed that the 'Predator and its kin were truly in the business of saving American lives wherever they flew'.[74] He was amazed at the 'schizophrenic' life he led, in which drone operatives would

> commute to work in rush-hour traffic [in Nevada], slip into a seat in front of a bank of computers, 'fly' a warplane to shoot missiles at an enemy thousands of miles away, and then pick up the kids from school or a gallon of milk at the grocery store on his way home for dinner.

When in his 'warplane' at the base, he felt 'like God hurling thunderbolts from afar'. After squeezing the trigger, he reflected that

> It had not been quite real, even afterwards . . . The ability to kill people from such great distances, playing God, widened the gap between the reality of war and out perception of it. It was almost like watching an NFL game of TV with its tiny figures on the screen . . . It could even be mildly entertaining.

But it wasn't that easy. Despite the fact that the US military 'went to superhuman lengths to avoid civilian casualties', Martin acknowledged that innocent people got killed. In the thirty seconds between launching a missile and it hitting its target, unintended victims could appear. On one occasion, this included two young boys on bicycles. The response of Martin and his colleagues to this collateral damage is striking. He starts by explaining that 'the responsibility for this shot could be spread among a number of people in the chain – pilot, sensor, JTAC [Joint Terminal Attack Controller], ground commander'. Nevertheless, 'gloom descended' on his team:

> Pilots and sensors congregated in solemn denial around the GCS screens, still in shock over what we had just witnessed – another of the dirty little horrors of war that lost none of its impact whether you were actually there or you viewed it all by remote.

The scene was disrupted when one of his colleagues told them:

> [B]reak up the pity party . . . No good can come from obsessing about it. It'll only distract us from doing our job . . . Things like this happen in war.

Martin recalled Secretary of Defense Robert McNamara's observation that 'you must sometimes do evil in order to do good'. Dead children were an unfortunately by-product of war.[75]

I began this chapter by asking what was the meaning of innocence. Do some people's suffering matter more than others'? With the rise of 'body bag' aversion, whereby Western powers seek to engage in war without any casualties on their own side, there is even a positive *preference* for civilian casualties. For human-hawks, innocence is often devoid of much meaning – at least when overlain by the idea of enmity. As Curtis LeMay bragged,

> we have burnt the belly out of Tokyo . . . We don't pause to shed any tears for uncounted hordes of Japanese who lie charred in that arid-smelling rubble. The smell of Pearl Harbor fires is too persistent in our nostrils.[76]

Iron Ass's belligerence may be too much even for many patriots to stomach: in peacetime at least, hawks rhetorically spare little children. For doves like me, however, it is even possible to ask a different question: on what grounds are combatants guilty, and therefore legitimate targets for mutilation and slaughter? In past wars, many armed personnel have been conscripts or draftees, rendered non-innocent simply by virtue of their gender, age and level of fitness. They don't want to be anywhere near the killing fields. Even today, who is to say that men and women serving in the armed forces are more responsible than other citizens for the fact that their government has declared war? Or, to put it slightly differently: who is to say that those of us who do not serve in the armed forces are not responsible for the wars waged in our name? Are we innocent?

CHAPTER FIVE

The Dark Art of Ballistics

'Through Science We Defend.'

This is the motto of the US Army Soldier and Biological Chemical Command at the Soldier Systems Center in Natick, Massachusetts.[1] Their mission statement promises to 'conduct research, development, acquisition and sustainment to maximize combat effectiveness and survivability of freedom's defenders'.[2]

Such a rhetoric of service and survivability is ironic given that weapons researchers, developers and instructors are dedicated to perfecting technologies that will most effectively wound and kill other human beings. Industrial barons, research scientists, technologists, engineers and computer and information specialists revel in their job: it is 'cutting edge', intellectually rewarding and, of course, lucrative. Of course, the role of science in war is much broader than the 'production' of wounds: it includes radar, cryptography, intelligence and so on. But I am interested in something more visceral: the intimate history of killing. When reading about the lives and intellectual passions of scientists who attempt to enhance the wounding and lethal capabilities of weapons, one question arises time and again: why do highly educated, urbane scientists devote their lives to devastating and destroying other human beings?

*

Professional military officers used to be reluctant to recognize that scientists might be central to the warring enterprise, a fact that mortified some practitioners of that esteemed discipline. Even within the category 'scientist' there were tensions between 'pure' theoreticians and 'applied' engineers. Although applied science had long been integral to the military, the idea that scientists would actually be given a role in making tactical and operational decisions was anathema to senior officers. Admittedly, not all 'pure' scientists were convinced that they should dirty their hands by engaging in the world of battle either. When scientists came to play important roles in war it led to explosive clashes over identity and authority. Nevertheless, by the 1950s science was firmly entrenched in the military. In 1961, a 'retrospective' concluded that

> The military have thoroughly accepted operations research, and not much of a 'selling' job remains to be done. Indeed, 'unselling' may be more needed in those instances where the customer [military officers] fails to distinguish between the difficult and the impossible.[3]

That was a judgement from hindsight. Things were not so rosy in 1914. During the First World War, anxieties that the British forces might be lagging behind their European foes in technological sophistication were very real. Clearly, something had to be done. Furthermore, many British and (a few years later) American scientists were keen to play their part in a war that they regarded as being waged by an aggressive nation bent on world domination. As historian Michael Pattison observed in his research on scientists, inventors and the military between 1915 and 1919, scientists increasingly 'sought to apply their knowledge to warfare, thus heralding the collapse of neutrality among the international scientific community'. This was a 'measure of the potency of nationalistic propaganda and the strength of social pressure in 1915'.[4] It was the beginning of a period which saw the militarization of science, and was to reach unprecedented heights during the 'wizards' war' of 1939–45. By the middle of the twentieth century scientists had been given a role in deciding the actual conduct of war, heralding a revolution in military affairs.

It is impossible to do justice to this revolution and its history in just a few pages. Furthermore, although I am primarily interested in only one aspect of this transformation within the military (that is, the science of wounding and killing), it is indisputable that other sciences were more influential in dictating the *course* of the war. Some argue that it was the scientists who developed radar, sonar and the A-bomb who 'won the 1939–45 war'. For my purposes, however, the focus will be on wound ballistics only.

In Britain, one of the leading scientists in this field was Solly (later, Lord) Zuckerman. Although the tag 'typical' could never be applied to Zuckerman, in Britain his influence on the science of wounding is undeniable. There are other contenders in the US, including Edmund Newton Harvey, Elmer Butler and John Fulton, all of whom could be called, as Zuckerman proudly described himself, 'professional students of destruction'.[5]

Zuckerman originally trained as an anatomist in Cape Town, where he developed a research interest in primate behaviour, before immigrating to Britain in 1926. He rose to become one of the leading scientists and political advisers in mid-twentieth-century Britain. Photographs show a stocky man, with rugged features. Even his close friends admitted that he was abrasive, vain and obdurate. They believed that he was being sarcastic when he chose '*Quot homines tot sententiae*' ('so many men, so many opinions') as the motto to adorn his coat of arms.[6] For Zuckerman, only one opinion mattered: his own.

Once British cities started to be bombed in 1940, Zuckerman turned himself into the leading expert on blast injuries. He did this by interviewing victims of the bombings, visiting mortuaries to examine dead victims, and animal experimentation. In one of his experiments he sought to calibrate the force necessary to induce concussion. To do this, he strapped rhesus monkeys to a board and caused a heavy pendulum, travelling at measurable velocities, to strike their unprotected heads. His notes describe how, in one instance, the monkey

> reacted to the noise [of the pendulum being released] by frowning heavily, and by moving its ears and head. After the third and subsequent blows the animal had bouts of violent shivering. Its pupils became somewhat dilated, and its nipples showed an extreme pallor which usually passed off in the intervals between blows.

After the sixth blow 'the animal closed its eyes as though fatigued but it still reacted strongly to the noise'.[7] On some occasions, the monkeys would be subjected to twenty-nine blows (each stronger than its predecessor) at three-minute intervals. Eventually, their skulls would fracture and they would die. Another series of experiments (shown in Figure 5.1, below) involved chaining animals, including monkeys, to the wall of a bomb shelter and igniting explosives.

Today, such experiments would be judged unethical. However, even in the late 1970s Zuckerman was proud of his scientific trials. In his autobiography *From Apes to Warlords* (1978), he described conducting research at a brickfield at Stewortby, near Bedford, which came to be known as the Oxford Extra-Mural Unit (OEMU) of the Ministry of Home Security's Research and Experiments Branch. On 'field days', Zuckerman (sometimes accompanied by Lady Joan Zuckerman, his young, aristocratic wife) and his team would transport monkeys and goats from Oxford to the brickfield. They would set up cages in the grounds, complete with pressure gauges to

measure the intensity of the blast, and place the animals inside them.
Then explosives would be detonated.

Afterwards, it was simply a matter of taking notes on the state
of the animals. Were they still moving? Wounded? Dismembered?
Dead? The corpses would be taken back to Oxford for autopsies
and tissue analysis. Even Joan Zuckerman overcame her 'natural
squeamishness' to help her husband examine the bodies.

Zuckerman recalled with relish that, on one occasion, some
monkeys and goats escaped. He and his wife chased them across
the fields; captured them; caged them; detonated the explosives.[8]

Figure 5.1. A close-up of Solly Zuckerman's experimental monkeys,
fastened to the wall of a shelter. Zuckerman is the man facing forwards
on the right of the photograph.

Zuckerman was not the first scientist or ballistic expert to test
the effectiveness of technologies for wounding and killing

people. Obviously, real battlefields were excellent opportunities for observing the lethality of various weapons. During the Second World War, distinguished physician Henry K. Beecher exalted in the fact that some of the most urgent problems in understanding wounding required 'human subjects'; in wartime, he noted, there was 'an abundance of material' at the 'active fronts'.[9] Beecher carried out his work observing injured soldiers in North Africa, Italy and France. In his influential article 'Pain in Men Wounded in Battle', published in the *Annals of Surgery* (1946), he reported that he had interviewed 225 recently wounded soldiers. He was struck by the significant differences in the amount of pain soldiers reported experiencing. The particular site of wounding was an important variable, he found. Penetrating abdominal wounds, for instance, were particularly painful: nearly half of men with such wounds admitted that their pain was 'bad', probably because such wounds caused blood and 'intestinal contents' to spill into the peritoneal cavity, spreading infection. In contrast, 12 per cent of men with penetrating wounds of the thorax said their pain was 'bad' and only 7 per cent of men with cerebral wounds. Beecher concluded that emotional responses played a crucial role in affecting the amount of pain felt.[10]

Not all periods of history created such a rich database of human casualties. As one expert grumbled in 1897, although small-calibre arms had been invented a decade earlier, there had been 'no great war in which the effects of the small-calibred bullet could exhibit its true properties on such an extensive scale'.[11]

Substitutes had to be found. As we have seen, for Zuckerman these were the bodies of animals – anaesthetized and unanaesthetized. This had been a common way of testing a weapon's effectiveness. In the 1890s, one ballistics expert bragged that he had been given 'material' by 'butchers who did their own killing' and so could test the effect of weapons on bodies that were 'in a perfectly fresh, often still warm condition'.[12] Others used human corpses.[13]

But did experiments on dead bodies accurately show the kinds of wounds that would be inflicted in real conflict situations? Would the injuries inflicted be 'as severe on the living body as it has been shown they are on the dead?', asked one surgeon in 1897.[14] In fact, as he and others discovered, cadavers were not an ideal medium. Rigor mortis was the chief problem, since it caused the flesh to coagulate, harden and lose its elasticity. The differences between living and dead bodies were even more obvious if the cadaver had been pickled in preserving fluids. The blood and other fluids that would transmit shock in living people was absent in the dead, creating very different wounding and lethal effects.[15]

There were, however, other ways to simulate the effect of a weapon on human flesh. Renowned nineteenth-century Swiss ballistics expert Emil Theodor Kocher tried them all. Convinced that deformation of the bullet was crucial in determining the severity of the wound, he tested the destructive effect of bullets and other missiles by shooting through books, lead and iron plates, stacks of fir boards, metal and glass bottles (sometimes containing water), blocks of soap, sandstone and metal cans filled with marbles. Animal organs also came in handy. He shot through the leg bones and livers of oxen, pig's bladders (filled, at different times, with water, sand, or air), and pigs' intestines swollen with water. When those tests came to an end, he turned to human skulls and whole human cadavers.[16]

It was unusual for a scientist to experiment with so many different materials. Most ballistic experts curious about the wounding potential and lethality of a weapon opted for simpler methods. In 'Remarks on Gunshot Wounds to the Head' (1915), the scientist Victor Horsley argued that modelling clay was an ideal medium for testing the ballistic power of high-velocity bullets as it 'roughly resembles the tissues in that it contains a considerable percentage of water in its interstices'.

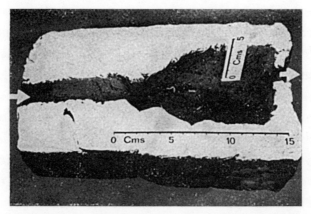

Figure 5.2. The shape of the temporary cavity caused when a 7.62 mm bullet was fired from a distance of five metres into a block of plasticine.[18]

However, its chief advantage was that when a bullet penetrated the clay it created a hollow space that mimicked the cavities formed in human flesh. Horsley only had to fill this cavity with plaster of Paris to reveal 'an absolutely accurate record of the whole effect of the shot'.[17]

Wood was also frequently used as a substitute for human tissue. Wooden soldiers, for instance, came to be called 'zuckermen'.[19] More typically, a series of one-inch pine boards, separated by a small air space of an inch, were stacked together and fired upon. Despite the popularity of wood, however, there were problems. Scientists recognized that there were too many textual variations to make the tests reproducible; experimenters couldn't control for the spin of the missile; and it was patently obvious that pine boards did not reproduce the effect of missiles hitting lungs, intestines, bones and blood vessels, all of which would produce a different wounding effect.

In 1962, the problems of using wood were clearly demonstrated during an experiment that went wrong. The mishap happened when Major Ralph W. French and Brigadier-General George R. Callender were demonstrating the effectiveness of shrapnel. On previous occasions, shrapnel balls had penetrated the pine boards deeply, implying a significant degree of lethality. However, on this occasion a projectile was accidentally detonated before the observers had taken cover. Shrapnel sprayed everyone in the room at close range. To the scientists' amazement, the only 'real casualty' was the man who had been holding the projectile, who lost a couple of fingers. There were a few bruises and a very embarrassed technician, but the fact that the balls had failed to even penetrate clothing demonstrated that, in battlefield conditions, this shrapnel would have been useless.[20] The pine boards were gathered up and reassigned to more constructive tasks.

French and Callender didn't remark on it, but the bruises that had been left by the pellets would have provided useful evidence if they had been interested in *dispersal* rather than *penetration*. Ingeniously, the head of the British Army Operational Research Group dealing with tank warfare in the 1950s used crayons. When fired in a single, long burst, where did machine-gun bullets fly, he asked. The question could be answered by taking some crayons (low-tech crayons were eventually ousted in favour of high-molecular-weight fluorescent dye),[21] marking the tips of the bullets and then firing them.[22] This was science mimicking the child's amusement of 'joining the dots'.

By the Second World War, such attempts to test the 'effectiveness' of weapons looked unscientific, even infantile. The time had come to place ballistics 'on a sound quantitative basis', as the scientists at the Wound Ballistics Research Group put it.[23] A revolution was underway. The WBR Group was run by physiologist Edmund Newton Harvey and anatomist Elmer Butler at Princeton University, and eventually included John Fulton's animal experimentation laboratories at Yale. They created a prestigious laboratory for the 'standardized production' of 'wound events'. Their tools were water, plasticine and blocks of gelatine, as well as live and dead animals, and they filmed the results using high-speed movie cameras, spark shadowgraphs, microsecond X-radiographs and pressure pulses by means of embedded piezoelectric crystals.[24] As Harvey commented, 'Without these modern techniques a knowledge of what happens when a high-velocity missile hits an object would be well nigh impossible.'[25] In other words, they used technology to make manifest the flight of death itself.

On a typical day, their research team in the physiology laboratories at Princeton would procure stray cats and dogs, give them a strong dose of a sleeping drug, place their legs (or other body part) in front of the muzzle of a rifle on a fixed stand and fire the shot. The bullets — which travelled at velocities of about three thousand feet a second — would have been scaled down to the size of the flesh-and-blood targets at which they were fired.[26] In their scientific style, they noted that

> a 0.4 gram missile moving 2700 f.p.s. and striking a 3-kg animal represents a situation, so far as mass of missile and mass of target are concerned, analogous to those of standard army rifle ammunition and the human body.[27]

Such prose brings to mind the language games I discussed in Chapter Two.

Motion picture or X-ray cameras would capture the result, revealing that, when the bullets hit the legs, there was 'a sudden bulging of the tissues along its path', faster than the human eye could see. The animal's tissue instantaneously 'leaped away from it in every direction, leaving an empty space for a minute fraction of a second. Blood vessels and nerves were pushed violently aside, often with rupture of the trunks.' It was, the scientist coolly recounted, 'very much as if a pinch of TNT had been planted inside the limb and then detonated'.[28] The result, at least, could be seen with the naked eye.

However, they discovered something else: a missile would typically lose 85 per cent of its energy as it ploughed its way through the body, leaving in its wake not only a permanent cavity of splintered bones, frayed nerves and mashed muscles but also a temporary cavity, which collapsed into the permanent one once the missile had passed. These experiments enabled them to conclude that the explosive damage done by modern missiles to the body was not due to the initial shock, nor to the burning heat of the missile, and not even to the wind pushed by the bullet. Rather, the damage was primarily caused by 'this transient, energetic cavity'.[29] This was what they meant by 'explosive wounds'.

It was awe-inspiring stuff. And the scientists became enormously excited. As the authors of an influential article in 1962 contended, 'pictures of rifle bullets in rapid fire' aroused 'admiration that so rapid a movement can be stopped in a photograph and the detail of events clearly visualized'.[30] The aesthetic pleasure in witnessing destruction – the trajectory, spin and yaw of a projectile – was literally breathtaking. Edmund Newton Harvey could barely contain himself. He boasted that the most modern high-speed camera could 'take moving pictures at the rate of 8000 frames a second and X-ray apparatus that requires only 1/1000 of a second for exposure'. In one swift technological surge, the barriers to understanding the mechanisms of wounding had been breached. It was, Harvey boasted, 'now possible to analyze events that are completed in a few thousandths of a second'.[31] For the first time, the very 'essence' of violence could be tracked, captured, measured, replicated and analysed. They had established the theoretical basis upon which the science of killing could be constructed.

The final revolution in ballistics research came in the 1970s, when a combination of advanced computing and ethical scruples over extensive experimentation on animals encouraged the development of abstract modelling in ballistics research. As one expert posited, it was surely possible to develop a mathematical theory capable of predicting 'the nature and extent of the injury from a knowledge of the physical parameters of the wounding agent and the circumstances of the wounding event'.[32] Until this time, assessing the probabilities of harm that would be done by various kinds of wounding had to be carried out by hand. The aim was to generate a 'numerical value expressing the mean percent incapacitation given a random hit on the human body by some ballistic projectile', researchers based at the Aberdeen Proving Ground in Maryland explained. Typically, this required eight steps. First, the expert needed to decide the 'shot line' of the projectile through each of the 108 cross-sections of human anatomy set out by Albert C. Eycleshymer and Daniel M. Schoemaker in 1911. Second, he had to identify the organs that would be affected. After calculating the velocity of the missile as it passed through these organs (stage three), he would define the size of the wound as a function of that velocity. The fifth and sixth stages involved coding each wound and then determining the 'wound effect along the track'. The penultimate calculation involved 'translating this wound effect through a sequence of correlations to an incapacitation value for that track'. Finally, he would combine all these incapacitation values into a single numerical value representing the degree of incapacitation expected from the projectile. Done manually, getting to this single numerical value would take three months. By automating it, this could be reduced to less than a day.

The result was 'The Computer Man'.[33] Calibrating death was as simple as uploading the data and pressing 'enter'.

By using such techniques, scientists were able to prove what everyone already knew: weapons have become progressively more devastating. We just have to think: atomic and nuclear bombs, fragmentation weapons, anti-personnel mines, biological and chemical toxins, rockets, flamethrowers – the list could go on and on. Even rifle fire has become more deadly. A simple comparison can be made between musket balls used in the eighteenth century and those used today. Figure 5.3 shows the injury caused by a musket ball hitting a man's upper femur, while Figure 5.4 shows the injury caused by being hit with a bullet from an AK47. Unlike the 'clean' wound created by the musket ball, in the latter case there was devastating muscle and bone damage caused by 'tumbling' and temporary cavitation.[34]

The seriousness of such wounds is largely the consequence of the amount of energy transferred from the missile to the body. The energy transfer of the musket ball to the femur was probably around one hundred joules. In contrast, at ranges of less than a hundred metres the AK47 transfers three thousand joules and even at long-distance ranges transfers significantly more joules than musket balls.[35]

Comparing the velocity at which missiles travel before hitting their target shows what dramatic change has taken place. Prior to the invention of gunpowder, missiles rarely travelled at more than several hundred feet per second (fps). Between the fourteenth century and the beginning of the twentieth century, this increased to 2000 fps and then jumped to 4000 fps just in time for the First World War. Even if we ignore atomic fusion, by the 1950s the velocity associated with gunpowder and related agents was 7000 fps.[37] Bomb fragments can travel at 9000 fps and may reach as high as 24,000 fps in certain circumstances.[38]

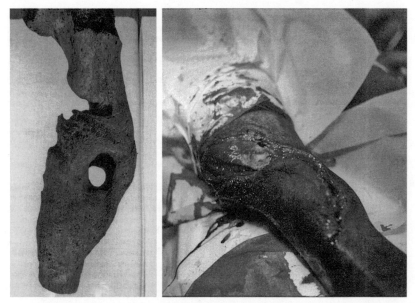

Figure 5.3. (left). 'Shaft of femur showing a cavity caused by a [musket] ball, with surrounding long-standing osteomyelitis.'
Figure 5.4 (right). 'The cavitational effects of an AK47 bullet on the vastus lateralis are in evidence.'[36]

The crucial point is this: once missiles exceed a certain velocity (generally 2000 fps) the severe shock wave creates a temporary cavity that wreaks terrible havoc. Such shock waves can exert pressures of up to 3000 pounds per square inch and, in volume, can create a temporary cavity that is twenty-seven to thirty times larger than the permanent cavity created along the track of the missile.[39] At higher velocities, even a fully jacketed missile (such as that used in the M16) will disintegrate inside the body, causing what is understatedly called 'lead splatter'.[40] The sub-atmospheric pressure also sucks clothing and dirt into the wound, contaminating it. Fractures routinely occur at some distance from the track of the missile, sending out fragments of bone that become secondary missiles. As the author of 'Wound Ballistics' (1977) reported, knowing that 'modest increases in velocity will result in tremendous increases in the kinetic energy of the missile' has led to 'the development of the new lightweight but powerful military rifles such as the M16, whose calibre (.223) is quite small'.[41] In other words, scientific knowledge is employed the better to wound and kill.

The mass of a missile cannot be ignored completely, however. For example, when it was found that the .38 special revolver was not sufficiently 'immobilizing' the enemy, ballistic experts substituted the 240-grain weight of the .45 automatic pistol, which has been standard issue of the United States armed forces since 1911. Put in their words, the .45-calibre pistol was developed to achieve 'the desired wounding effect'.[42] The importance of mass can be seen by comparing the .357 magnum and the .44 magnum, both of which travel at the same velocity (about 1500 fps). However, because the .357 bullet weighs 158 grains compared with 240 grains of the .44 bullet, the muzzle energy values are 845 ft-lbs and 1150 ft-lb respectively.[43]

There are other 'design features' intended to inflict terrifying wounds. Examples can be chosen from any period. For instance, as we have seen, hollow or soft-point bullets were invented in the late nineteenth century in order to inflict worse injuries. In the mid-twentieth century, cast-iron grenade cases were designed to break into deadly fragments. As Eric Prokosch tells us in *The Simple Art of Murder* (1972), by the early 1970s the M26 grenade was 'made of notched steel wire that breaks into more than a thousand fragments', each having a 'velocity of over 4000 feet per second upon explosion'.[44] So-called frangibles (or advanced energy transfer rounds) were also invented with maximum destructive capacity in mind: they are bullets made with small metal fragments either pressed together at high pressure or held together with a nylon or epoxy resin. Their fragmentation properties cause horrific injuries. Similarly, the fearsome Black Talon round manufactured by Winchester, has a jacket that peels away, forming six 'claws'. These are design features that tear, crush and stretch tissues, muscles and organs.

As I argued in an earlier chapter, these weapons circulate back home. When athlete Oscar Pistorius killed Reeva Steenkamp on St Valentine's Day 2013, he used an expanding bullet or 'black talon' ammunition. In the words of forensic pathologist Gert Saayman at Pistorius's trial, when this missile hits human flesh it 'folds out like the petals of [a] flower'.[45]

Other projectiles are deliberately made unstable so that they yaw, or tumble end over end inside bodies, causing greater damage. Flechettes are a well-known example. They are small dart-like missiles that are packed into a cartridge. While they don't have 'any greater penetration power *per se* than conventional missiles of the same make and velocity', they tend to 'lose their fins on entering tissue and so become unstable and tumble', following 'long and torturous paths within the body'.[46] Still other projectiles are designed to travel only specific distances within their victim's body. In order to hit the most vital organs, it is estimated that the 'ideal' distance is fifteen centimetres.[47] To cause the greatest damage, the bullet should dissipate all of its energy inside the body; there should be no 'residual exit energy'.[48] This is why bullets that deform upon impact are especially dangerous.

For ballistic scientists, knowing the impact of various weapons on human victims can have humanitarian consequences. There can be significant benefits in weapons research for victims, or, at least, those on 'our side'. In the words of Harry Cullumbine, the head of the Physiological Section at Porton Down in 1946, the 'offensive tests' (that is, experiments that seek to develop the most devastating chemical weapons) were a

necessary preliminary to experiments designed to evaluate protective measures and equipment; the possible hazards had

first to be determined before methods of defence could be
formulated.[49]

It is probably more accurate to argue that these benefits are a
form of collateral *data*. In part, the problem is the one identified
by Cullumbine: so much of military research is 'dual use'.[50]
Porton Down spokesmen constantly struggled with this issue. In
the words of a 1968 news report on the Microbiological Research
Establishment (MRE) at Porton Down, their research into how
diseases may be spread by aerosols was problematic. 'Viewed in a
humanitarian light', the report began,

> this could mean finding out more about the way in which
> coughs and sneezes spread disease. But it could also mean
> discovering how best to disable an enemy by spraying his
> troops with a solution from the air. Since much of the research
> in this field deals with methods of promoting the survival of
> bacteria by adding protective mixtures to the suspending fluid,
> it is difficult to show that it is not offense-orientated.[51]

Defenders of the research facility were in a difficult position for
two reasons. First, they were part of the Ministry of *Defence* rather
than of Health. Second, they were committed to sharing all their
findings with the American Army's research institution at Fort
Detrick, the centre of the US biological weapons program and
one that openly conducts research for 'offensive purposes'.[52] The
view of officials at the MRE was 'what Fort Detrick does with the
information . . . is Fort Detrick's business'.[53]

The problem of dual use research can be illustrated by turning
to Zuckerman's work on the effect of blast. In an attempt to
understand what made some people vulnerable, he and statistician
Frank Yates devised standardized casualty and kill rates. Although
these rates were used in arguments about which shelters were the

most protective, they also had offensive applications. As a result of the rates, they made a surprising discovery: 'ton for ton, 50 kg bombs produced significantly more casualties than did 250 kg or 1000 kg bombs'. As Zuckerman explained,

> The basic reason why smaller bombs were more effective in causing casualties was clearly the larger number of strikes that they implied for the same weight of aircraft load. Moreover, because of the smaller radius of effective action, a larger proportion of people at risk when 50 kg bombs struck were exposed with little, or only light protection between them and the explosion. A bigger bomb might have a bigger radius of action, within which, however, thick walls might protect some people who would otherwise be at risk. It also turned out that the number of casualties caused by fragments of the metal casing decreased, aircraft load for aircraft load, as the size of the exploding weapon increased . . . This was only one of the significant conclusions that were reached as a result of the air-raid casualty survey on which I had embarked.

It was a finding that was to be used when bombing German cities. As Zuckerman later admitted, 'By that stage of the war, I had become inured to the idea of casualties, whether our own or the enemy's.'[54]

There was another problem, though: academic researchers might not even be *aware* of the military application of their findings. The disjunction between their aims and that of the armed forces was exposed in an investigation carried out in 1971 by students at the Stanford Workshops on Political and Social Issues. They published a two-volume report entitled *Department of Defense-Sponsored Research at Stanford* in which they listed over one hundred research contracts held by academics at Stanford that were fully or partially funded by the US Department of Defense.

This constituted one quarter of all contracts or grants held by the university. Because defence contractors discouraged scientists from stating the military uses of their research, the students gained access to in-house statements about these contracts stored at the Defense Documentation Center (DDC). While the academics described their research in one way (as improving traffic, reducing pollution and so on), DDC statements gave very different accounts of the military potential of their research. For example, one contract based in the Department of Electrical Engineering was entitled 'High-power broadly tunable laser action in the ultraviolet spectrum', and the academic investigator correctly stated that ultraviolet lasers were 'needed in the areas of medicine, long-distance communication, and high-energy physics research'. However, the Office of Naval Research, which was funding the project, gave it a different title: 'Weaponry – lasers for increased damage effectiveness'. In a paragraph describing the research, the DDC stated that,

> Damage mechanism allowed by laser weapons is under intense investigation. However, it is known that within a range of frequencies the amount of damage for a given power increases with frequency. The highest frequency, shortest wavelength, is thus desirable.

In another example, a contract carried out by psychologist Philip Zimbardo was described as 'Individual and group variables influencing emotional arousal, violence, and behavior', but the DDC title gave the research a different spin: 'Personnel technology factors influencing disruptive behavior among military trainees'.[55] This level of military involvement in university research came to be known as the military–industrial–academic complex.

Furthermore, defence industries were quick to threaten to 'pull the plug' if the research became too 'soft'. In the UK, the

Chemical Defence Experimental Establishment faced this risk. It had been established in 1956 when Cold War hysteria, coupled with the Suez crisis and heightened IRA activity, meant that 'information was required by weapons assessment and design authorities (e.g. Ordnance Board, AORG and ARDE) on the wounding power of small missiles of various shapes and velocities'.[56] By 1965, however, the main task of the Army Wound Ballistics team involved infecting goats with gas gangrene in order to explore the progress of infection. As a result, W. S. S. Ladell, Assistant Director (Medical), wondered whether 'now that its experiments have been diverted from ballistics to what amounts to a study of wound healing and experimental surgery', it was worth considering whether the Ministry of Defence should continue to invest in the unit.[57] As I argued in Chapter Three, they were, literally, saved by the Troubles in Northern Ireland.

Perhaps the relative weight of humanitarian and anti-humanitarian objectives can best be summed up by Major Ralph W. French and Brigadier-General George R. Callender's contribution to one of the most influential books in the science of wound ballistics. After genuflecting towards its humanitarian aims (that is, such knowledge will help Medical Officers treat the wounded), they quickly turned to its darker goals. 'This knowledge', they bragged, 'permits the design of ordnance material for antipersonnel purposes on scientific grounds.' It 'also lessens the need for costly rule-of-thumb or "cut and try" methods by either the military surgeon or the ordnance engineer'.[58] In other words, the 'fog of war' could be dispelled once weapons designers, engineers and mathematicians had perfected the killing machines.[59]

Finally, in the late twentieth and early twenty-first century, scientists, technologists and engineers spawned a new Revolution in Military Affairs (RMA), which they claim is as important as previous RMAs (which included the invention of gunpowder, of

armoured vehicles and of aerial flight). Given the common sub-
stitution in military circles of the term 'warfighter' for what used
to be known as soldiers, sailors and airmen, I have dubbed this the
birth of the 'post-human warfighter'. The armed forces of
advanced Western states, particularly the US, were responsible
for conjuring up its existence, funding the scientific technology
required for its birth, sponsoring its proliferation and subsidizing
the diversionary apparatus (such as within entertainment industry,
which I explore in the next chapter) that has been central to its
infiltration into the popular imagination. The crushing force with
which the military complex has grasped the destructive potential
of this militarized post-human points to a new, more destructive
wounding of the world.

As two spokesmen from the US Naval War College put it in
2013, the military forces of advanced states had to maintain 'a
technical edge over potential adversaries . . . by fielding systems
that enable [American forces] to deliver lethal force while mini-
mizing the risk to their own forces'.[60] To do this, they needed a
militarist post-human who was dependent on external extensions
(technological 'add-ons') as well as internal modifications of the
physical body. The range of these modifications can be illustrated
by looking at what is currently being funded by the US Defense
Advanced Research Projects Agency (DARPA), a central organization in the post-human military project. DARPA is dedicated to
developing 'materials and devices inspired by living-systems and
using these new technologies to create new military systems'.
They feature a formidable arsenal of post-human enhancements,
from the 'Warrior Web' (an under-suit that enhances the ability of
soldiers to carry heavy gear for long periods) and prosthetics
controlled by brain–machine interfaces to robots, microelectro-
mechanical systems and nanotechnologies.[61] They insist that
'DARPA is well on its way to creating a Bio-revolution' which will
'help warfighters'.[62]

For advanced military nations, scientists, computer specialists and engineers have been responsible for waging new armed conflicts with the aid of humachines. Drones, robotic weapons, unmanned vehicles and suchlike are at the heart of twenty-first century aggression. In the words of a headline in *The Economist*: 'The Future of Warfare: Select Enemy. Delete'.[63] During 'Operation Enduring Freedom' and 'Operation Iraqi Freedom', unmanned aircraft systems flew almost half a million hours and unmanned ground vehicles conducted more than thirty thousand missions during which they detected and neutralized over fifteen thousand IEDs (improvised explosive devices) as part of the US-led coalition.[64] While the US Department of Defense had only fifty unmanned aircraft in 2000, by October 2009 they had 6800 and were still expanding. In 2010, the Department requested a further $6.1 billion from the US government for new unmanned systems.[65]

From the tiny 'Wasp' drone, which is small enough for a soldier to toss into the air like a mobile aeroplane to discover what might be behind a wall or hill, to the 44-foot long Global Hawk, which flies at sixty thousand feet and can remain airborne for thirty hours, human–machine systems dominate '*Bellum Americanum*'. The drone pilot, operating thousands of miles from his target, is a networked being, connected to local, national and global computer and satellite systems, including direct streaming into the offices of the US Secretary of State for Defense and the President.

As a result of this scientifically driven RMA, warfare loses a sense of boundaries. One of the most basic ways in which this happens is by the failure of contemporary militarists to recognize state borders. Drones conduct their killings without regard for national territories or liberal notions of sovereignty. They exercise persistent surveillance over large areas of the globe. As long ago as 2006, the Department of Defense's *Quadrennial Defense Review*

Report decreed that its goal was to 'establish an "unblinking eye" over the battlespace' – note, not battlefield – through 'persistent surveillance'. This would

> support operations against any target, day or night, in any weather, and in denied or contested areas. The aim is to integrate global awareness with local precision.[66]

This new form of warfare has significant implications for the traditional legal constructions of human rights and for humanitarian law that I discussed in Chapter Three. As Hannah Arendt astutely observed in *The Origins of Totalitarianism* (1973), human rights have customarily been associated with nation states: personhood is both conferred and revoked by sovereign leaders.[67] However, if the human of 'human rights talk' is defined by citizenship, the post-human military state denies this by eradicating the relevance of national boundaries or categories of citizens.

In other words, the crisis I discussed in Chapter Three has been further exacerbated by contemporary scientific technologies. Humanitarian law falters under this new, post-human form of warfare. In *Wired for War: The Robotics Revolution and Conflict in the Twenty-First Century* (2009), P. W. Singer quoted a proponent of military robotics as saying that 'the robot is our answer to the suicide bomber'.[68] His comment was taken up in 2011 when a commentator in the *Harvard National Security Journal* noted that this 'analogy between a robot and a suicide bomber is a chilling portent of post-human warfare'. He explained that

> both are the extremities of war: present in combat, lethal, and neither is entitled to the protections of IHL [International Humanitarian Law]. In short, they are objects of war not contemplated by humanitarian law, and place discourses of 'humanity' in question. They are post-humanitarian concerns.[69]

In other words, the '*jus in bello*' in humanitarian law is based on the idea of an active, willing human agent who can be held accountable for lethal decisions made in war. Scientists and robotic experts have fundamentally changed the entire scene. With the increase in semi-autonomous machines – and the future risk of fully autonomous machines charged with making decisions about who to kill – the basis of humanitarian law is undercut. In this way, the post-human has liberated itself not only from the constraints thrown over it by 'nature' but also from the constraints of humanist ideology that insists (in theory, if not in practice) on the application of humanitarian law in armed conflicts.

Deterritorialized warfare is not the only similarity between the post-human military and the terrorist: the other is the absence of temporal limits. For both, the aims of armed struggle are unlimited (thus precluding any decisive victory – indeed, rendering the concept of 'victory' redundant) and the means are bounded only by capacity and imagination. Both terrorists and science-driven, advanced militaries understand that their violence is futile in a liberal human sense: the suicide bomber who kills revellers in a Bali nightclub and the drone pilot who targets his victims from sixty-thousand feet in the sky are not attempting to change people's minds. Their state of war is indefinite; it is criminal action and police reaction masquerading as war. It is a form of warfare without bounds.

In addition to technological extensions to the human, which enable 'warfighters' vastly to exceed previous physical capabilities, contemporary science has also been employed to chemically alter brain states. Psychopharmacology has become a significant area of research and practice in post-human militaries. Among other things, it involves administering steroids to enhance physical traits like strength and endurance, and 'go pills' which contain the stimulant dexamphetamine. The latter are commonly used in the US Air Force. Although these pills are said to be voluntary (and pilots have to sign a document to that effect), refusing to take them could result in a pilot being banned from flying, thus jeopardizing his career in the Air Force.[70] Research is also being conducted into what is popularly known as the 'anti-remorse pill', aimed at eradicating the fear of engaging the enemy as well as the guilt arising from killing. As Leon Kass, chairman of the President's Council on Bioethics, explained, 'It's the morning-after pill for just about anything that produces regret, remorse, pain, or guilt.'[71] A national coordinator for Vietnam Veterans Against the War put it more succinctly: scientists were creating an 'anti-morality pill'.[72] This is the military–scientific complex taking charge of systems of ethics that have traditionally been the preserve of religion and philosophy.

I started this chapter with the US Army Soldier and Biological Chemical Command in Massachusetts, who believe that it is their duty to serve national interests through the application of science. One of the striking features of their service is their belief that, through developing weapons of individual, group and mass destruction, they are in fact promoting peace. Many scientists sincerely believe that by inventing more terrible weapons they will inhibit nations from going to war. Alfred Nobel, the inventor of dynamite, claimed that this was his motivation. He informed his friend Bertha von Suttner that he 'would like to produce a substance or a machine of such frightful, tremendous, devastating effect, that wars would become altogether impossible'. He believed that his dynamite factories would

> put an end to war even sooner than your [peace] congresses: on the day that two army corps can mutually annihilate each other in a second, all civilized nations will surely recoil with horror and disband their troops.[73]

Similarly, Richard Gatling (the inventor of a 250-shot-per-minute hand-cranked black powder gun) declared that when a man invents a process 'by which a whole army could be killed', then

> the lion and the lamb will lie down together . . . Wars among civilized nations would cease forever . . . The inventor of such a machine would prove a greater benefactor of his race, than he would should endow a thousand hospitals.[74]

More recently, drone pilot Matt Martin echoed the sentiment that

> If we who operated battle machines did our job properly, wars would be shortened and fractured societies rebuilt more quickly and securely . . . Machines would make warfare less destructive, not more.[75]

The problem is that at the same time Nobel was penning such life-affirming words to von Suttner he was also writing to others about his hope that the War Office would find his research into improving ballistics useful.[76] When Gatling invented his new weapon, he invented the 'first weapon of mass destruction'.[77] And when Martin claimed that high-tech weapons would 'driv[e] our adversaries to the bargaining table rather than the battle-field', he was thinking like the 'terrorists' he was seeking to exterminate. In each case, the 'dark science' of ballistics was creating what Zuckerman proudly called 'professional students of destruction'.[78]

PART FOUR

Militainment

CHAPTER SIX

Playing War

Why would someone *choose* war?

Fourteen years after volunteering to serve as a Marine in Vietnam, William D. Ehrhart attempted to explain why he had actively sought combat. He had been just seventeen years old at the time, and while he recognized that some volunteers had been naive, dim-witted or seeking an alternative to borstal or prison, those explanations did not apply to him. In 'Why I Did It' (1980), Ehrhart casted a calm, forensic eye over what had motivated him to put his young life at risk by volunteering to be dispatched to a particularly brutal war zone.

Ehrhart admitted that he had grown up in the all-white, 'hick', Pennsylvanian town of Perkasie, where people worked hard and 'never questioned the meaning of Duty, Honor, and Country'. Each school day began with the Lord's Prayer and the Pledge of Allegiance; every Memorial Day bicycles were decorated with red, white and blue crêpe paper; on Armed Forces Day school-boys openly admired the 'dazzling dress blue uniform with red trouser stripes and gold piping' of the Marines. Military recruiters understood the psyche of adolescent males sufficiently to know that telling potential recruits that they would be sent into real war zones would be enticing rather than alarming. Everyone in

Perkasie assumed that America was the 'greatest and noblest nation on earth'; everything America did was right.

However, there were more subtle forces that Ehrhart believed made enlisting in the Marines attractive. Even before undergoing Basic Training, Ehrhart was fully conversant with all things military. Since childhood he had immersed himself in war games, films and literature. Actors like John Wayne (who starred in some of the most classic war films of all time) and William Holden (hero of *Stalag 17* and *The Bridge on River Kwai*) were his idols. He knew all about the exploits of the First World War fighter ace Eddie Rickenbacker, as well as of the two most highly decorated American soldiers of the First and Second World Wars, Alvin York and Audie Murphy. Prior to being hanged as an illegal combatant during the American Revolutionary War, Nathan Hale famously quipped: 'I only regret that I have but one life to give for my country' – and the adolescent Ehrhart could be heard echoing Hale's sentiments. He had spent hundreds of hours constructing miniature battleships, fighter planes and bombers from model kits. His most memorable Christmas presents were a life-sized plastic .30 calibre machine gun and a .45 calibre automatic cap pistol, complete with a leather holster embossed with USMC (US Marine Corps). Joining the real thing was a defiant 'I'll show them' to his parents and community. It encapsulated his teenage dream to become 'a man no one would dare to mess with'.[1] And so Ehrhart enlisted and was sent to Vietnam where his life changed for ever.

If we are to understand Ehrhart's rash decision – and those of millions of other volunteers – we have to understand the pleasures of imaginary violence. We have to know why violence is so easily turned into a game.

Ehrhart was a fairly typical young man. He loved playing war. The title of a book published in 2009 echoes the lie that the young

Ehrhart bought into: *War Isn't Hell, It's Entertainment*.[2] As Ehrhart discovered, this is only true for people a long way from the killing fields.

Within the cosy confines of 'hick' towns and suburbia, however, war-themed toys enthral many children and even adults. Although some girls enjoy playing with model soldiers (the young Charlotte and Emily Brontë were fans), war toys have mainly been marketed to the male sex. Men as diverse as warmonger Winston Churchill, socialist and pacifist-sympathizer H. G. Wells and heart-throb Douglas Fairbanks, Jr., were all keen war gamers. Robert Louis Stevenson even composed a poem celebrating uniformed soldiers and their miniature accessories. In it, he conjured up the image of a boy lying sick in bed with 'all my toys beside me lay / To keep me happy all the day'. Then,

> sometimes for an hour or so
> I watched my leaden soldiers go,
> With different uniform and drills,
> Among the bed-clothes, through the hills.

Through play, the boy could imagine himself

> the giant great and still
> That sits upon that pillow-hill,
> And sees before him, dale and plain,
> The pleasant land of counterpane.[3]

It was a glorious fantasy in which the enfeebled child was able to wield power over a Lilliputian world. In a less poetic vein, this was also what the British sculptor of toy soldiers Roy Selwyn-Smith was alluding to when he attempted to explain the 'charm of the old toy soldier'. Its allure, he concluded,

lies in its simplicity of shape, which verges on that of a cari-
cature. With his doll-like rosy cheeks and small black-dot
eyes – unblinking, wide-awake – he seems to be awaiting
your command in a fantasy world where his only claim to
individuality is the slight variation of his bright, glossy uniform
supplied by the painter's hand.[4]

In other words, the charm of the toy-soldier lay in the players'
ability to subject it to whatever fantasy they want to conjure up:
alert, obedient and armed, the miniature figure will perform any
desired task.

As playthings, toy soldiers are an eighteenth-century invention.
Of course, miniature soldiers had been made in ancient Rome and
chess (a war game) originated in eastern India before the sixth
century AD, but significant production of toy soldiers started in
the 1730s. Originally, these German figures were flat, only
becoming fully rounded replicas near the end of that century.
From the 1760s, Andreas Hipert of Nuremberg began making tin
imitations of the much more expensive silver or lead toy soldiers,
however their widespread appeal had to wait until the development of mass-production techniques and the rise of large
department stores in the nineteenth century.

Until the 1890s, British and American children were
dependent upon exports of toy soldiers from Germany and
France. In 1893, William Britain, Jr. proposed improving on
his father's technique of manufacturing tin soldiers by introducing hollow casting. The result was a commercial success:
compared with their predecessors, Britain's toy soldiers were
lighter, cheaper to make and distribute, and, most importantly,
were considered to be aesthetically more agreeable. Despite
some anomalies (Fusiliers and Scots Greys were oversized,
while lancers and infantrymen of the Royal Sussex Regiment
were undersized), his toy infantrymen were made to the scale

of 1:32. Each stood a proud 54 millimetres tall without their headdresses.[5]

Over time, other innovations were introduced. Inflexible limbs and fixed weapons were gradually jettisoned; moveable parts became *de rigueur*. The ceremonial poses of earlier soldiers were increasingly regarded as old-fashioned (albeit popular with collectors): they lacked the authenticity and energy of toys that could crouch behind walls, leap from trenches, wield bayonets and fire miniature pellets.

In more recent decades, G.I. Joe is one of the most representative of the new breed of such toys. America's Movable Fighting Man, G.I. Joe was designed by Larry Reiner for Hasbro in 1965. In its first year, it brought in $23 million in sales, becoming the top selling toy for children between the ages of five and twelve years.[6] Why was this 'action figure' (in advertisements and packaging, he was never called a doll) so popular? Crucially, G.I. Joe was supple: he could be bent into active postures and he was able to carry a range of weapons. Children were able to choreograph his movements: at one moment, he could bayonet an evil enemy, while the next moment he could crouch behind a boulder and use his machine gun to mow down an entire battalion. No longer spectators, children were able to actively live out their war fantasies. Indeed, in its earliest incarnation, G.I. Joe actually stood nearly one foot tall. It was the anti-war sentiment arising out of the war in Vietnam that resulted in him being cut down to size: by 1977 he was only eight inches tall, and was reduced to only three-and-a-quarter inches in 1982.[7] There is no need to invoke Freud to know that this was an inglorious end. G.I. Joe was gradually usurped by more aggressive action figures such as *Star Wars* figures (1970s) and the Mighty Morphin Power Rangers (1990s).

It is important to observe that such toys and action figures did not only appeal to children. Adults also took delight in these miniature men, although they call it 'collecting' rather than 'playing'. Often, a defensive note can be heard. In the after-math of war, revering toy soldiers came with a whiff of warmongering. In 1935, one collector felt the urge to plead with readers of *The Times* to 'relieve the collectors . . . of the reproach of being bloodthirsty ruffians'. Their passion for minia-ture soldiers was not about 'putting in the path of innocent youth the warlike toys whose brutalizing influence can infect an other-wise lamblike infancy with an incurable itch for carnage'. Collectors were not nostalgic for 'old wars', but were as peace-loving as other men.[8]

Writing in the context of the conflict in Vietnam, the author of *Collecting Toy Soldiers* (1967) also sounded a little defensive. The first sentences in Jean Nicollier's book asked, 'Is collecting a nerv-ous affliction? And is a collector, therefore, a kind of hypochondriac?' Collecting some things might 'invite ridicule', he admitted: being obsessive about train tickets, restaurant menus or cigar bands was beneath contempt. There was also the risk that adults who collected military figurines would be accused of mil-itarism. Unthinking acquaintances might wonder: 'Is there in him a dormant yet bloodthirsty general, doing his best to alleviate his bellicose tendencies?'

Nicollier batted away such anxieties. The man who collected model soldiers was nothing short of a 'visualizer', he insisted. He seeks to

> reconstruct, at little cost, very realistic scenes of to-day and yesteryear. He exhibits these in showcases fitted with appro-priate lighting . . . trees, hills, houses, fences and guns, all in their proper scale, contribute a sense of reality to the scene.

Soldiers 'appeal to eye and heart'. The collector was attracted to the aesthetics of the splendid coats and jackets of the National Guard, the armour of Marignano, the sumptuous clothing of Charles the Bold or the Sun-King, Louis XIV. And to complete all this pomp and circumstance, the standards and colours bring their coats-of-arms, devices and wide expanses of green, blur or red fields, where shot and shell have left their mark.

As a result, even in the most 'workaday homes' miniature soldiers bring to life 'a past whose lustre and heroism are no longer a closed book'.[9] Or, as another collector put it, through handling these simple figurines, men could retreat nostalgically to child-hood, often in the company of likeminded friends.[10] This nostalgia for a more chivalric, glamorous past, as well as for the innocence of childhood, permeates much of the literature on collecting.

Of course, even Nicollier admitted that he was also passionate about reproducing 'very realistic scenes of *to-day*', as well as 'yes-teryear'.[11] This was certainly the case with prolific collector M. Leicester Hewitt, who in the 1930s could boast of a collection of toy soldiers that consisted of fifty thousand pieces ('representing a replica in miniature of an Army Corps of the British Expeditionary Force'). He thanked the military authorities for their 'encouragement', acknowledging that their advice had enabled him to 'keep closely acquainted with Army developments so that I have been able to bring my army bang up to date in all detail outlines'.[12]

Whether melancholic about the romance of past martial tra-ditions or admiring present-day militarism, collectors of miniature militia agreed that their pastime was aesthetically pleas-urable and manly. This was obviously the case for men who collected guns. In the words of one avid collector, its

aura of mystery enhances fascination, and differentiates gun collectors from, for example, stamp collectors, who find family and group encouragement at an early age, often from female relatives. Involvement with guns connects the boy to older, admired males, and differentiates him from women.[13]

For this collector, stamp collecting was scorned because of its association with 'female relatives'; the hyper-masculine leisure pursuits associated with weapons brought pleasure.

Not only manly, it was also a healthy pastime, deeply embedded in the triumphant stride of human civilization. Time and again, collectors emphasized that just as it was 'in the nature of man to be warlike both as a hunter of animals and as a killer of his own species', so too it was 'in his nature to paint likenesses and make models of his everyday life'.[14] Or, as another put it, 'fighting is one of the laws of Nature', which was why it was 'unlikely that the cult of the military toy will ever die out altogether among children young or old'.[15] In such a way, war and war-play were inextricably linked and naturalized.

The 'cult of the military toy' is also a lucrative business. As I was writing this chapter, a single plastic Jawa figure (from *Star Wars*), complete with weapon, and made by Palitoy in Coalville, Leicester, was sold for £10,200.[16] The purchaser was obviously a wealthy collector, but even toy companies devoted to promoting cheap, recreational combat for young children make vast profits. Their range of products is immense: after all, toy soldiers are only one of hundreds of imitation war objects promising hours of fun. Fake guns, for instance, are extremely popular. Some are mute, requiring players to utter the ferocious war cry 'rat-a-tat-tat!' Other models are charged with a fulminating compound or fire blank .22 cartridges. Sales of both are impressive. In 1950, the President of the Carnell Manufacturing Company bragged to the *New Yorker* that 'Last year there were enough holster sets manufactured to supply every male child in the United States three times over. I don't know where they go.' His plant in Brooklyn produced between nine and fourteen thousand holster and pistol sets a day yet still could not meet demand.[17] He was right to be amazed: according to another calculation, between 1944 and 1951 American toy companies sold more than 160 million pistol and holster sets.[18] By 1962, toy guns were the largest category of toys for boys, with American sales exceeded one hundred million dollars annually.[19] Two decades later, nearly 10 per cent of all toys available for sale in the United States were war toys.[20] In 1986, nineteen million toy guns were sold in the United States; a number that had soared to thirty-three million by 1997.[21]

The child-consumer (and his parents) was inundated with choice. When William D. Ehrhart, with whom I started this chapter, was a child, an arsenal of toys catered to his obsession with the Special Forces. He would have been able to spend his pocket money on Green Beret action figures, books, records, comic strips, bubble gum and puzzles. The Sears catalogue offered a Special Forces outpost, complete with machine gun, rifle, hand grenades, field telephone and, of course, replica soldiers wearing berets. The whole thing cost only ten dollars. It was a bargain. Not to be outdone, Montgomery Ward's Christmas catalogue promised to send a Green Beret uniform for half that price, with (for an additional six dollars) an AR-15 rifle, pistol, flip-top military holster and a green beret.[22]

Of course, there were lots of imitation 'sci-fi' weapons on the market, but there was even greater demand for weapons that mimicked real-life conflicts. Perhaps the most controversial genre played with atomic destruction. In the late 1940s and 1950s, for example, children might have an Uranium Rush board game, a seven-foot-long Polaris Nuclear Submarine (which fired rockets and torpedoes), a Lone Ranger Atomic Bomb Ring, a toy Geiger Counter and models of the bombs dropped on Hiroshima and Nagasaki. While playing, they could suck on Atomic Fire candy.[23]

Figure 6.1. The novelty toy company A. C. Gilbert Company released the 'Atomic Bomb Dexterity Puzzle' (*c.* 1947), which consisted of a small box covered with a glass top, inside of which was a map of Japan. Players were told to shake the box so that two bomb-shaped missiles came to rest in the indentations beside the cities labelled Nagasaki and Hiroshima.[24]

In 1981 a similarly controversial game was released by Waddington's House of Games in Leeds, entitled Bombshell. It sold for £6.49 or less, and was described by its manufacturer as an 'explosively funny game' for children aged over six years of age. At a time when IRA bombs were killing people – including military personnel engaged in defusing the devices – in Northern Ireland, Ireland and mainland Britain, Bombshell encouraged children to play at defusing bombs. Players took on the character of 'brave but bungling' soldiers (they could take up the identity of Major Disaster, Sergeant Jeremy Jitter, Private Tommy Twitter and Piper Willy Fumble) who would creep up to an unexploded bomb (a red plastic shell with a spring inside) and attempt to defuse it. Players would turn the top of the shell until it 'exploded', after which they would clip on plastic badges showing how injured they were. After four injuries, their character would be deemed 'out'. As can be seen in the television advertisement for Bombshell, the game caused children and grandfathers to laugh and clap excitedly.[25] Understandably, families of bomb-disposal experts killed by IRA bombs were appalled and the game was withdrawn,[26] but not before the normalization of deadly violence had been noted.

Finally, the normalization of violence through embedding it in toys and other games was significantly boosted from 1999 when the Institute for Creative Technologies at the University of Southern California began formally coordinating links between weapons manufacturers and commercial toy companies. This enabled commercial toy makers to produce imitation weapons that exactly matched their lethal counterparts.[27] In fact, the exchange when both ways: real-life weapons were also modelled on toys. Thus, when the Marines used the Dragon Eye remote-controlled air reconnaissance vehicle in Iraq they were probably unaware that model planes had inspired the bungee cord that launched it.[28]

An army of psychologists stepped up to insist on the value of war-play. In the context of the bombing of Britain during the Second World War, psychoanalysts such as Anna Freud (daughter of Sigmund) had a therapeutic reason to encourage children to play at death and destruction. She gave war toys to traumatized young children in an attempt to help them master their anxiety or, at the very least, to provide temporary relief while they were coming to terms with the destruction and death they had witnessed.[29]

In a very different way, during the Cold War some psychoanalysts promoted war-play as a way of allowing young boys to act out their aggressive impulses, thus warding off communist impulses.[30] Others simply noted that such games 'let off steam'.[31] Patriotism and manliness were fostered; effeminacy and moral weakness dealt a fatal blow.

Other champions of militaristic toys went much further, claiming that young children were innately murderous and these toys simply allowed them to express this natural impulse. The author of 'Warlike Children: Frightfulness in the Nursery' (1915) was particularly forthright. Children possessed 'belligerent imaginations', he claimed. He conjured up an image of a typical living room, on the floor of which lay

> a dozen overturned soldiers of wood of varying degrees of dismemberment, and we were told on no account to touch them. 'Don't touch those; they're dead.' We thought it right to ask what had killed them. 'The poison gases.' And a disused gramophone was pointed out, supposed to be exuding fatal fumes. But wasn't it horrid? Wasn't it rather cruel? No — obviously it was great fun . . . They want 'more men' as we do, more guns, more ammunition . . . They want fatal effects, fatal mechanisms.[32]

Gas had only been used against real Allied positions in December 1915, less than six months before this account, but it had already been incorporated into children's play.

Equally rapid was the militarization of play at the start of the Second World War. Two months after the British declaration of war on Germany in 1939, an editorial in *The Times* entitled 'Toy Soldiers for Christmas' echoed the view of the author of 'Warlike Children' that the nation's youth possessed 'belligerent imaginations'. The editorial was a response to an unnamed correspondent who protested against the sale of 'toy tanks, bombing aeroplanes, reproductions of the Siegfried Line, etc.' on the grounds that they 'familiarize our babies with such horrible things'. Nonsense, the editor exclaimed: 'it is they [the 'babies'] who familiarize us'. He insisted that even very young children

> have an instinctive craving for these most obvious and mani-
> fold means of exercising power; and on the nursery floor the
> most frightful weapons, the bloodiest massacres, the most
> crushing defeats are innocent of all pain and of all horror . . .
> Toy soldiers are always the best of fun because . . . no other
> game so richly and harmlessly satisfies the infant craving to
> destroy.

He admitted that there had to be some limits to this instinct – children must be taught not to attack other children, punch animals or throw plates, for instance. Nevertheless,

> There is nothing in the world toward which to guide it better
> than ranks of gallant soldiers who can be mown down with
> lethal weapons of thrilling power and then stood up again not
> a penny the worse.

In other words, children were to be taught to direct their aggressive impulses against 'gallant soldiers' rather than other children, animals or inanimate objects. Somewhat optimistically, the editor concluded that giving toy soldiers to children would not 'induce the spirit of militarism' because that 'spirit is there already, and the more it can work itself off in the nursery the stronger the hope for the peace of the world'.[33]

By evoking the 'natural' belligerence of infants and children, these commentators were suggesting that war-play was benign, and probably even desirable. Not everyone agreed. At one extreme, some psychoanalysts and psycho-historians drew lurid conclusions

from the fact that the young Adolf Hitler had been a passionate
player of war games.[34] Less hysterical critics identified questions
of taste as being the problem (the Bombshell game is an obvious
example), while others simply lamented the poor quality of mass-
produced toy weapons. This seems to have been the point of a
reporter in 1969, who lauded the revival of high-quality toyshops
where an aesthetically sensitive parent could buy a 'beautiful
wooden shotgun' for his or her children. It was a gun that 'could
not offend even the most ardent campaigner against war toys', she
observed.[35]

Morally conscientious parents needed a different kind of reas-
surance. Scares about the effect of weapon-play flared up in the
context of violence in real human encounters, particularly during
the war in Vietnam and after mass shootings at schools and in
other public places. Anti-establishment movements from the
1960s onwards frequently protested against the militarization of
childhood. Between the 1960s and the 1980s, feminist voices
became especially forceful, arguing that playing with weapons
served as a form of basic training for the future role of boys within
patriarchal, capitalist society. Their fears generated a vast amount
of research exploring the relationship between war games,
aggression and increased testosterone in young males.[36] There
have been periodic bonfires lit for toy guns and war books.[37]
Many crèches and schools responded by introducing 'zero toler-
ance' for such games within their premises.[38]

Unfortunately, the social-scientific evidence behind much of
the research linking specific acts of violence and playing war
games is patchy. For every study showing a positive correlation,
there was another showing a negative one. Methodological rigour
was often lacking. Lines of causality were confused. For example,
while some violent adolescent males who engaged in school
shootings were obsessed with war-play, it is also clear that many
similarly obsessed young people did not go on to kill their

playmates. Examples include Eric Harris and Dylan Klebold, who were responsible for the shootings at Columbine High School on 20 April 1999. When some journalists used the provocative photographs of Harris and Klebold pretending to fire guns as evidence of a link between play- and real-violence, others quickly pointed out that the uncropped photograph actually showed at least five other adolescent boys and girls in the same pose. None of those young people confused pretended belligerence with real violence.[39] It is difficult to avoid the conclusion that pre-existing political outlook, rather than scientific rigour, continue to dominate the debates.

I also believe that attempting to find a direct link between war-play and personal aggression is misguided. If we are to understand the pervasive militarism of modern society, we won't find it by exploring the psychological make-up of individual perpetrators. The problem is much bigger.

Rather than turning to individual psychology, there are other ways to suggest that militaristic play may be harmful. First, it is important to note that the military establishment has good evidence that war-games, especially video games and shooter-play, greatly improve the 'lethal effectiveness' of their armed personnel. This is why these games are used extensively in military training. I turn to this evidence in the next chapter. Of course, this is not to say that playing such games lead to violence, merely that they provide training in violence and they impart skills that can be utilized in belligerent contexts.

Second, some toy weapons cause injuries. Notoriously, non-lethal weapons such as airsoft firearms and paintball markers, which are marketed towards older adolescents, have led to serious injuries.[40] Many imitation guns are almost identical to real-life ones, and can damage tissue. For instance, the MP5K BB gun is the same shape and size as its real counterpart. The only differences are that it is slightly lighter, fires 6 mm pellets instead of

9 mm bullets, has a slightly lower rate of fire (750 pellets/min versus 900 rounds/min), and has a muzzle velocity of 90 metres per second rather than 400.[41] Replica BB weapons can be purchased without age or security checks, yet, when fired into a person, cause multiple pellets to hit a relatively small area of tissue. When some surgeons tested on the weapon on the carcass of a chicken they were shocked by the injuries inflicted. Of course, they observed, 'there are many differences between a supermarket-purchased fresh chicken and a human', but 'modern, electric-powered BB guns are almost indistinguishable from the weapon on which they are based and have the ability to fire pellets at a high rate and penetrate tissue'.[42]

The third danger of play weapons is the ease with which they can be converted into lethal ones.[43] This has become an increasing problem in the inner cities. 'Zip guns' – or improvised firearms – are relatively easy for a 'curious youngster' to make.[44] For instance, Brocock air-powered pistols (which can be purchased by mail order or in shops to anyone over the age of seventeen years in possession of a hundred pounds) can be converted in less than an hour into a pistol capable of firing live ammunition.[45] Because Brococks use metal parts they can withstand being fired with live ammunition without shattering.[46] In 2002 and 2003, a series of killings in Manchester, Bristol, Strathclyde, Birmingham and Nottingham using the air-pistol Brocock led to their subsequent banning in the UK.[47] This has not happened in the US.

The final reason militaristic play can become dangerous is that it encourages children to play with real weapons. This is a particular problem in America, where between 20 and 37 per cent of American homes possess guns and as many as 18 per cent of owners admit to keeping their firearms unlocked and loaded.[48] Between 1979 and 1994, firearms killed nearly twelve thousand American children under the age of fifteen years.[49] In the 1990s,

one in every six American adolescents had seen or known someone who had been shot.[50]

Some American commentators have responded to these
killings by calling for children to be taught firearm safety at
school. The solution to gun accidents, in other words, is *more*
training in gun use, not less. The National Rifle Association
(NRA) has led this argument. The NRA's interest in children's
enjoyment of weapons forms part of their belief that guns are an
American right. Billing themselves as 'America's Longest-
Standing Civil Rights Organization',[51] the NRA encourages
children as young as eight to be taught how to handle and fire
weapons. The 'golden rule of handling firearms', a NRA
spokesman insisted in 1964, is 'Never point a gun at any person or
living creature – unless you intend to shoot it – even if the gun is
a toy'. While a six-year-old child might look 'cute' when he runs
out '"shooting" people with his toy cap pistol . . . he is not so cute
if he finds a real gun in the closet'. Parents

> should expect a child to treat a real gun in the same rough
> careless way he has been handling his toy gun . . . One needs
> only to watch children playing 'war' or 'sniper' to realize
> how often the muzzles of their toy guns point directly at each
> other . . . Basic gun safety codes can be taught easily to the
> small fry with his cap pistol, so that when the time comes for
> him to have his own rifle, he knows a few rules.[52]

In other words, play-shooting *is* preparation for its real-life
counterpart.

Historically, play-shootings and lethal-shooting *were* connected:
encouraging young boys to play with weapons was considered an
important part of their preparation for manhood. From the conquest of Native American lands through to periods of imperial

invasions, children (again, primarily but not solely boys) had to be socialized into the use of violence. Land was conquered, leaving homesteads in need of defence; hunting was a source of protein as well as a popular pastime; being an effective marksman was a crucial stage in the development of a virile masculinity. Such arguments were spelt out in detail by 'L. B.', writing during the Second Boer War. He praised the interest that boys and men in Britain had for cricket and football and argued that it was important not to 'extinguish an interest in these games which are so useful in developing a keen eye, swift feet, and skilful arm'. Nevertheless, he urged men to 'divert' such sporting interests to 'other games which may serve a more practical purpose': that is, 'how to handle a gun, how to shoot, and how to manœuvre'. Only this would protect Britain in the case of future wars.[53] From the late nineteenth century onwards, an astounding range of politicians, lawyers, physicians, writers and martial leaders devoted their formidable talents to promoting military drill in schools, both to improve public health and to ensure that citizens were prepared.[54]

Weapons manufacturers energetically marketed guns to children. From the 1860s onwards, the craze for guns in the US was helped by their declining price as a result of escalating manufacturing capacity during the American Civil War. In Canada, too, guns aimed at the children's market were inexpensive. By the 1880s, revolvers sold for $1.50 or less.[55] Eaton's (Canada's large department store) offered .22-calibre rifles for only two dollars in 1899.[56] Air guns were sold in the toy section of Eaton's catalogue in 1892–3, and even when they shifted them to the firearms pages in 1902 they continued to refer to weapons such as the King Air Rifle as 'a splendid rifle for boys'.[57]

Masculine values, as well as good manners, would be promoted by training children in the use of firearms and marksmanship. Or so it was argued. In the words of Robert Baden-Powell in his phenomenally popular *Scouting for Boys*

(1908), 'every boy ought to learn how to shoot and to obey orders, else he is no more good when war breaks out than an old woman, and merely gets killed like a squealing rabbit'.[58] Magazines routinely portrayed the connection between boys and weapons as the most 'natural' thing in the world,[59] such as in an advertisement in *Arms and the Man* (1918): 'Let *Your* Boy Try for the Famous Winchester Medals' because 'every natural boy wants a gun'. It was part of a man's 'instinct' and

> allowed to develop naturally it will make a man out of him. Sooner or later he is going to get hold of the thing his manly instinct leads him to want, so the sooner you put a gun in his hands and teach him how to use it correctly, the better for both of you.[60]

This was a masculine rite that linked sons to fathers. Indeed, it was the paternal duty of fathers to teach their sons how to wield 'the fine, accurate Winchester .22'. As a bonus, 'You and he can have a lot of fun together.'[61]

Interestingly, in recent years, pro-gun lobbyists have supplemented this argument that guns are a form of father–son bonding with a parallel one in which mothers play a significant role. The catchword is family values. Thus, the NRA website features a video promoting gun use as a healthy family activity. In it Lisa Looper, a mother of three boys aged from two to eight years, talks about guns designed for 'concealed carry' by women, arguing that she started wearing a gun after she had children because 'it helps me to protect my boys – and that's what a mom is supposed to do'. She also believes that guns reinforce family life, arguing that so many family activities are

> geared towards just adults or just kids, but shooting sports is something that the whole family can be involved in. Being on

the range definitely causes everyone to focus. You don't have the video games and the cell phones with there with us. We focus on each other; we focus on the experience. It is definitely a chance to bond.[62]

That is, the good mother removes her children from the pernicious playing of videogames and the isolating effects of mobile phones in order to engage with the outdoor sport of shooting. Neoconservative values and the wielding of weapons of destruction are mutually reinforcing.

Appealing to family values was only one of many neoconservative principles important to pro-gun lobbies. Patriotism was also crucial. War-play was an important recruiter for the armed forces. Each of the military services recognized the importance of 'fun and games' in encouraging young people to sign up. This was as true during the First World War as it is today and can be illustrated in one of the most influential recruiting posters distributed in Britain during the First World War. It was designed by the popular book illustrator Savile Lumley in 1915, at the height of the crisis over recruitment to the war. The initial idea came from printer Arthur Gunn, shortly before he volunteered to serve in the Westminster Volunteers. 'One night', Gunn's son explained,

> my father came home very worried about the war situation and discussed with my mother whether he should volunteer. He happened to come in to where I was asleep and quite casually said to my mother, 'If I don't join the forces whatever will I say to Paul if he turns round to me and says, "What did you do in the Great War, Daddy?"'[63]

And that became the slogan for the famous recruiting poster. But the story does not stop there. In the final version, the poster shows a father sitting in a chair with his young *daughter* on his lap. The most striking thing about the poster is not the mortified father, nor the fact that Lumley understood that it would be more effective to have a daughter, rather than a son, ask the question. Instead, the most interesting aspect is the image of the father's young son. He is sitting at his father's feet, completely absorbed in playing with toy soldiers. Unlike his shirking father, the son knows what is necessary in order to be a real man: he is already in training.

In the next chapter, I explore the link between video games and recruiting more thoroughly. For now, I want to note that video games are not the only form of pleasure that military recruiters seek to exploit. Like the young son with his toy soldiers in Lumley's poster, in modern recruitment advertisements toys are prominent. For instance, the US air force's 'Cross into the Blue' ad is a classic example of the evolution of a young boy into an adult war pilot. In seeking to attract young people into the air force, this commercial posits a seamless transition between the pleasures of playing with toy aeroplanes and operating unmanned drones. The advertisement begins with a young boy playing with a paper aeroplane. As the boy grows older his playthings also evolve: his Styrofoam glider becomes a powered model airplane, then a radio-controlled one and, by the time he is an adult, he is manning a Predator drone. The transformation from boy to man is complete: the words 'We've been waiting for you' appear on the screen. Such promotional films not only capitalize on nostalgia, but they also erase the distinction between innocent play and the job of dropping lethal missiles.

The message in such recruiting campaigns is clear: the armed forces are fun. Along with war as a 'humanitarian' enterprise, it is a message promoted in many of the forces' public relations campaigns. Vast sums of money and energy are exerted in entertaining both potential recruits and their families. As early as

1968, for instance, visitors to Chicago's Museum of Science and Industry could sit in a Bell UH-1D (Huey) helicopter simulator and fire an electronic machine gun at Vietnamese homes.[64] On a lighter note, the military invests significant time and money in military bands, skydiving teams, aerial demonstrations, talent competitions, re-enactments and so on. Through fun and games, they seek to bring the war home.

One of the most influential ways in which the armed forces insinuate themselves into popular culture is through cinema. War and films have always been intimate. Indeed, it is no coincidence that we talk about 'shooting' films. The first proto-motion picture camera was Étienne-Jules Marey's 1882 chronophotographic rifle, which was a camera mounted on an actual rifle stock. Gelatine plates were situated in the magazine of the gun and when the trigger was pulled images were captured on the plate.[65]

Of course, Marey's version of 'shooting' films was mechanical and metaphorical. In the context of real military conflicts there was more at stake than capturing moving images: manpower and morale could be manipulated through the cinematic image. One of the most effective was the *Why We Fight* series of seven films produced during the Second World War. It was to become the blueprint for subsequent endeavours. Promoted by General George C. Marshall, the US Army Chief of Staff, and directed by innovative filmmaker Frank Capra, these highly moralistic films were shown in cinemas throughout America as well as to the troops. They were a propaganda triumph. Opinion polls revealed that troops who had watched these films and the biweekly newsreels issued by the War Department were significantly more pro-war than those who had not seen the films.[66]

This was one of the reasons the US Department of Defense attempted to replicate their formula during other conflicts.

Examples include the *Why Vietnam?* film, released in 1965, which spread a strong anti-Communist message to troops as well as to young people in high schools and colleges. The filmmakers ignored the violence of that conflict in order to emphasize the importance of American aid to the Vietnamese. Similarly, in *The Unique War* (1966) and *Vietnamese Village Reborn* (1967), Americans were invited into villages and encouraged to see the war as one of liberation and freedom. Even those films addressed to servicemen – such as *Your Tour in Vietnam* (1970) – had strong patriotic and aesthetic elements. *Your Tour in Vietnam* luridly evoked the thrills of combat and gave out tough advice, but it also ensured that the explosions of bombs dropping from B-52s were timed to the rhythm of a jazz score.[67]

It would be wrong, however, to place too much weight on films that were explicitly intended as propaganda. The relationship between the cinema and the armed forces is much more subtle than that. Even during the early years of cinema, senior military officers recognized that they could benefit from sponsoring productions. In 1915, the US Secretary of War ordered the army to provide over one thousand cavalry troops and a military band to help make the pro-Ku Klux Klan epic *The Birth of a Nation*. Half a century later, *The Green Berets* (1968) benefited from the loan of military airplanes, helicopters, weapons and troops. The Special Forces provided advisers and allowed the film crew to spend 107 days filming inside Fort Benning. There was a public uproar when it was discovered that the government received only $18,600 for the use of the military equipment, facilities and manpower (at a cost to the taxpayer of around one million dollars). However, the protests were swatted away with the explanation that working on the film had 'training benefits'.[68]

In recent years the relationship between the three military branches and the film industry has been formalized. There is a symbiotic relationship between the film industry and the military complex. On the one hand, the film industry has a lot to gain from the armed forces. All films that have a military component are dependent upon material support from the armed forces to add the authenticity that is essential to such productions. The loan of personnel might be essential, as in *Top Gun* and *Iron Eagle* (both 1986), when highly trained military pilots were needed to perform some of the aerial manoeuvres. In the *Transformer* series (2007, 2009 and 2011), director Michael Bay required the help of military personnel and airbases. He recalled that, 'The military adds such credibility. It adds to the realism of the movie and . . . it's always an amazing experience and I never even thought they would give us approval for this movie but the Pentagon was really into it.'[69]

On the other hand, the only reason the military cooperate is because they, too, benefit immeasurably. The US navy loaned the makers of the film *Behind Enemy Lines* (2001) a vast array of equipment (including the supercarrier USS *Carl Vinson*, fighter planes and Apache helicopters) as well as personnel. In return, they were allowed to make significant changes to the script and were able to use clips from the film in their 'Navy: Accelerate your Life' recruitment campaign. Similar negotiations took place with other films. Thus, Master Sergeant Larry Belen, superintendent of technical support for the Air Force Test Pilot School, noted that he auditioned as an extra in the film *Iron Man* to ensure that audiences would gain

> a really good impression of the Air Force, like they got about the Navy seeing *Top Gun* . . . This is a chance to show people what we're made of and what we're able to do.

Air Force Captain Christian Hodge (the Defense Department's project officer for *Iron Man*) agreed, pointing out that one of the biggest gratifications of his job is getting to see real servicemen and women bringing their expertise to a movie that bolstered the reputation of their service. 'This movie is going to be fantastic,' he bragged. 'The Air Force is going to come off looking like rock stars.'[70] It is no wonder that during showings of war films such as *Top Gun* and *Behind Enemy Lines*, the US Navy set up recruiting stations in the lobbies of movie theatres.

This point is neatly summarized by the US Air Force Entertainment Liaison Office, which boasts about its role in producing feature films. According to their website, they are 'the primary contact for processing documentary/television/film and music video production requests seeking support from The United States Air Force'.[71] The Liaison Office is 'the industry's gateway to an extraordinary arsenal of aircraft, equipment, incredible personnel, and locations'. Their mission is to protect and project the air force in entertainment media, including film, television, video games, music videos, comic books and more. They encourage producers to come to them 'at the earliest possible stage', so that 'we can be having a dialogue about what works for us and what works for them long before their production deadlines'.[72] In the words of Philip Strub, Director of Entertainment and the Media at the Department of Defense, 'When filmmakers come to us and seek our assistance in the production of feature films and television programs and those sorts of things, we see this as an important opportunity to tell the American public something about the US Air Force.'[73] Of course, there is another side to this: the military can deny support, as it did with the film *Thirteen Days*, on the grounds that it gave unflattering portray of Curtis LeMay. As Strub said in another interview, 'Any film that portrays the military as negative is not realistic to us.'[74]

By the time of the Iraq War in 2003, the military–entertainment complex had taken yet another turn. Real-time war was marketed as entertainment for *two* audiences, the victims as well as those at home. 'Shock and awe' was all about giving the Iraqis 'a big production number' so that 'their hearts and minds will follow', as Stephen Stockwell and Adam Muir put it.[75] A senior White House official had a message for the home front: 'Boom, boom, we're going in hard and fast,' he exalted, adding, 'By this time next week, sit by your TV and get ready to watch the fireworks.'[76]

This emphasis on deliberate attempts to promote militaristic values and imagery is fairly blunt, which is why it is interesting to observe that even *anti-*war films can end up bolstering aspects of the military–entertainment complex. This happens in at least two ways. The first includes the way anti-war films promote the myth of universality, as can be illustrated by the film of Erich Maria Remarque's novel *All Quiet on the Western Front*. The film was released in 1930 (one year after the novel became an international best-seller) and tells the story of a group of German schoolboys who enlist in the army and, one by one, are disillusioned and then grossly mutilated or butchered. In the most famous scene, the lead character Paul Baumer (played by Lew Ayres) bayonets a French soldier and is forced to spend three days and nights in a crater while his victim slowly dies. He pleads for forgiveness, crying that all men are all alike and none wanted war. Baumer is killed in October 1918, just before the Armistice, as he reaches out to touch a butterfly.

All those involved in making *All Quiet on the Western Front* lauded its emphasis on universal experience of war. Ayres claimed that the film set out to show

> the Germans as having the same values that you and I have . . .
> just people caught in this thing that's bigger than all of us . . . *All Quiet on the Western Front* became one of the first voices for universality . . . [it said] that unity was possible within the world.[77]

Similarly, Carl Laemmle (founder of the studio that made the film) asserted that the film 'indicts no nation, no individual, but . . . records an international human experience'.[78]

This is a problematic politics, however. War as universal suffering serves to naturalize war. Although the film does include scathing attacks on teachers, fathers and other male authority figure, unlike the novel it is silent about the political and military elites who instigated the conflict. There is no sense of *why* war broke out. The war is stripped of human agency. Audiences are left with the empty cliché 'war is hell', devoid of political or ideological context.

In addition, the insistence on universal suffering is misleading. For American and British audiences, the graphic presentation of harrowing scenes of suffering was only possible because the protagonists were German and French: it would have been impossible to produce such a film with American infantrymen. As historian Guy Westwell astutely observes in *War Cinema* (2006), 'the critical view of war offered in *All Quiet on the Western Front* is allowed because it defers to the more important task of contrasting the vitality of American liberal democracy with the dead end of European militarism'.[79]

This bias was even stronger in the 1979 television remake of the film, which was directed by Delbert Mann and starred Richard Thomas (famous for playing John-Boy in *The Waltons*) and which played to anti-war American sentiment after the war in Vietnam. In 1979, the First World War was an easy target for sentiments about the pointlessness of war: such a film would not have been possible about the 'Good War' of 1939–45. Indeed, the 1979 version of the film even included a reference to American troops making a major stand to defend the French, thus undercutting any sense of war as futile and based on destruction only. In 1979, the Americans were needed to rescue the hapless, militarist Europeans.

The second problem with some of the most prominent anti-war films is their assumption that people and nations will be deterred from waging war if they (cinematically) witness its horrors. This is patently not the case. Indeed, it is more correct to observe that spectacles of horror and displays of romantic heroism coexist, feeding off each other and creating the thrill and enthralment that is inherent to war representation. In other words, war films – whether propagandist or anti-war – still fetishize machines, technology and manliness. They effectively glamorize war. Indeed, displays of suffering and death are what actually bring value to the warring enterprise. Horror is not antagonistic to the adventure story of combat, but is an intrinsic component of it. This unfortunate aspect of war representation is obvious to anyone watching children playing war games or adults attending combat films.

Indeed, graphic descriptions of carnage might even incite desire to emulate the perpetrators. Young men who watched anti-war films were often thrilled by the brutality and wanted to sign up in order to prove their manliness in an effete society. Violence generated excitement; filmic and fictive genres provided men with a way of legitimizing murderous conduct. Even gruesome, anti-heroic films could be included in the romanticized canon of war. As Vietnam War veteran Philip Capulo recalled in *A Rumor of War* (1977), he 'wanted the romance of war, bayonet charges, and desperate battles against impossible odds', adding, 'I wanted the sort of thing I had seen in *Guadacanal Diary* and *Retreat, Hell!* and a score of other movies'.[80] This was also the argument of Anthony Swofford in his best-selling memoir *Jarhead: A Marine's Chronicle of the Gulf War and Other Battles* (2003). Reflecting on his early period in the force, he described how Marines would watch scenes from the anti-war movie *Apocalypse Now* in order to hype themselves up for combat. In his words, all Vietnam war films are pro-war, no matter what the supposed message, what Kubrick or Coppola or Stone intended. Mr and Mrs Johnson in Omaha or San Francisco or Manhattan will watch the films and weep and decide once and for all that war is inhumane and terrible ... but Corporal Johnson at Camp Pendleton and Sergeant Johnson at Travis Air Force Base and Seaman Johnson at Coronado Naval Station and Spec 4 Johnson at Fort Bragg and Lance Corporal Swofford at Twentynine Palm Marine Corps Base watch the same films and are excited by them, because the magic brutality of the films celebrates the terrible and despicable beauty of their fighting skills. Fight, rape, war, pillage, burn. Filmic images of death and carnage are pornography for the military man; with film you are stroking his cock, tickling his balls with the pink feather of history, getting him ready for his real First Fuck.[81]

Other men have made similar comments about the effects of witnessing *Saving Private Ryan*. It was precisely the horror that thrilled (largely male) audiences and readers: gore and abjection *were* the pleasure, subverting any pacific moral.

Strangely, perhaps, the influence of fictive and filmic modes of seeing war could survive well into an actual conflict. When young men engaged in real wars they sometimes continued to see the event through the eyes of war-play. It is almost a cliché for combatants to describe combat using analogies drawn from childhood games, television and the cinema. In *The British Soldier* (1915), machine gunners were depicted as 'cinematographing the grey devils' who were sheltering in a farmhouse. In the words of the author,

The picture witnessed from the farm on the 'living screen' by the canal bridge was one that will not easily be forgotten.

The 'grey devils' dropped down in hundreds. Again and again they came on only to get more machine murder.[82]

Similarly, during the Second World War, an unnamed Canadian combatant described aiming his machine gun on thirty Germans as being 'like one of those movies when you see troops coming at the camera and just before they meet it, hit it, you see them going off to the left and right, left and right'.[83]

A similar thing can be observed in the context of the war in Vietnam. For instance, in his diary on the 1 July 1966 bomber pilot Frank Elkins reflected that 'I keep reacting as though I were simply watching a movie of the whole thing'; the 'torn limbs' of his victims, 'the bloody ground, the . . . guts in the mud' elicited no strong feelings. His anguish, though, was palpable: 'The deep shame that I feel is my own lack of emotional reaction.[84] Jacques Leslie was also curious about his response to watching a B-52 strike in Vietnam. He felt 'no horror, no pain': 'Had men been killed beneath the smoke? . . . I know I should be appalled, but I felt only numbness: it was like watching people die on television.'[85] Or, as he put it on another occasion when being attacked with a M16 and rocket, 'I couldn't believe it was real; the soldiers looked like my childhood friends playing war.'[86] In *Nam. The Vietnam War in the Words of Men and Women Who Fought There* (1982), an eighteen-year-old radio operator confessed that he

loved to just sit in the ditch and watch people die. As bad as that sounds, I just liked to *watch* no matter what happened, sitting back with my homemade cup of hot chocolate. It was like a big movie.[87]

Or, as Philip Caputo put it, killing Viet Cong was enjoyable because it was like watching a movie: 'One part of me was doing something while the other part watched from a distance.'[88] A similar observation is made about twenty-first-century warfare, especially for crew of unmanned aerial vehicles or drones. As the drone navigator Matt J. Martin admitted in his autobiography, he 'enjoyed a fine box-set view of the fireworks' from the safe setting of the military barracks in Nevada.[89]

This argument can be taken further. As I contend in *An Intimate History of Killing*, combatants were tempted to mime the actions of their favourite movie stars. During the Vietnam war, 'grunts' could be observed doing 'little guts-and-glory Leatherneck tap dances under fire, getting their pimples shot off for the network ... doing numbers for the cameras,' Michael Herr complained. They were 'actually making war movies in their heads'.[90] In Grenada in 1983, soldiers charged into battle playing Wagner, in imitation of Robert Duvall, the brigade commander in *Apocalypse Now* (1979).[91] Films *created*, as well as represented, combat performance. As I will argue in the next chapter, this is even more the case with video games.

We are routinely entertained by representations of war. These everyday objects are highly gendered (note the absence of Barbie dolls in this chapter), enabling ideology to permeate into everyday life. Toy soldiers and replica weapons, allow many of us to re-enact wars we have seen, heard about and imagined. Combat cinema (and by 1985, a quarter of all movies shown in the United States were war movies)[92] has fundamentally influenced the way we think about modern war. Sometimes, it is impossible to know what is fiction and what is real, as in the case of the infamous scene in *The Battle of the Somme* (1916) that shows men going over the top. Although this was only one of very few scenes in the film that was staged, it routinely appears in documentaries as footage signalling the beginning of the battle. Episodes in *All Quiet on the Western Front* have suffered a similar fate. Not only is Remarque's novel often called a 'memoir', but scenes from the 1930 film set are often presented as actual footage from 1914–18.

Humans are playing animals. Illusion, imagination and feigning terror as well as pleasure occupy central positions within our culture. This is why fun is political. This is also why we should be wary when powerful institutions such as the military invest billions of dollars in entertaining us. As much as we may continue to entertain our own imaginaries in the pleasurable aspects of the military–entertainment complex (even if we do while risking our own psyches and well-being), fantasies of war often had a short life. Josh Cruze, who joined the Marines at the age of seventeen and served in Vietnam, had this to say:

> The John Wayne flicks. We were invincible. So when we were taken into this to [sic] the war, everyone went in with the attitude, 'Hey, we're going to wipe them out. Nothing's going to happen to us.' Until they saw the realities and they couldn't deal with it. 'This isn't supposed to happen. It isn't in the script. What's going on? This guy's really bleeding all over me, and he's screaming his head off.'[93]

This was also the lesson learnt by William Ehrhart, the seventeen-year-old volunteer with whom I started this chapter. Instead of excitement, honour and glory, he found himself pitched into a war where killing was not courageous, simply filthy. His ideals of 'Duty, Honor and Country' were snuffed out 'under the terrified and hate-filled gaze of human beings who wanted little else but for me to stop killing them and go away'.[94]

CHAPTER SEVEN

Violent Gaming

Thirteen months ago, I had never killed anyone. Today, I can boast about a dozen or so confirmed hits.

I never expected murder to be such fun. After all, I am a peaceable woman: I don't have a temper, rarely feel resentful and have never struck anyone in anger. My parents taught me to be polite, even when upset.

I blame a good friend of mine for this extraordinary (and thankfully temporary) change in my character. We were exchanging the usual grumbles about the tedium of marking exam scripts when he exclaimed, 'Let's unwind!' and introduced me to *Sniper Elite V2*. When it was first released the game won praise from *GameSpot Review* for being 'delightfully gory', as well as 'gruesome and gratifying'. The *Official Xbox Magazine* raved that it offered 'buckets of red awesomesauce'.[1] It does exactly what one of its earliest reviewers promised: its 'hyper-realistic, surgically accurate' kill-camera (KillCam) 'takes you inside your victim's body to see precisely how your bullet will end his life'. The reviewer breathlessly observed that

> You could see the bullet rotate, see the waves like dreamy smoke rings, left in its wake. The music muted slightly . . .

The bullet splattered though the cornea, shattering the bones
of the eye-socket and cheek, broke through the blood vessels
at the back of the eye, burst backwards through the brain
cavity and punched a hole in the back of the skull, its course
realistically altered by its journey. Blood and bone shot
upwards, outwards, backwards.[2]

I was hooked – not to the game and certainly not to killing
(virtual or otherwise) – but to what it told me about the aesthetics and language of violence. As in this reviewer's account, bullets
were portrayed as dancing 'dreamily' towards their victims; music
was delicately muted; targeted body parts were disembodied
from real people (*the* cornea rather than *his*); disembowelled victims simply uttered restrained grunts before collapsing.

It surprised me to discover how difficult these games are to play.
Even the simplest ones require an enormous range of skills. I am
not referring here to hand–eye coordination (although that, too,
proved challenging) but to the military knowledge and martial discipline needed to survive beyond a few minutes on the virtual
battlefield. Firing weapons requires more than simply pointing and
pressing. For one thing, I had to choose my preferred weapon. Was
it to be a rocket-propelled grenade (RPG), sniper rifle or a machine
gun? If I chose the RPG, I had to know that I needed to balance the
weapon against a firm object to absorb its powerful kickback. The
first dozen times I used a machine gun I ended up firing into the air.
What is the best weapon to use if I am running? How often do I
need to reload it, how long will that take and what ammunition
does it require? Different weapons have to be picked up if I am
trying to kill my enemy at short range (a shotgun or even a knife
may come in handy, but a sniper's rifle would be useless). When I
first saw a heavily armoured tank thundering towards me, even I
knew that my pistol was not going to save me. And what about the
direction and speed of the wind? I had to learn to keep an eye on a

tiny flag blowing in the breeze on the front of a vehicle that would give me this information. On other occasions, it was necessary to avoid giving away my location, but where (and how) could I pick up a silencer? On more occasions than I care to recall I inadvertently committed suicide by firing a rocket launcher too close to myself or failing to lob a grenade in time.[3]

The twenty-first century commitment of gamers to the minutiae of weaponry, battle tactics and warring environments is what some theorists called the 'fetishization of the real', or an obsessive attention to 'authenticity'. Obviously, though, computer games are just entertainment. On a real battlefield there is no 'KillCam' following the bullet as it leaves the sniper's gun and 'invades the body – with all the bone-crushing, organ-bursting blood-spewing destruction that entails'.[4] We don't get rewarded with a digital trophy in the corner of the screen.

Furthermore, despite all the attention paid to verisimilitude in these games, not all facts are equally weighted. In *Medal of Honor: Rising Sun* (2003), finicky details such as the atomic bomb and Japanese internment camps are ignored. In other games, especially those geared towards younger players, grotesque images of pain and gore have to be minimized if the producers are to obtain the necessary 'T' (for 'teen') rating. In the words of Chris Chambers, who was the deputy director for *America's Army* (one of the most widely played games), 'We have a Teen rating that allows 13-year-olds to play, and in order to maintain that rating we have to adhere to certain standards . . . We don't use blood and gore and violence to entertain.'[5] For this reason, bullet wounds in *America's Army* (2002) only cause a small red blotch to appear. There is no screaming; no dismemberment. Bodies simply fade into the virtual landscape.

The obsessive attention to 'authenticity' has not always been a prominent aspect of video games. Early generations of these

games were highly unrealistic. For instance, *Wolfenstein 3D* (1992)
is often credited with being the 'grandfathers of first-person
shooters'. Players are invited to choose between generic weapons
(machine gun, pistol or knife) and their avatars or 'skins' could
carry a veritable arsenal of weapons at the same time. When
Doom was released the following year it was equally short on realism: players could even use chainsaws to slaughter the enemy in
highly imaginative, grisly ways. Blood splattered dramatically over
the virtual ground. The game was also naively atmospheric, complete with dark corners full of nasty surprises.

In contrast, to fully enjoy *Brother in Arms: Road to Hill 30* (2005)
players must choose the correct ammunition for the MI carbine
semi-automatic rifle, the German MP40 sub-machine gun or the
M1918 Browning automatic rifle. Extreme precision is demanded
of players of *Battlefield Vietnam* (2004). Are they going to carry a
M1911 pistol, M14 assault rifle, or M72 LAW rocket launcher? If
players pick up the heavy assault kit of a US Marine, they need to
know that their sidearm is a M1911, their primary weapon is the
M60, and they will have either a LAW. or a M79 grenade
launcher. In contrast, simple assault kits contain the M1911
sidearm, a Mossbery 500 or M16 and grenades. Each of these
weapons obliges players to carry the appropriate ammunition, of
course. Players are also required to employ different tactics when
they enter the Mekong Delta in Operation Game Warden (15
January 1965), attack the city of Quang Tri (31 January 1968) or
participate in covert operations in Cambodia (1 May 1970).[6]

In addition, there is a light-hearted tone in earlier games,
which is absent from later ones. In *Wolfenstein 3D* the gamer's
avatar is William 'BJ' Blazkowicz, playfully dubbed 'the Allies'
bad boy of espionage and a determined action seeker'. He is
attempting to escape a medieval castle that, for reasons unknown,
is inhabited by Nazis. Blazcowicz has super-human powers and is
capable of single-handedly massacring a hundred elite Nazi troops.

When even one of these nasty Nazis is killed, a text pops up onto the screen exclaiming 'Let's See That Again!' The gruesome killing is then repeated in slow motion to a soundtrack composed by Bobby Prince (aka Robert C. Prince III, a prolific sound engineer who had also served as a platoon leader in Vietnam). Hitler's appearance in the game is also jokey. In the words of one keen gamer, Hitler is

> portrayed as the short-legged, moustachioed, nasty-looking man that he was and barking out German phrases like Scheisse (Sh*t) and Die, Allied Schweinehund (Die, Allied pigdog) to try and incite you. The big difference to his real world persona was the fact that he started the battle in a mechanical suit, and then burst out of it in full Nazi regalia armed with chain guns on the end of his wrists.[7]

When killed, Hitler shrivels up and liquefies into a pool of blood before his head rolls away from his body, settling at a comical angle.

Twenty-first century players are spared the farce of a Hitler in a robotic suit. Authenticity pervades all production decisions. The creators of *Sniper Elite V2* even ensure that the wallpaper is typical of 1940s German homes.[8] In *America's Army*, novice players are required to go through basic training in barracks and pitches that have been painstakingly created as exact replicas of the US Army post at Fort Benning. Weapons and other equipment fastidiously replicate their real-life counterparts. Even the sounds made when weapons are fired attempt to reality: depending on the type of grenade thrown, for example, a different explosion is heard. War wounds are carefully calibrated; the extraordinary vigour of avatars in earlier games has been jettisoned. Wound ballistics is taken seriously, its knowledges migrating from real-life battlefield research to computer-game programming. A reviewer of *Sniper Elite V2* was impressed, noting that its creators ensured that

> The primary subject of research for the [production] team
> was . . . internal: what happens when a sniper's bullet enters
> a human body? They consulted medical experts, ex-military
> snipers, photography of real-life gun-shot victims, X-rays of
> bone fractures, gathering a mountain of data and funnelling it
> through the incredibly powerful software and hardware used
> to create today's video games.[9]

As a result of this emphasis on accuracy, gamers are required to digest a vast amount of technical knowledge about weapons and ballistics. It is taken for granted that novice players know what is meant by military terms such as 'suppressing fire', 'situational awareness' and 'base of fire'. However, even experienced players need considerable help in understanding many of the technical, logistic and strategic intricacies of battle. This is why there is a formidable industry, both online and in published formats, dedicated to imparting this information, often using methods that exactly reproduce the way soldiers are trained in non-virtual garrisons.

Twenty-first-century war games include other features that distinguish them from earlier incarnations. To bolster claims of authenticity, recent games typically incorporate 'featurettes' or short documentaries cataloguing 'real-life' happenings. Interviews with veterans, as well as structured online visits to battle sites, are especially prominent. For example, both *Medal of Honor: Rising Sun* (2003) and *Brother in Arms: Road to Hill 30* (2005) use historical photographs and newsreel, site studies and eyewitness accounts to reinforce the verisimilitude of their games.

Achieving this level of authenticity necessitates considerable cooperation with the military. Military consultants and immersion experiences have become *de rigueur* for gaming production teams. In creating the *Medal of Honor* series, Steven Spielberg found expert advice indispensable: he employed Captain Dale Dye (a retired combat Marine Corps veteran) and other military experts as consultants. He even insisted that the design team undergo boot camp. How else would they truly appreciate the weight, texture and sound of weapons, or know how soldiers/avatars might respond in demanding and traumatic environments?

Similarly, the civilian designers of *America's Army* are regularly sent on 'Green Up events' – that is, occasions in which they immerse themselves in military life. Colonel Casey Wardynski, the director of the Army's Office of Economic and Manpower Analysis at West Point and originator of *America's Army*, explained that

> the whole idea is for the designees to get a feel of what it's like to be with soldiers, what they do for a living, what it sounds like, what it feels like, even what it smells like . . . The experience helps make the game more realistic.[10]

When designing and producing the original *America's Army*, the civilian team visited nineteen army posts, handled and fired weapons, travelled in military vehicles and inspected rifle ranges and barracks. They shot videos to help construct animations, recoded thousands of sound effects and paid avid attention to the texture, spatial orientation and sensory affect of combat environments. They rode in Black Hawk helicopters, witnessed the 'fireworks' of live shelling, practised parachuting, and joined soldiers in military drill and exercises. There was a fanatical concern to ensure that even fairly simple procedures such as throwing a grenade or erecting a bipod were 'performed strictly according to doctrine'.[11] As the designers and producers at the Modeling,

Virtual Environments and Simulation Institute (MOVES) at the
Naval Postgraduate School in Monterey, California, bragged,
careful attention was paid to 'games physics'. As a result, players
find that

> When shooting . . . the weapon sways slightly with the avatar's
> breathing, recoils on discharge, and occasionally jams. Bullets
> penetrate or ricochet depending on the makeup of the target
> (e.g., wood, adobe, dirt, glass, or steel), distance from target,
> and the weapon's calibre, type, and firing velocity. The target's
> composition also determines depth of penetration, and dis-
> tance and angle of reflection.[12]

Insight into 'Green Up' events for civilian producers and designers can be gauged by reading Seth Schiesel's *New York Times*
account of accompanying game designers while they developed
America's Army. Special Forces: Overmatch in 2005 (the game was
released the following year). Schiesel was struck by the gaming
specialists' expressions of 'pure wonder (tainted by hints of
queasiness)' as they flew in a Black Hawk helicopter at a hundred
miles an hour. 'You can't buy this!' shouted Eric A. Battner,
America's Army's quality assurance director. They fired weapons,
took apart assault rifles and raced around at night wearing night-
vision goggles. Kitted up in camouflage uniforms, black balaclavas
and pouches, some of the game developers actually seemed 'more
military than the soldiers'. They engaged in impassioned discussion about the forthcoming introduction of the 249 machine gun
and whether it would use the advanced combat optical gunsight (it
didn't: the M4 uses the ACOG, but the 249 would normally use
a M145 gunsight). The creators of *Special Forces: Overmatch* claimed
to have learnt from their immersion in military life. As a result of
their experiences, one developer decided that

he wanted to add a jostling video effect when the players were in the back of a truck. After spending a few minutes under the targets at a 100-meter firing range, another developer said he would change the 'whizzing' sound effect when a bullet passed by to a more realistic 'crack' that emulates the miniature sonic boom that a military round really creates.

A Special Forces commander who liaised between the Army and the game's team proudly claimed that the programmers were 'passionate about their work . . . It's their way of contributing to the war effort.'[13] In the 'war without end' that has been initiated by the 'war on terror', the development of war games is part and parcel of the larger war effort.

What lies behind this fetishization of authenticity? Why has it become the keyword in computer gaming? Game designers may simply quip that gaming has morphed into something much more detailed and complex simply 'because we can'. Immense kudos is attached to developing superior graphics and enhancing the speed and 'feel' of games. 'Making it real' is the ultimate goal. This has been greatly helped by the symbiosis between games and cinematic productions. The technologies used in the emotionally raw combat scenes at the opening of Spielberg's film *Saving Private Ryan* (1998) were also exploited in war games. Indeed, players increasingly *expect* their games to mirror the production standards and tropes of cinematic representations: war films are the 'gold standard' by which combat in computer games as well as 'real combat' is judged.

Ideologically, this emphasis on 'authenticity' makes sense in the context of the 'new militarism' of the post-9/11 world. The bellicosity of Western nations in conflicts in Iraq and Afghanistan, as well as the ubiquitous nature of the 'war on terror', has given a new salience to concepts such as 'freedom' and 'liberty'. The last time these concepts were banded about with such gusto was during the war against Hitler and National Socialism. It comes as no surprise, in fact, that the twenty-first century has witnessed a dramatic rise of computer games set during the Second World War. In the decade since 2000, more than a hundred Second World War-themed computer games have been released.[14] Unlike most war games prior to this date, these typically include prominent dedications to the men who fought between 1939 and 1945. *Medal of Honor: Allied Assault* (2002) proudly claims to be dedicated to 'all the men, women, and their families who gave the ultimate sacrifice for our freedoms. You will always be remembered.' *Call of Duty* (2003) lauds 'The men and women around the world who gave their lives in defense of our freedoms'. *Brothers in Arms: Road to Hill 30* (2005) upped the ante in terms of specificity. It is dedicated to

> The veterans of the 101th Airborne, The Greatest Generation, for having the courage to stand against evil and win the war against fascism, and all those who have fought and died in the defense of human freedom.

Such statements are most prevalent in games with Second World War themes, but even computer games set during the Vietnam War – that most contentious of American conflicts – increasingly feel the need to include hallowed words about freedom. Thus, *Battlefield Vietnam* is 'dedicated to the men and women of the Armed Forces who served with honor and bravery in the Vietnam War. Your sacrifices were beyond measure.'[15] Such inscriptions further justify the jettisoning of slapstick humour that characterized earlier games: faced with the need to valorize those heroes who saved the Western world from Nazism and Communism, dry, sardonic wit is acceptable so long as a respectful tone is unfailingly maintained.

Computer gaming has always been enmeshed with military networks. Admittedly, it can be too easy to exaggerate the connections, both from the perspective of the civilian producers and the military promoters of the games. In the first instance, hackers have been responsible for many of the most extraordinary innovations in gaming. They are often spurred on by a geekish passion for technical virtuosity rather than ideological posturing. When representatives of the armed forces initially contacted these counter-culture programmers, they were surprised by the amount of resistance they encountered. In 1980, for instance, the Army's Training and Doctrine Command approached the pioneering electronic entertainment company Atari about creating a more realistic version of *Battlezone* to use in training soldiers to effectively use the Bradley Infantry Fighting Vehicle. Talented game designer Ed Rotberg was more than queasy about cooperating with the military. He explained that in the late 1970s,

> there were any number of jobs to be had by professional programmers in military industries or in military-related industries. [For] those of us who found our way to video games . . . it was sort of a counter-culture thing. We didn't want anything to do with the military. I was doing games; I didn't want to train people to kill.

He eventually agreed to cooperate, but was 'vehemently opposed to Atari getting into this sort of business at all'.[16] The result was *Army Battlezone*.[17] Many others designers simply refused outright.

It also is important not to exaggerate the extent to which the military has embraced such technologies. As late as 2010 a battle command officer who had been in charge of army simulations for eleven years admitted that he still had to fight what he called the 'parent effect'. In his words,

> It is hard to walk past a soldier on this site and not associate it with your 18-year-old playing Xbox when he should be doing

his homework . . . The hardest part is to see this as valid training enablers, and not just playing a game.[18]

This generational gap is fast closing, as soldiers with extensive
gaming experience as part of their life's basic toolkit are being
promoted.

Indisputably, though, the relationship between the armed
forces and the entertainment industry has become closer, denser
and more direct in recent decades. In December 1996, the
National Academy of Sciences hosted a workshop on simulation
aimed at encouraging cooperation between the defence and
entertainment industries. In the subsequent report, the value
of such cooperation was comprehensively spelt out and, in
1999, a $45 million partnership was established between the
army and the University of Southern California to establish
the Institute for Creative Technologies (ICT).[19] In 2011, the US
Department of Defense extended ICT's contract to 2014,
giving it a further $135 million.[20] The ICT brought together
military specialists, computer scientists, social scientists, writers, artists and cinematographers. Although the aim was to
improve military modelling and simulations, the initiative was
also part of an attempt to give a more modern face to the
armed services. By 2011, the ICT estimated that more than
seventy-five thousand soldiers had been trained using the innovative ICT-developed technologies.[21] As the US Secretary of the
Army Louis Caldera boasted in 1999, the ICT was 'a joint
effort of the Army, the entertainment industry and academe –
an innovative team to advance dazzling new media and ulti-
mately benefit training and education for everyone in
America'.[22] Significantly, Caldera did not see the cooperation
as benefiting the military forces solely, but all of society. It was
a typical assumption, and not unrealistic given the snowballing
militarization of American life.

What was so pioneering about the ICT initiative? Prior to its establishment, military simulations had focused primarily on developing applications that could advance strategic planning, improve procedural systems and introduce guidelines concerning military doctrine. In contrast, ICT researchers recognized that humans were emotional beings. They sought to inject feelings and interpersonal relationships into decision making and battle conduct.[23] They believed that efficient military organizations needed to be sensitive to the emotional lives of everyone, from the raw recruit to the most seasoned commanding officer. Environmental thrills, emotional reactions and intellectual challenges were necessary to spur service personnel to effective operational engagement with the enemy.[24]

In September 2004, the ICT released the first military training application developed for a commercial game console: *Full Spectrum Warrior*, a squad-based, tactical-action game. They developed this game in close cooperation with the US Army Infantry School at Fort Benning 'to ensure content fidelity', but they also filmed real-life soldiers in order to create their computer character animations.[25] It was no coincidence that the game was set in a fictional place in the Middle East and was based on the 'war against terror'. Its purpose was to train infantry soldiers in asymmetrical warfare. As ICT spokesmen repeated time and again, a new kind of war demanded different interactions within gaming environments.

Full Spectrum Warrior was one of many games that served a dual function as training programme for the military and entertainment for a wider (primarily male) public. Its commercial release by the game publisher THQ became a critical and commercial success. When playing it, critics bragged that 'you felt like a reporter embedded with a US Army division' and praised its 'stunning realism – just watch the tree branches sway as your chopper lands'.[26] It was a clear winner, and was judged the Best

Original Game and the Best Simulation Game at the 2003 Electronic Entertainment Expo (E3)'s Game Critics Awards.[27]

Full Spectrum Warrior is one of the more successful crossover training/entertaining games, but there are numerous others. *Spearhead II* (2003) simulated a real-time tank battle and had been designed to train tank commanders. It was also released commercially to give non-military citizens an opportunity to explore their skills in armoured warfare.[28] *Real War* (2001) is another such game. It was initially built under contract by the Joint Chief of Staff as a way to teach coordination across different branches of the military. The military version of the game is called *Joint Forces Employment* (2000) and has been used for training purposes at the US Joint Forces Staff College, Joint Special Operations University and the Air University. Since it was developed by defence contractor OCI and the video-game developer Rival Interaction, it has also been released commercially.[29]

Interestingly, war gaming did not only move from barracks to bedrooms. It also moved in the other direction: commercially available war games were adapted for military use. On occasion, the threat of such crossovers caused an international furore, as in 2000 when Sony's PlayStation 2 console was banned from Japanese export because of worries that its components could be used as a missile guidance system.[30] More typically, war games were adopted by military training regimes. War games – and especially first-person shooters – have become important yet inexpensive training devices in all branches of the military.[31] In 1996, Marine Corps Commandant General Charles ('Chuck') C. Krulak was responsible for the effective adaptation of *Doom II: Hell on Earth*, a hyper-violent video game, for training purposes. The result was *Marine Doom*, which turned monsters into terrorists, transformed the settings into real terrestrial battlefields and simulated first-person, team-based combat in both offensive and defensive situations. For the price of the game CD-Rom (less than fifty dollars in 1995),[32] the Marines had an effective training product. *Steel Beasts II* was another successful adaptation, and was used in military training by the Finnish Combat School, Dutch Cavalry School, Swedish Combat School, Danish Army Combat School and Spain's Ejército del Tierra, as well as at the United States Military Academy at West Point.[33] The air force also quickly recognized that recruits could benefit from playing first-person shooter games. British and American militaries are currently seeking to recruit keen video-gamers, on the grounds that their skills at the console will be useful in controlling unmanned planes and 'killer robots'. Military 'toys', such as the Dragon Runner robot, are guided by a six-button keypad deliberately modelled after Sony's PlayStation 2 controller. A 2005 study of the effect on 413 people playing first-person shooters found that the games were very important in developing skills that could be transferred to real-life situations in the military. In the words of one cadet, 'My attention to detail when under stress has increased, and my target-acquisition skills have increased.'[34]

I have already mentioned *America's Army*. It is the *Why We Fight* for the digital citizen-consumer.

It is interesting, therefore, to look at exactly how this game came to be conceived, produced and marketed. *America's Army* was built as part of a $2.2 billion cache allocated by Congress to boost recruitment in the armed forces, which had reached its lowest point in thirty years.[35] Its funding authorized by the Assistant Secretary of the Army for Manpower and Reserve Affairs, the game was originally designed and built by MOVES under the direction of Dr Michael Zyda. *America's Army* took three years to produce and initially cost $7.5 million, which was three times the industry average.[36]

America's Army is widely regarded as the most influential military-themed game in the world. It was launched on Independence Day

(4 July) 2002 and can be downloaded for free by anyone thirteen years or older. It won Guinness World Records for its popularity, having been downloaded more than forty-two million times. In 2009 alone, it was the most downloaded video game, the largest virtual army, the game with the most hours spent playing a free online shooter, the earliest military website to support a video game and the largest travelling game simulator. The game is rated 'T', meaning that the Entertainment Software Rating Board has deemed it suitable for teenagers. In fact, most players are aged between thirteen and twenty-one. It costs the US government $2.5 million annually and welcomes sixty thousand visitors daily.[37] Currently there are over ten million registered users.[38]

Despite these impressive statistics, its creation myth is surprisingly modest. In some accounts, Colonel Casey Wardynski claims to have come to the idea at a cocktail party,[39] while elsewhere he relates how he first conceived of the game on a trip to the electronics retail store Best Buy, after his sons told him that the most popular video games were devoted to military themes.[40] Whichever version is correct, Wardynski recognized that 'with game technology we can make something very vivid; we can deliver it into pop culture; we can structure it in a way that was designed for teens 13 and above'. Instead of being the last career that young people thought about, the game would mean 'we'll get there about the same time as other ideas for what to do with lour life'.[41] In other words, through this computer game the military could put itself at the forefront of the minds of teenage boys at precisely the age when they were making career decisions.

In conjunction with Michael Zyda at the MOVES Institute, they set about creating *America's Army*, convinced that, for some of their young players, picking up M16s, firing sniper rifles and throwing grenades would prove mesmerizing. The website promises gamers that they will 'discover a life filled with adventure and meet other smart, motivated people like you'.[42]

It was a top priority, then, to ensure that the game was as realistic as possible. As Wardynski, David Lyle and Michael Colarusso noted in their article in the Officer's Corps Strategy Series in 2010, *America's Army*

> places the Army squarely inside youth popular culture. It allows players to test-drive the Army ... *America's Army* exposes users to the organizational values, opportunities, and requirements of military service with sufficient vividness to separate the gist of serving in today's Army from the gist of service conveyed by the media or Hollywood. It embodies teamwork and draws upon realistic mission scenarios, teaching young adults lessons about Army culture within an engaging pop culture format that resonates with them.[43]

In achieving this aim, a balance had to be struck between educating and entertaining. As researchers at the MOVES Institute acknowledged,

> All parties understood that setting the right tone was key to avoiding public-relations disaster. The army could not be perceived as celebrating trigger-happy Rambos, nor, by downplaying lethal force, be guilty of deceit and hypocrisy; must not pander to the testosterone of the demographic, yet must keep teens engaged; must avoid charges of jingoism, mesmerism, cynicism, cliché, exploitation of vulnerable youth, incitement to violence, or a hundred other incorrectnesses.

As they drolly exclaimed, 'one postmodern excess and the game was up'.[44]

The result – the outcome of the labour of talented technicians, creative directors, design consultants and a veritable army of graduate students and military officers – was a game that sought to impart 'core army values'. Crucial was the rewarding of good soldierly behaviour. As an internal document written at MOVES explained,

> Out on mission, your buddy collapses in front of you. You can attend him, which earns points for loyalty and honor, or keep running, which scrubs points. If you do stop, you become a target yourself, which takes courage, and if you're hit, your health will suffer, so you need the integrity to inform your actions with sound judgment. Doing your duty and saving both your lives wins the most points. Just like in combat.[45]

Of course, this was unadulterated spin, as any grunt will tell you – in real-life battle, rewards don't come so easily. But this game is propaganda masquerading as infotainment.

There was one momentous advantage to developing *America's Army*: enticing new recruits through computer games was cheap. The initial investment in the game and its subsequent maintenance and development is inexpensive. Because of the game, the army saves between $700 million and $4 billion a year in recruitment costs.[46]

The cheapness is even more important given the vast number of young people – that is, potential recruits – who play these games. War gaming is a major form of pleasurable consumption. According to the Electronic Software Association's 2010 statistics, video games are played in 68 per cent of American households, and 60 per cent of these players are men. A Pew Study focusing on Americans aged between twelve and seventeen revealed that gaming was ubiquitous: 99 per cent of American boys of those ages played video games and more than half listed games rated 'M' (mature audiences) or 'AO' (adult only) as their favourites. Given these rating codes, it is fair to assume that most of these games would be violent.[47] Indeed, the second most popular game is the first-person shooter *Halo* (the first in the series was released in 2001).[48] Some of the online multiplayer games have player populations the size of small nations. In 2011, for example, *World of Warcraft* (2004) had 10.3 million active accounts.[49] In 2007, industry sales of consoles, hardware, software and accessories generated nearly $19 billion in revenue in the US.[50] Popular video games routinely overtake film releases.

Military spokesmen for *America's Army* frequently claim that it was not designed for recruitment. Wardynski insists that the game is nothing more than a 'communication tool designed to show players what the army is – a high-tech, exciting organization with lots to do'.[51] Nevertheless, there is considerable evidence that *America's Army* has been remarkably successful in attracting young men to the army. People logging on can click through to the recruiting website goarmy.com: 28 per cent of visitors do so.[52] In 2008, a survey by the Massachusetts Institute of Technology found that nearly a third of all Americans aged between sixteen and twenty-four years expressed a more positive impression of the army because of the game.[53] In another survey, 4 per cent of new recruits claimed to have joined specifically as a result of playing *America's Army*, while another 60 per cent of new recruits had played the game more than five times in the week prior to enlisting.[54] Young men who played *America's Army* at US army recruitment fairs were 30 per cent more likely than adolescents who never played the game to consider the army as a possible career option.[55]

We must be cautious about such statistics. After all, adolescents who already have a favourable impression of the military are more likely to go to recruitment fairs at which the game is available and are also more likely to play it at home. Nevertheless, the results are significant. At the very least, as one army recruiter concluded, *America's Army* 'is never going to overcome someone's trepidation and fears regarding the ongoing war on terror. But it does get some people talking to recruiters who might not have otherwise. It opens a window, and if they look in and they decide to join, great.'[56]

In terms of military training, gaming trains young people in some highly valorized military skills. Colonel Anthony Krogh, director of the National Simulation Center acknowledges that 'soldiers are familiar with these programs . . . They are digital natives who have grown up in a digital world.'[57] Indeed, the ICT admits that one of its main goals in providing cutting-edge training technologies is to reduce 'the need for expensive live simulations and human role players'.[58] As Marine Corp Commandant General James L. Jones admitted, there should be a balance between live and simulation-based training, but the latter was 'more expensive, if you are shooting a very expensive shell'.[59] In the words of Lieutenant Scott Barnett, project officer of the Marine Corps Modeling and Simulation Management Office,

> Every marine is a rifleman. The problem is that with budget cuts, we don't have the money to pay for the ammo and field time we need to keep ourselves in practice. So for a few years now, the corps has had to scramble to find cheaper, more efficient ways to train marines and keep them in fighting trim.[60]

It made economic sense to train men in simulation, which will 'actually result in higher scores when they go out and do live fire', according to Marine Corps Commandant General James L. Jones.[61] While dome-based simulators with 'motion-base and full wrap-around imagery' cost between five and ten thousand dollars an hour to operate, PC-based ones using the internet costs only twenty-five cents an hour.[62]

These games also offer cheap ways to deal with the aftermath of recruiting and combat. They are employed to help men whose military experiences have been psychologically scarring. Instead of expensive psychotherapy, video games have been developed to help soldiers suffering from post-traumatic stress disorder (PTSD).[63] Soldier-patients are given a head-mounted display to wear, which are customized to the individual's unique involvement in battle. The soldier is gradually immersed in the combat scenario, including specific experiences (such as type of attack and weapons employed) and the environment (weather, terrain and so on), that was thought to have triggered the PTSD.[64] Given that 35 per cent of veterans of the war in Iraq are thought to have suffered PTSD, this is regarded as a valuable new tool.[65]

What does it mean to shoot at lifelike images of people?

Crucially, players do not shoot at generic 'people': they shoot at *specific types of people*. They shoot at the 'enemy'. These opponents are often highly racialized, and occupy worlds that mirror imperial environments. War gaming typically takes place in the new empire, complete with headscarves, turbans, scimitars, camels, caliphs, djinns, deserts, belly dancers, minarets, bazaars and harems. Take *Full Spectrum Warrior*, for instance. Except for the Osama bin Laden figure (Mohammed Jabour Al-Afad), all other opponents are nameless and faceless. When identified, they are called Zekes, Motherfuckers and Tangos (from 'T for target'). Similarly, in *Call of Duty: Modern Warfare*, the enemy are clearly Middle Eastern: their faces are often covered and, if seen, they frequently sport unruly or 'swarthy' beards. The 'insurgents' are scruffily dressed, often not even in a uniform, in stark contrast to the tidy, uniformed American soldiers. The 'good guys' (and there are very few women in these hyper-masculine environments) are professionals: they are emotionally sturdy, fond of cracking dry witticisms and have a strong sense of loyalty to their comrades. While the British and American soldiers simply fall down when shot, Middle Eastern and Russian soldiers dramatically jerk, shriek and fling their weapons in the air.

These war environments are not only devoid of many (or any) women, they are also generally cleared of civilians. When civilians do appear, it is usually against the rules to attack them; and anyone who does so in *America's Army* is automatically sent to a correctional facility.

On those occasions when the prohibition of killing civilians is ignored, rationalizations are readily proffered. An illustration of this can be taken from the Virtual Army Experience (VAE), a mobile mission stimulator that was launched in January 2007. The VAE travels around fairs, festivals and air shows, encouraging attendees to play *America's Army*, handle military equipment and participate in kinetically engaging battle simulations. Anthropologist Robertson Allen attended a VAE as a participant-observer. He described being in the battle simulator when the screen showed civilians running away from their vehicle. The instructor ordered the players not to fire at the civilians but to wait for the appearance of bona fide terrorists, but Allen observed that the players ignored the order and enthusiastically discharged their weapons at the fleeing women and children. Disappointingly, he reported, the 'virtual civilians . . . do not react in any way and keep on running'.

How did Allen explain this tendency for those in the simula-tor (including himself) to deliberately target civilians? He admitted that some of his readers might 'find the idea of shoot-ing at civilians appalling, whether or not they are virtual', but insisted that most of the players were not firing out of 'spite' or due to the 'corrupting' influence of video games. Rather, he explained,

> visitors do it to test the limits of believability in this virtual environment, to push back against and reappropriate the scripted narrative that is thoroughly entrenched at the VAE. The act of shooting at civilians was the most powerful and

common mode of speaking back to authority I witnessed inside the VAE.

Disobeying orders from the army instructor not to fire on the virtual civilians was posited as an act of resistance. It also shows the work of the superego. Behind every prohibition there is a silent voice is saying 'do it', enjoy the sense of guilt.

Allen continued, adding that the 'inability of civilians' to die was 'disappointing to many[,] especially regular gamers'. Why? Because it 'punched through the logic of the claim I often heard during my time at the VAE that "this is as close to realistic combat as you can get outside of going to war"'.[66] The statement is revealing, showing the fetishization of 'authenticity' mentioned earlier, in which the failure of the game-producers to allow the virtual civilians to 'die' is regarded as a form of fraud. Gaming technology had to be true to the world it was mirroring in order to be psychologically satisfying.

As must be obvious by now, war games come heavily freighted with ideological messages. Playing is always an interaction between self and world. Gamers and their virtual worlds are always embedded in a political space. In the case of war games, this political space is remarkably sanitized: games rarely mention politics, hint about the legitimacy of killing, or admit to 'collateral damage'. They are saturated with talk of 'our troops', habituating civilians with an armed version of themselves. Combat legitimacy is resolutely jettisoned for player proficiency.

In fact, playing these games is a form of participating in war. Promotional materials often claim that gaming is a type of volunteering. For example, the *America's Army* website boasts that the game 'provides civilians with an inside perspective and a virtual role in today's premier land force: the US Army'.[67] Or, in the words of Chris Chambers, a retired army major who was *America's Army* deputy director in 2005,

> We don't expect that a young person is going to play the game and run out and join the Army . . . That was never the point. We want the game to help us form a more long-term connection with the young person.[68]

Computer gaming creates citizens who are much more than spectators of war: the player is an active consumer and creator of combat worlds. Immersed interaction is not only desirable; it is required. The player's dynamic consent is necessary for the game to progress. The player must perform certain acts and make particular inputs. Of course, game designers attempt to direct action and provide strong messages about what ought to be done next, but it still depends on the player interpreting the action and responding in diverse ways. The player of first-person shooters, for example, is *required to* align him- or herself with the military. Furthermore, they teach a particular *kind of war*: war is perpetual, indeterminate, it erodes all civil rights and is banal. This is a war of 'no surrender'. As *Conflict: Desert Storm* (2002) announces on its cover: 'No Diplomats. No Negotiations. No Surrender'.

Video games do not only impart ideological content about war. They also teach gender. Thus, when the US Army Chief of Staff General Ray Odierno visited the ICT in June 2012, he was introduced to the 'Gunslinger saloon' where 'computer-generated characters take on the iconic roles of the Western bartender, bad guy and damsel in distress, while a real person plays a Texas Ranger who must save the day.'[69] Such gendered stereotypes are hardly surprising. After all, violent games and first-person shooters are very much a masculine game. While two-thirds of American boys aged between twelve and seventeen play first-person shooters, only 17 per cent of girls of similar age play them.[70]

Perhaps as importantly, these games teach a certain kind of discipline, including masculine comportment and efficiency. It increases the cultural capital of the military. It teaches proficiency with technology, ruthlessness and the ability to process vast amounts of data quickly and accurately. Recent games emphasize proficiency over heroism, which is exactly what the 'new military' does.[71]

These games provide young men with a way to play with and test their masculinity: are they really tough enough, knowledgeable enough, smart enough? Of course, there are different models of masculinity that a gamer can choose – players can even experiment with different personae. Rambo-types can grab the bazooka or Mossberg 500; those proud of their cool, Bond-like detachment can take up the M16 Sniper; practical types choose engineer kits, complete with acetylene torches to dismantle vehicles, spanners to disable mines and claymores to dismember enemy troops.

Games also teach real soldiers how to make war more game-like. Real soldiers attempt to make their experiences in combat resemble those in the games and vice versa. For example, twenty-year-old Specialist Alfred Trevino recalled the first time he shot an Iraqi using a M16A4 assault rifle. 'You just try to block it out,' he said,

> see what you need to do, fire what you need to fire. Think to yourself, This is a game, *just do it, just do it* . . . Of course, it's not a game. The feel of the actual weapon was more of an adrenaline rush than the feel of the [video-game] controller . . . But you're practically doing the same thing; trying to kill the other person. The goal is the same. That's the similarity. The goal is to survive.[72]

Trevino and his mates would often play war-games until the early hours of the morning and then go on patrol. As Sergeant Sinque Swales put it,

> We're doing this stuff for real and we're playing it on [*sic*] our spare time . . . And yeah, it was ironic. But it was so normal, we didn't think nothing about it.[73]

It reduced the men's inhibition. When mock M16s were used in training, Lieutenant-Colonel Scott Sutton of the technology division at Quantico Marine Base observed, soldiers 'probably feel less inhibited, down in their primal level, pointing their weapons at somebody'. It 'provides a better foundation for us to work with'.[74]

A similar effect was observed by men who piloted or navigated drones. In the words of one, it was

> a surreal experience. Almost like playing the computer game *Civilization*, in which you direct units and armies in battle. Except with real consequences. I also felt electrified, adrenalized. My team had won. We had shot the technical college full of holes, destroying large portions of it and killing only God knows how many people. It would take some time for the reality of what happened so far away to sink in . . . I had yet to realize the horror.[75]

In such ways, gaming becomes profoundly relevant to the citizen's political life. By blurring entertainment and war – 'militainment' or, in J. Der Derian's coinage, the 'military–industrial– entertainment–complex'[76] – citizens come to expect war without end. Entertainment has become a way of creating militarized citizens. The war is digested for easy consumption. We are all turned into citizen-soldiers, no longer viewing the war but embedded in it, albeit virtually. This brings war closer in some aspects, but at the same time further decontextualizes it.

Computer games can be understood in the context of their discursive and representational meanings. However, they must also be approached as a game. They are an activity that involves imagination in the creation of fantastical worlds. For me, the important point in this context is that play is an 'event' and players undergo a metamorphosis in the act of playing. In playing games, we see the fluidity of the self/ego as well as the malleability of the body. As such, play is creative — it works on the self and the body. The question becomes: who is the self when playing first-person shooters? What kind of space is being entered? How does the transitioning into a different space and a different body take place? It is important to note that the player is not passive, but brings his or her fantasies and beliefs to the game. Indeed, first-person shooters can even require players to position their bodies in alignment with the hand and weapons that the avatar is carrying, that is, their hands grasping the weapon.

Both in terms of the game and its meanings, players are required to have a material, ideologically situated body that is engaged in killing. As we have seen, gaming enthusiasts fastidiously follow the latest trends in weapon development and their journals are packed with real-life applications. Many popular video games are produced by the military (often for military training purposes) and then adapted for general release. Boundaries are increasingly blurred as, on the one hand, games become more realistic and, on the other, live warfare grows ever more remote through the use of sophisticated long-range ballistic weaponry and drones. In other words, developments in gaming and weaponry inspire, inform and validate one another. Access to combat is open to anyone with an internet connection and a computer, and it proving a popular way of participating in the war without end. As retired Marine Colonel Gary W. Anderson, former chief of staff of the Marine Corps Warfighting Laboratory, argued, the twenty-first-century soldiers are 'new Spartans':

> Remember the days of the old Sparta, when everything they did was towards war? . . . In many ways, the soldiers of this video game generation have replicated that, and that's something to think about.[77]

The warfighter is enhanced by post-human technologies and pharmaceuticals forged in the military–industrial complex of the twenty-first century. However, this aggressor is encouraged to view his *victims* as post-human too. Seen through the pixelled computer screen, the distinction between the life of the sentient body and the avatar is blurred. Biological and simulated existence become interchangeable. In front of his computer screens in Reno, Nevada, drone navigator Matt J. Martin reflected on how it felt to be 'among the first generation of soldiers working with robots to wage war'. He confessed to feeling a

> thrill . . . at the moment I prepared to squeeze the trigger . . . It had not been quite real, even afterwards . . . The ability to kill people from such great distances, playing God, widened the gap between the reality of war and out perception of it. It was almost like watching an NFL game of TV with its tiny figures on the screen . . . It could even be mildly entertaining.[78]

He admitted that this kind of killing was indistinguishable to 'simulated combat, like the computer game *Civilization*'.[79] When he launched a missile, he 'experienced the by-now-familiar pixilation of the screen as the missile launched from its rail to briefly interrupt the return link' before, thirty seconds later, 'the Papa streaked straight down to impact between [two men]. They never knew what hit them.' He admitted, 'Sometimes I felt like God hurling thunderbolts from afar.'[80]

Sergeant Sinque Swales, from Chesterfield, Virginia, made a similar comment. He observed that war gaming was crucial to his ability to shoot a .50-calibre machine gun at Iraqi insurgents in the northern town of Mosul. He recalled that

> It felt like I was in a big video game. It didn't even faze me, shooting back. It was just natural instinct. *Boom! Boom! Boom! Boom!* . . . I couldn't believe I was seeing this. It was like 'Halo'. It didn't even seem real, but it was real.[81]

As David Bartlett, former chief of operations at the Defense Modelling and Simulation Office and the creator of *Marine Doom*, explained, when the time came for Swales to kill in real life

> he was ready to do that . . . His experience leading up to that time, through on-the-ground training and playing 'Halo' and whatever else, enabled him to execute. His situation awareness was up. He knew what he had to do. He had done it before – or something like it up to that point.[82]

The post-human gaze streamed through entertaining, and spectacular war games united cybernetically enhanced super-soldiers in Halo and Reno, Mosul and Chesterfield.

PART FIVE

The End of War

CHAPTER EIGHT

Protest

We can stop wounding the world.

We are a peaceful people. Few of us actually enjoy hurting others; even enthusiastic sadists ensure their partners have a safe-word in case delight turns into distress. Most people recognize the look of pain on other people's faces, even if they are strangers. Many of us actively seek to reduce or eradicate other people's suffering. One of the ways we can do this is by resisting the militarization of our society.

The first step is acknowledging that it doesn't have to be this way: we can decide not to remain helplessly enthralled to military ideologies, practices and symbols. One of the most debilitating myths for people seeking to forge more peaceful worlds is the assertion that armed conflict is inevitable. So many times when writing this book I have been told that wars have 'been part of the human condition since the struggle between Cain and Abel, and regrettably they are likely to remain so'.[1] Pacifist pronouncements are often portrayed as hopelessly utopian, and one strand of the political left worry that they forestall the possibility of armed struggle *from below*, or by the oppressed.

Does this make me a naive romantic? No. I am optimistic for three reasons. The first is that the history of humanity has been one of cooperation more than competition. Armed conflict between nations is not inevitable. It is helpful to remind ourselves that conventional wars today are creations of sovereign states. Equating international wars with spontaneous individual aggression is simply wrong. Wars serve instrumental purposes; they involve the investment of trillions of dollars, pounds, euros, roubles or yuan. They are a social activity. As such, they can be unmade as well as made.

But secondly, I don't think that pacifism is a dangerous fantasy that will hamper the struggle against tyrants. Armed struggle by the oppressed is no longer the way in which revolutions take place. There is no Bastille or Winter Palace to storm. In the twenty-first century, radical change of the social and economic order demands different approaches.

The final reason it is not a utopian dream is because disobedience and defiance are what it means to be human. As political philosopher Costas Douzinas reminds us, 'Humanity starts in disobedience. Adam and Eve defy God's command and leave the Garden of Eden. Prometheus steals fire from the Olympian Gods and gives it to men alongside writing, mathematics, agriculture, medicine, starting civilization ... Humanity is born in acts of disobedience, defiance, and resistance.'[2] Throughout human history, wherever there is power there has been resistance.

If the first step requires acknowledging that we don't have to passively accept the inevitability of war and violence, subsequent steps are more difficult to identify. Personally, I don't have any patience for dogmatists. Activists who insist on laying out rigid blueprints for a better world fail to engage with the awe-inspiring, creative diversity of human existence. Their cardboard cut-out figures are easily squashed by the vast corporate interests involved in armament design, production and use. We don't all have to join a peace movement (although I believe it is a good idea) nor should we expect everyone to demonstrate vociferously in the street, camp outside nuclear bunkers, boycott products sponsored by the military or engage in sit-ins, pray-ins, occupations, lock-downs, radical street parties or e-campaigns. In the three-volume *The Politics of Nonviolent Action* (1973), Gene Sharp catalogues nearly two hundred different ways people can engage in non-violent protest.[3] The strategies open to us are legion.

Each of us possesses proclivities, skills and spheres of influence that enable us to make a difference in our own local contexts. Wherever we are situated – as homemakers, academics, labour-ers, shopkeepers, secretaries, publishers, journalists, civil servants, teachers, entertainers, novelists, artists, lawyers, doc-tors, scientists, unemployed and so on – we can make a difference globally. The only crucial element is this: a refusal to outsource political engagement. As philosopher Slavoj Zizek, speaking during Occupy Wall Street in 2011, warned:

> After outsourcing work and torture, after marriage agencies are outsourcing our love life ... we can see that for a long time, we have allowed our political engagement also to be outsourced. We want it back.[4]

I can't deny, however, that that some forms of action are likely to be more effective than others. This is a pragmatic assessment only. For example, I do not find it helpful to engage with *one strand* of debates about the militarization of toys and games. For too long, feminists and other activists have been caught up in an argument about whether a seven-year-old boy's interest in plastic Kalashnikovs, a young man's obsession with violent video games and an adult man's enthusiastic recitation of firearm calibres encourages individual male aggression. The idea that these (especially first-person shooters) are 'murder simulators' is exag-gerated.[5] The fact that so many 'normal' young people enjoy

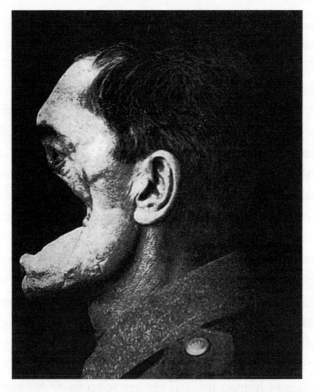

Figure 8.1. The original caption of this photograph in Friedrich Ernst's *Krieg dem Krieg (War against War*, 1924) reads: 'The "health resort" of the proletarian. Almost the whole face blown away.' His book is an influential example of the 'war as horror' genre. Ernst's technique was to juxtapose comments about heroism and glory with mutilated bodies – creating an incongruous, macabre and terrorizing critique of the First World War. By 1930, the book had been published in forty languages but, given the absence of politics and human agency, the emotional reactions it generated were impotent in the face of the rise of National Socialism.[6]

these forms of entertainment is proof enough that the games can't be as effective in creating assassins as their critics suggest. More to the point, censorial tactics that attempt to outlaw things that give some people pleasure are counterproductive. Young people enjoy war toys and militaristic games in inverse proportion to their elders' disapproval. Of course, I do believe that we should worry about the military–entertainment complex, but not because it has a potential to brutalize our young people. We should worry because it has global consequences in real-life military conflicts.

I also find the universalizing tendency of much anti-war commentary unhelpful. During the commemorations around the centenary of the First World War we heard a great deal about the unspeakable misery inflicted on people and animals between 1914 and 1918, as well as the devastation caused to environments worldwide. There are three problems with this emphasis: first, suffering was *not* evenly distributed; second, it elides those occasions when 'we' are the perpetrators of violence; finally, relentless emphasis on gut-wrenching horror is more likely to encourage a turning-away from military realities than any engagement with them. 'War is hell' is both true and meaningless. It is an impotent creed. It embraces a politics that lacks wider perspectives, political dimensions and human agency. As a result, war (in all its reified glory) is given agency: it steps out of time, place and the specificities of human lives. If we are to make a difference, we need to remain true to these specificities.

How do we resist the militarization of our worlds? This question has stimulated the imaginations and excited the energies of millions of individuals and thousands of political movements. Entire libraries (both bricks and mortar as well as online) are devoted to describing and analysing the results. Here I will briefly sketch out some examples that I have found interesting.

In my past research, I was curious about men who, in the cauldron of battle, decided to 'just say no'. Given the rigours of combat, the dependency of combatants on their comrades and the often-overwhelming sense of camaraderie engendered by sharing life-threatening experiences, it takes a lot of courage to refuse to conform. Throughout the centuries, however, numerous war memoirs recount times when combatants looked into the eyes of enemy soldiers and recognized them to be like themselves. In the commemorations associated with the centenary of the First World War, we heard a great deal about such occasions. On 3 November 1917, for instance, Charles Stewart Alexander admitted feeling 'fiendish joy' at the prospect of combat in France, but baulked when he encountered a German soldier begging for his life. He wrote:

> There was one incident that I saw that I will never forget. A Hun of about 18 years of age lay on the ground & one of our boys stood over him with the point of his bayonet on the Huns [sic] stomach & he was saying. 'I am going to kill you you—' The look of terror on that boys face was awful & he was screaming for mercy. I could not see him killed. It was too much like murder. I knocked the bayonet aside & dragged the Hun to his feet. That incident I will never to my dying day forget.[7]

Cecil H. Cox told a similar story. Cox was serving in Northern Italy at the time, and described the moment when he looked into the eyes of his enemy and could not shoot:

> I saw a young German coming towards me and at that moment I just could not murder him and lowered my gun, he saw me do so and he followed suit, shouting 'What the h— do you want to kill me for, I dont [sic] want to kill you.' he [sic] walked back with me and asked if I had anything to eat? At once the relief inside me was unspeakable, and I gave him my iron rations & my army biscuit.[8]

State-legitimatized killing was understood as 'murder' in a moment of epiphany that was 'unspeakable' at the time.

We must remember, of course, that such forms of defiance are extremely limited. Alexander and Cox were immersed in a global, military slaughter in which their individual refusals to kill were a drop in an ocean of blood. But if it had been one of my loved ones whose life was saved, their courage would have been momentous. Indeed, the slaughter of loved ones has spurred many people to protest against war. Vera Brittain, author of the best-selling *Testament of Youth* (1933), whom I discussed in Chapter Three, turned to pacifism in an attempt to give meaning to the deaths of her fiancé, two male friends and her brother. The authority of millions of war-resisters has been premised on the fact that they endured personal losses in military conflagrations.

In recent years, grieving families have sought to limit the representation of war within popular entertainment. This was what the gaming company Konami discovered when they planned to release *Six Days in Fallujah*. Members of Military Families Speak Out and Stop the War Coalition were appalled, and set out to resist this commercialization of their loved ones' deaths. Joanna Polisena, sister of Edward Carman, who was killed in Iraq on 17 April 2004, bitterly complained that

> When our loved one's 'health meter' dropped to '0', they didn't get to 'retry' the mission. When they took a bullet, they didn't just get to pick up a health pack and keep 'playing' . . . They suffered, they cried, they died. We – their parents, siblings, spouses, children and friends – absolutely find it disgusting and repulsive that those so far detached (and clinging to denial of reality) find it so easy to poke fun at such a thing.

Joan Maymi, whose nephew Ernesto Manuel Blanco-Caldas was killed in Iraq on 29 December 2003, echoed these sentiments. 'To trivialize it in a video game and continue to desensitize our society from the scope of violence war entails goes beyond words,' he reminded people.[9] Their messages included: cherished lives had been violently snuffed out; don't play with our grief.

I can only guess how members of Military Families Speak Out might respond to anti-war activists who seek to sabotage the logic behind violent video games such as *Six Days in Fallujah*, but *from within*. These activists accepted the plea to respect the men and women who had been killed, but the activists did so by playing the games. This represents a shift from more traditional artistic and literary forms of protest. In the post-modern (and I claim that we are at the beginning of a post-human) phase of warfare, interventions are increasingly occurring in public spaces outside the traditional *agora* or town squares. They are happening in public, virtual realms.

A formidable number of permutations exist, so I will merely give two examples that I find both fun and subversive: the creative engagements of Joseph Delappe and Anne-Marie Schleiner.

Delappe is inspired by a belief in the power of 'ludic activism' (that is, playful dissidence) to challenge the militarized environments of computer war games. One of Delappe's early performance pieces, which took place in 2003, involved him entering *Medal of Honor: Allied Assault* to recite the angry anti-war poetry of Siegfried Sassoon.[10]

More creatively, on the third anniversary of the war in Iraq (March 2006), Delappe entered *America's Army* as a peace activist. After logging in under the name 'dead-in-iraq', he would immediately drop his weapon and then use the game's messaging system to type in the name, age, service branch and date of death of Americans killed in the conflict. It was a 'fleeting, online memorial'.[11]

Other gamers were not happy. Typically, they would attempt to get him to stop, by abusing him in the messaging system, 'vote-kicking' him out of the game for violations of the Code of

Conduct (he was accused of engaging in 'chat spam'), or killing
his avatar. Although not all players were negative – on one occasion, two players even stood in front of Delappe's avatar in order
to take the bullets[12] – most gamers regarded his actions as
provocative: he was not 'playing the game'. Delappe was breaking the magic circle inherent to gaming; that is, its alleged
separateness from the 'real world'. This is ironic, given the fact
that *America's Army* is a recruitment tool, meaning that the 'outside' political world is an integral part of the game. An exchange
with other players – including typos and abbreviations – read:

> [US Army] dead-in-iraq messaged: CHARLES A HANDSON
> JR, 22 MARINE NOV 28 2004
> [ENEMY]{UN}(USA)Richdog messaged: dead- Plese this is
> not the formu to do this
> [Enemy] Hadestortures messaged: I DON4T GIVE A ****
> [US Army] srgntpepper messaged: man will all the fn hackers
> goplay ping pong or something.[13]

The following year, Delappe rectified his earlier emphasis on
commemorating only 'our' deaths. His iraqimemorial.org was
an online forum drawing attention to the thousands of Iraqi civilians who had been killed since the invasion by the US and its
allies. This initiative was a response to the launch of the World
Trade Center Site Memorial Competition, which sought to commemorate 'the thousands of innocent men, women and children
murdered by terrorists' in the 1993 and 2001 attacks. Why
should the innocent victims of 9/11 be memorialized at precisely
the time when 'many thousands of people, arguably just as innocent, were being killed in order for us to "fight terrorism",
"protect our freedoms", and "spread democracy abroad"' he
asked. These were the crucial questions: 'Who is remembered?
Who is mourned? Who is responsible? How do we, as artists,

choose to respond?' With this in mind, Delappe invited artists, designers, architects, musicians, dancers and other creative individuals or groups to submit proposals to iraqimemorial.org for ways to remember those 'victims of a war who will likely never be recognized through official processes'.[14]

The second anti-war gaming tradition I find interesting is very different from Delappe's forceful interventions. These anti-war video-gamers recognize that in order to counter militarist tendencies it is not enough to simply expose the *facts* of militarization of games; they must also confront its *pleasures*. One way gamers have done this is by reconfiguring commercially released computer games in order to introduce different (that is, non-violent or pacifist) characters, sounds and graphics.[15] This process – called modding – can fundamentally alter the content and ideological message of the entire game.

Of course, like the other interventions, modding is not *inherently* opposed to the military–entertainment complex. Corporations, as opposed to local authorities, own the online spaces in which these activities take place and there are fierce debates about copyright. Some proponents have even observed that mods can increase demand for the original game, in part because they update and 'refresh' it.[16] This seems to have happened with the release of mods for *Half-Life* and *Doom III*. But for many anti-war activists, modding has been a powerful way in which players (especially those politicized by feminist, anti-globalization and anti-war movements) can subvert or reappropriate the content of games.

A prominent proponent is Anne-Marie Schleiner, a gaming designer, artist, critic and writer. She is an astute observer of game-play and activist art, as well as computer-gaming cultures, and delights in uncovering 'the specific tactics and modes that have been developed by activists, artists, and ordinary citizen-players to counter the hold of the game'.[17] Schleiner's initial interventions were inspired by a workshop on modifying computer games that she attended a few weeks after the 9/11 attacks. To entertain the participants, the organizers had uploaded a 'new demo' of *Return to Castle Wolfenstein* to all of the PCs. While trying out the game, Schleiner learnt that the US had declared war on Afghanistan, and as she heard this news, the 'sounds of the [virtual] weapon-fire echoed off the concrete walls of the workshop warehouse space', transforming what she had 'approached with playful macho geek irony . . . into uncanny echoes of real life violence'.[18]

This experience led to her and fellow 'media interpreter' Joan Leandre into discussions about creating an anti-war mod. The result was a 'programme patch' for the first-person shooter *Counter Strike*. Called *Velvet Strike*, it gives players the capability to paint anti-war and non-violence graffiti on the floors and walls of *Counter Strike*. Players can draw hearts, write 'peace' on walls and insert flowers or children into the virtual landscape. It was the first major example of how violent games could be undermined from within. One of the sprays available through *Velvet Strike* is called 'Make Love, Not War'.

The creative responses to militarization of Delappe and Schleiner were twenty-first-century examples of something that has a distinguished history. Poets, artists, satirists, filmmakers and musicians have always played significant roles in resisting the 'warification' of society. This should not surprise us: art is a cultural practice like any other and, as such, is infused with moral values. The fact that millions of schoolchildren can recite Wilfred Owen's 'Dulce et Decorum Est' (1917) is evidence of the power of poetry to question the militarist heroics of war. Powerful images of war's carnage range from John Singer Sargent's *Gassed* (1919) (which was voted Picture of the Year by the Royal Academy of Arts) to Pablo Picasso's *Guernica* (1937), which

Figure 8.2. 'Family lying dead in their home as a result of poison gas'. Coloured lithograph released by the Women's International League for Peace and Freedom, *c.* 1920s.[19]

brought the Spanish Civil War to the world's attention. Less well-known examples of artistic disruptions include the strong anti-war tradition in working-class amateur theatre, as well as more organized groups (including, in the 1930s, the Federal Theatre Project and the Workers' Theatre Movement). In my view, some of the best responses to the Gulf War of 1990–1 were theatrical. For example, Trevor Griffiths's *The Gulf Between Us* (1992), which opened on the first anniversary of the attack on Iraq, has a particularly searing indictment of the aggressors. One of the characters, Dr Aziz, looks down at the bodies of dead children and says,

this will not be justified by invoking the evil of my rulers or
the unavoidability of your 'collateral damage'. This world is
full of evil rule . . . As for the unavoidable, how stupid, how
very stupid you must think us, to imagine a decent human
being believing you for one second, when you have told us and
you have shown us your ability to tell the time on a child's
wristwatch from one hundred miles, the side a woman parts
her hair, the stubble on a man's face. We have a holy place, a
place of worship, a place your cameras tell us every day are
filled with children, and you send a missile, not a wayward
bomb, to burn it up . . . In the name of God? In the name of
humankind?[20]

Griffiths was committed to exposing the lunacy of killing one
quarter of a million people and bombing Iraq back five thousand
years in an attempt to create a better world. The cruelty was
even worse because Iraq was the 'origin of so much that we in the
West have inherited in the way of art, science, mathematics, medicine, literature, language, and even our alphabet'.[21]

Satirists have sought more mischievous ways to subvert militarist encroachments into everyday life and undermine militarist
hubris. Jon Stewart's *The Daily Show* has a deserved reputation for
reminding viewers of the military–industrial complex while still
making us laugh. In the words of Stewart's fellow comedian Ed
Helms, miniature soldiers being marketed to children as
Christmas presents come with 'everything a peacekeeper could
possible want – border shells, machine guns, high-powered sniper
rifles . . .'[22]

Feminists, too, have revelled in satirizing and subverting norms
of womanhood for anti-war aims. Again, there are numerous
examples, but I want to briefly mention three: Code Pink, the
Raging Grannies and the Missile Dick Chicks. They couldn't be
more different. Code Pink is a feminist anti-war group established

in 2002, with eighty branches throughout the US. Dressed in bright pink, they call on 'ordinary outraged woman willing to be outrageous for peace'.[23] While waving banners with words like 'Make Love, Not War', Code Pink stage kiss-ins at military recruitment fairs; they parade with giant puppets and effigies dripping with fake blood. They also organise major protest marches and routinely heckle leading politicians and others who support the war. The Raging Grannies also parody femininity by wearing floral dresses and elaborate, old-fashioned hats. They engage in 'grannying' – that is, doing things like visiting military barracks, offering soldiers homemade cakes and tea, and sweetly spreading their anti-militarist message in words and song.[24] In stark contrast to both Code Pink and the Raging Grannies, the Missile Dick Chicks strut about in shiny red, white and blue costumes with strap-on missiles jutting from their groins. In bitter satirical language, they describe themselves as 'pissed-off housewives' who have 'conspired' to drag themselves 'away from our martinis and over-the-counter pharmaceuticals and into the streets' to protest everything from the proliferation of missiles to patriarchal 'ramblings'.[25]

In Chapter Seven, I explored the dependency of filmmakers on the military establishment. It is an influence that could be resisted. Most notably, Oliver Stone refused military assistance when making *Platoon* and *Born on the First of July*. He reasoned that the military sought to

> make prostitutes of us all because they want us to sell out to their point of view . . . They want a certain kind of movie made . . . They don't want to deal with the downside of war. They assist movies that don't tell the truth about combat, and they don't assist movies that seek to tell the truth about combat. Most films about the military are recruiting posters.[26]

Film is a powerful medium with which to criticize the military. Like music, it arouses political as well as aesthetic emotions: just as music can be used to make people conform to military ideologies (as in the call-and-response running cadences of military training grounds), it can also be used to counter militarism. The composition and lyrics of songs like Bob Marley's 'Get Up, Stand Up', Cat Stevens's 'Peace Train' and Joni Mitchell's 'One Tin Soldier' are examples, along with festivals such as Woodstock in August 1969 and more recent compositions such as Erik Hillestad's 'Lullabies from the Axis of Evil' (2004). Perhaps no one identified the power of the arts more eloquently that that great poet Adrienne Rich. She observed that it was important to

> define the 'aesthetic' not as a privileged and sequestered rendering of human suffering, but as news of an awareness, a resistance, which totalising systems want to quell: art reaching into us for what is still passionate, still unintimidated, still unquenched . . . when poetry lays its hand on our shoulders we are, to an almost physical degree, touched and moved.

In contrast to Margaret Thatcher's famous assertion, 'There is no alternative' (which earned her the nickname 'TINA'), Rich argued that 'The imagination's roads open before us, giving the lie to that brutal dictum, "There is no alternative".'[27]

To make a permanent difference, however, individual resisters need other resisters. People have to join together and organize. Anti-militarist protest movements date back to classical times and have been inspired by a daunting range of threats. Some distrusted the economic rationales for putting their own (and other peoples) lives at risk; others fretted over the possibility that standing armies might one day endanger peacetime constitutional democracy. For some, wars are always civil wars of the ruling classes for world domination. Critics have long suspected that the armaments industry might encourage militant, expansionist desires simply in order to test their weapons and increase their profits. Feminists united over concerns about the high levels of domestic violence on military bases and sexual violence in wars, while eco-warriors rallied around the fact that the military is the largest single polluter in the world and a significant contributor to global warming.

Peace movements have espoused a vast range of ideologies. They include pacifists like the Quakers who, from the seventeenth century onwards, warned against the pernicious influence of militarist values and practices of whatever incarnation. At the other extreme, some critics simply limited their opposition to specific conflicts: this war, but not that one, is wrong. Anti-war campaigners devoted to radical feminism are a world apart from their libertarian sisters and brothers. Some protesters are dedicated to internationalism or solidarity with the oppressed worldwide; others serve the interests of right-wing libertarianism. For Antiwar.com, for instance, 'non-interventionism abroad is a corollary to non-interventionism at home'.[28] Nonviolent organizations such as the War Resisters' League and the religious-orientated Fellowship of Reconciliation have motives different from more militant anarchist, syndicalist and Marxist movements. Many groups seek to persuade men and women not to join the armed forces (in 1934, the Peace Pledge Union famously encouraged men to sign a pledge to 'renounce war and refuse to support or sanction another'). Others urged enlisted men to desert. The latter strategy was adopted in the 1970s by the veteran British anti-war campaigner Pat Arrowsmith. She was prosecuted under the 1934 Incitement to Disaffection Act for distributing leaflets to army bases, encouraging soldiers to leave the armed forces or to refuse to serve in Northern

Ireland.[29] 'Unarmed interpositionary peacekeeping' – the creation of 'human barriers' – also has a long history. In the words of Dr A. Maude Royden, suffragist and follower of Mahatma Gandhi, writing in 1931,

> I would like now to enrol people who would be ready if war should break out to put their bodies unarmed between the contending forces, in whatever way it be found possible.[30]

It was a strategy that was attempted by the English group Non-Violent Action in Vietnam who, in 1967, drew up plans to place volunteers in areas in North Vietnam that were being attacked by American forces. They wanted to show solidarity with the Vietnamese people, as well as to disrupt the bombing.[31] 'Body barriers' attracted worldwide attention in 2003 when American activist Rachel Corrie, acting in solidarity with the Palestinians in Rafah, was crushed by an armoured bulldozer belonging to the Israel Defense Forces. Although Corrie's death evoked passionate debates about the role of privileged white men and women showing solidarity with the poor and oppressed, no one doubted her integrity and passion for justice.

Organized resistance *within* the military has been particularly effective, in part because military personnel can claim a moral authority that is not available to 'doves' who have never risked anything for the values they hold dear. They can also expose realities that our governments seek to conceal. Two prominent examples are the photographs that army photographer Ronald Haeberle took at My Lai on the 16 March 1968 and those leaked by personnel at Abu Ghraib prison from 2004. In both cases, revelations of mass murder and torture galvanized anti-war sentiment throughout the world.

In *An Intimate History of Killing* I wrote about some courageous

individual soldiers during the two world wars and the war in
Vietnam, but only briefly touched on organized movements such
as Vietnam Veterans Against the War (VVAW), which was established in 1967 and boasted a national membership of twenty-five
thousand by 1972.[32] VVAW engaged in a range of activities, from
support groups for veterans to mass rallies. They understood the
function of spectacle, as in Operation RAW ('Rapid American
Withdrawal') in September 1970, when hundreds of veterans,
wearing combat fatigues and sporting toy weapons, dramatically
marched eighty-six miles from Morristown, New Jersey, to the
Valley Forge State Park in Pennsylvania. En route, the Philadelphia
Guerrilla Theatre Company and the veterans conducted 'search
and destroy' missions in neighbourhoods and towns. While passing through communities,

> they cordoned off the villages, 'interrogated', 'tortured', and
> 'shot' the actors posing as civilians, and in general tried to
> recreate the brutal realities of war. The towns and roads were
> mapped out in advance and the skits were pre-arranged so that
> as the company surrounded a home or a village – with walkie-
> talkies screaming and vets running all over the place, blood
> capsules bursting on library steps or in front of stores – there
> was a sense of realism in the air as these safe rural hamlets
> were 'invaded'. The veterans terrified and shocked some
> people, challenging many others.[33]

On reaching their destination, the veterans (110 of whom had
earned Purple Hearts) broke their plastic weapons and chanted
'Peace . . . Now'. The following year, veterans threw their medals
over the fence and on to the gardens and building of the Capitol as
part of the Dewey Canyon III demonstrations in Washington, DC.
   VVAW also staged the Winter Soldier Investigations of 1971
and 1972, at which veterans spoke about their experiences of

war and combat. Ex-servicemen confessed to having committed or witnessed atrocities. They testified that their training had been dehumanizing; senior officers brutalizing; racism and misogyny rampant. In 2008, this Winter Soldier event was restaged by Iraq Veterans Against the War (IVAW), with the testimonies streamed live online, gaining an audience not only in the US but also among men and women serving in Afghanistan and Iraq.[34]

IVAW is one of nearly twenty anti-war organizations founded to protest against the wars in Iraq and Afghanistan and linked to military personnel and their families.[35] Slogans such as 'Don't Send My Son to War for Oil' (by Military Families Speak Out) and 'Support the Troops? We Are the Troops!'(IVAW) were regarded as particularly credible. In the words of Mike Hoffman, co-founder of IVAW, it was relatively easy to dismiss many anti-war protesters with the words, 'Oh he's just some college-educated tree-hugger that doesn't really know what's going on in the world.' In contrast,

> when the average American hears a veteran – be it from this conflict, Vietnam, WWII, Korea, whatever, somebody who has seen combat and knows what it means – people listen, more than they do to anyone else, because this is somebody who has been on the ground, knows what the realities are, knows what these things mean.[36]

Disrupting pro-war rhetoric cost veterans a great deal. Their careers stalled abruptly; they forfeited educational and health benefits; in some cases, they were vindictively assigned additional tours of duty. Their families were also punished by being ostracized from non-peace veteran movements and denied physical and psychological support. Perhaps most painful for anti-war families were anxieties about whether their spouses or children would be punished for their activities.[37]

For many, though, it was worthwhile. Lives were at stake — and not only in Iraq and Afghanistan. This was the view of Garett Reppenhagen, who served in Iraq and belongs to the IVAW. Despite the traumas of war service and the ordeal of being a soldier-protestor, he was keen to emphasize that American personnel were not the chief victims of the war. They were the 'victimizers'. Talking about his colleagues as well as himself, he argued:

> I think [a serviceman] feels like a criminal, honestly. He feels like the killer and the rapist and the thief, and he comes back to America and it's 'Thank you for your service.' But we're, like, 'You have no idea what you're thanking me for. You don't know what I did.'

Despite suffering from post-traumatic nightmares, Reppenhagen refused to take 'happy pills'. He explained that he was 'flat against' taking medication because

> I don't want to separate myself from my war experience. I think my war experience is part of who I am now, and I've got to learn to carry that. My healing comes from helping other veterans, being part of the movement.[38]

Members of the armed services are not the only 'insiders' with strong links to the military. Scientists are another prominent group with a public responsibility to resist military encroachments. Like servicemen, scientists also have a long history of anti-war opposition. In the modern period, an important intervention came from J. D. Bernal, one of the most influential British scientists of the twentieth century. In *The Social Function of Science* (1939), Bernal appealed to his colleagues to think more seriously about the social implications of their research as well as its potential applications. He was dismayed by the amount of scientific energy that was diverted into armaments development and production, and warned that the cost of this misallocation of resources was too high.[39] In *World Without War* (1958), Bernal went even further, making a cogent argument that the best ways to improve the world were world disarmament and the reallocation of military R&D.[40]

Similar sentiments were echoed in the constitution of the Society for Social Responsibility in Science when it was established in 1949. They sought

> to foster throughout the world a . . . tradition of personal moral responsibility for the consequences for humanity of professional activity, with emphasis on constructive alternatives to militarism; to embody in this tradition the principle that the individual must abstain from destructive work and devote himself to constructive work, according to his own moral judgment.[41]

It was a position that Albert Einstein endorsed in a letter published in *Science* the following year. As he put it,

> In our times, scientists and engineers carry particular moral responsibility, because the development of military means of mass destruction is within their sphere of activity . . . This society, through discussion of the inherent problems, will make it easier for the individual to clarify his mind and arrive at a clear position as to his own stand.[42]

The same industries that make war — which include the scientific–military–technological complex — bore responsibility for unmaking it.

In fact, it is a responsibility borne by *all* academics and educators. In my own field of the arts and humanities, the militarization of universities is frightening. Prominent cultural critic Henry Giroux has been involved in the analysis of universities for decades. To counter this militarization, he advises academics to refuse to 'instrumentalize the curriculum', lobby to give the humanities 'a larger role in educating all undergraduate students', and introduce courses that 'stress a critical education over job training; and enabling students to learn how to read the political and pedagogic forces that shape their lives not as consumers and soldiers but as critically engaged citizens'.[43]

Such sage advice is equally relevant when educating school-children, as many British historians have observed in connection with the recent 'history wars' (in which senior politicians have attempted to shift the curriculum into a nation-building enterprise). In fact, there have been times in the recent past when peace activism was prominent in schools. In 1937, for instance, high-school teacher Ellen Lamar Thomas published a heartfelt plea for children to be taught about the effects of war. In her words, 'We know that no war would be popular if it were known that it was fought even in part to increase the profits of a newspaper or a steel corporation'. She asked teachers to remind their students of

> the hundred-million-dollar orders placed by the Allies for Bethlehem Steel, the five-hundred-million-dollar loans arranged for the Allies by the Morgans ... The expressions 'making the world safe for Wall Street', and 'putting the dollar sign on the American flag' are worn-out phrases now – but the chances are that most students have never heard them.[44]

Admittedly, peace education has undergone a crisis in recent decades. It developed in the late nineteenth century when peace societies – many of which had strong feminist input – throughout Europe and the US sought to encourage internationalism through education. From the 1970s to 2000, however, there has been a significant narrowing of focus, with increased attention being placed on individual responses *to* violence rather than structural sources *of* violence. Peace has come to be seen as something that is only relevant in the context of the *local* community or even simply the school itself. Global history, internationalism and systemic inequalities have been jettisoned for vague slogans about the need to give peace a chance.[45] Let's all stand and sing, 'Imagine all the people/Living life in peace'.[46] Thankfully, this is a trend that can be reversed.

In *Philosophy and Resistance in the Crisis* (2013), Douzinas insists that 'Ours is the age of resistance. The possibility of radical change has been firmly placed on the historical agenda.'[47] If this is to become true, one central task is to reaffirm our right to engage in the public sphere. As sociologist Sasha Roseneil advised, it is important to challenge the 'geopolitical privacy' surrounding defence issues. In other words, it is not the case that debates about the military should take place in certain contexts only (in Parliament or in the mainstream media, for instance) rather than others (the home or immediately outside the perimeter fence).[48]

This is why the two-decade women's peace camp at Greenham Common was so important. These women were spurred to action after Prime Minister Margaret Thatcher backed the 1979 decision to base ninety-six cruise missiles in Britain. On Thursday 27 August 1981, thirty-six women, four men and a few children left Cardiff to walk to the American base in protest against the nuclear missiles. En route, they handed out a leaflet. On one side, it asked 'Why are we walking 110 miles across Britain, from a nuclear weapons factory in Cardiff to a US base for "Cruise" missiles in Berkshire?' On the reverse: a photograph of a badly deformed, dead baby from Hiroshima. Calling themselves Women for Life on Earth, these protestors chained themselves to the fence around the base and settled in for the long term. The movement attracted enormous crowds, notably on 12 December 1982 when thirty thousand women turned up to protest.[49] The women embraced tactics traditionally associated with femininity: they encircled the base, holding hands, singing and dancing; they attached dried flowers, paper birds and ribbons to the fence; they keened in grief. The camp at Greenham Common became synonymous with the peace movement of the 1980s. Long after the missiles were removed, the protest continued, extending its focus to the Trident missile programme. Their actions led to a wave of similar camps across the UK (Molesworth in Cambridgeshire, Upper Heyford in Oxfordshire and Faslane on Clydeside), Western Europe and the US (including the famous camp at Seneca Falls). But Greenham Common was always to be associated with the threat of cruise missiles.

I admit to being impressed by the women of Greenham Common. They represent just one example of a vast movement of marching and protesting. In recent years, this has included the worldwide network of 'women in black'; the saucepan revolution in Iceland; riots in Tunisia, Egypt, Spain and the US; the Arab Spring; Occupy Wall Street; and Occupy London. This is also what we learnt by participating with the *aganaktismenoi* in Greece, the *indignados* in Spain and joining the millions who went to the British streets to protest against the 2003 invasion of Iraq, supported by the British Prime Minister Tony Blair (or '*Bliar*', as witty poster-designers put it). Such public spectacles have been immeasurably helped by new technologies such as the internet, satellite television, e-petitions, and podcasts. Although some activists sneer at engaging with new media such as YouTube and

Twitter, claiming it is 'political engagement as fast food', there is no doubt that it has enabled many protestors to build different and vibrant communities of resistance in global as well as local ways.

These technologies won't make physically present forms of resistance redundant: they facilitate and supplement, rather than replace, the power of people massing together to protest. The presence of recalcitrant bodies linked together in solidarity has a subversive force that cannot be trumped. This has long been recognized. Indeed, it was a major part of the appeal of anti-nuclear protests in the mid- and late twentieth century, where women would march to the perimeter of weapon test sites, plant crosses and loudly wail in mourning for what was being done inside. The contrast between their display of 'hysterical' sorrow and the abstract reasoning of weapons scientists engaged in MAD (mutually assured destruction) was viscerally arresting.[50] The physical presence of likeminded people galvanizes protestors and is responsible for emergent feelings of solidarity. In other words, solidarity may not *precede* protest, but emerge from it. This was what a demonstrator at the World Trade Organization protest in 1999 was alluding to. He explained that

> Each of us came to Seattle for different reasons . . . When we filled the streets of Seattle, there was a power in our bodies that we didn't know we had. In this city, for this moment, our lives were our own. Who can say at what precise location, exact hour and date, this global movement began. In Seattle we were just a small part of the movement, but in the gas and bullets our memory returned. For that moment our history was made clear to us. We felt the edges of our skin marked by global and historical struggle. We stopped waiting for our world to be legislated or prescribed to us. This time we did not ask for permission to be free.[51]

In order to explain this emergent sense of the collective, we don't need to appeal to any 'primordial connection to the past that can be accessed in moments of crisis'.[52] As choreographer Susan Leigh Foster rightly reminds us, a vast amount of 'physical labor . . . goes in to establishing the connection among bodies that protestors experienced'. Non-violent protestors have to discipline their bodies: they learn not to hit back, to be polite when sworn at and how to hang limply when arrested. They undergo training to 'pattern their pacifism' and this 'cultivation of physicality' prepares bodies 'to apprehend the like-mindedness of adjacent resisting bodies'. It instils 'the potential to feel connected as a community of bodies partaking in a common effort'. This is not a matter of 'transcending cultural and historical specificities'. Rather, the physical act of non-violent protest 'instantiated differently in each political setting' serves to build 'an articulated network of resistance'.[53] In other words, bodies are actively engaged in processes of resistance; the social interactions that emerge in relation with other bodies during protests are in themselves political. As philosopher Maurice Merleau-Ponty argued, 'a body is not just something we own, it is something we are'.[54] Bodies influence the way people think. Recalcitrant bodies spawn recalcitrant politics.

But the body is important for another reason: we need to revive a politics of fear. Those of us who are well off and living in affluent environments have made ourselves too comfortable. We have buried our heads in the sand and there is only one way out: to return to a politics that recognizes that in wounding the world we wound ourselves and our loved ones. As I stated in the Introduction, by passively accepting militarist encroachments we also close down encounters with strangers we might have learnt from, laughed with and loved.

A decade ago, I wrote *Fear: A Cultural History*, in which I observed that people in terrifying, life-threatening situations turn time and again to one question: what does it mean to be human?[55] Sometimes they answered this question in violent and damning ways; more often, their answer spurred them to engagement with other frightened or oppressed people.

I was also struck by the way people made strategic decisions about what they were going to be frightened of. Faced with a horde of risks and threats, they made deliberate choices about what would provoke their anger. They used fear in creative ways. Fear led people to strive to reduce inequalities in local or global communities; it led others to engage politically with feminism, eco-movements, anti-racism, gay movements and equity initiatives.

There is nothing inherently wrong about fear. It can be – and faced with militarization of our society I believe it *is* – an appropriate emotion to incite. We can't pretend that scientific research into more effective ways of maiming and killing other people is none of our business. Our taxes pay for their experiments. Their formulas for calculating how best to kill and injure others are at the heart of our democracies. The militarized logic they apply to their work can be beguiling, since they speak the language of (post)modernity, progress, rationality, freedom and humanism. But if our children or lovers were being conscripted to their service, would we remain mute?

History also tells me that we should fear the militarization of our society. We just have to think about the rapidity with which advanced democratic nations descended into the most barbarous forms of war in 1939. We have to recall how precariously close the world came to mutually assured destruction during the Cold War. In *Welcome to the Desert of the Real* (2002), philosopher Slavoj Zizek made this argument in the context of the terrorists attacks of 9/11. He noted that

The USA, which, until now, perceived itself as on island exempt from this kind of violence . . . is now directly

involved . . . Either America will persist in – even strengthen
the deeply immoral attitude of 'why should this happen to us?
Things like this don't happen *here*!', leading to more aggres-
sivity towards the threatening Outside . . . Or America will
finally risk stepping through the fantasmatic screen that sepa-
rates it from the Outside World, accepting its arrival in the
Real World, making the long-overdue move from 'A thing
like this shouldn't happen *here*!' to 'A thing like this shouldn't
happen *anywhere*!' That is the true lesson of the attacks: the
only way to ensure it will not happen here again is to prevent
it from happening anywhere else.[56]

Combined with a powerful sense of hope – 'it doesn't have to be
this way' – fear can be beneficial. It can stimulate attention,
sharpen wisdom and energize activism. It can promote better
behaviour, encouraging us to act in cooperative ways. The military
is not as powerful as it wants us to believe. The rich tapestry of
public and private resistances open to us is inspiring: fear can
build on these resistances and turn them into the principle of
hope.

Notes

INTRODUCTION

1 G. C. Spivak, 'Can the Subaltern Speak?', in Patrick Williams and Laura Chisman (eds), *Colonial Discourse and Post-Colonial Theory: A Reader* (Hemel Hempstead: Harvester, 1993), 93.

2 GunPolicy.org, at http://www.gunpolicy.org/firearms/region, viewed 17 January 2014.

3 See GunPolicy.org, at http://www.gunpolicy.org/firearms/region/united-states. For the UK statistics, see http://www.gunpolicy.org/firearms/region/united-kingdom.

4 Gallup, 'Guns', at http://www.gallup.com/poll/1645/guns.aspx, viewed 14 January 2014.

5 Ministry of Defence, 'Monthly Personnel Report' (1 December 2013), at http://www.dasa.mod.uk/publications/personnel/military/monthly-personnel-report/2013-12-01/1-december-2013.pdf, viewed 19 January 2014.

6 Sam Perlo-Freeman, Elisabeth Sköns, Carina Solmorano, and Helén Wilanhn, 'Trends in World Military Expenditure, 2012', *SPIRA Fact Sheet* (April 2013), at http://books.sipri.org/files/FS/SIPRIFS1304.pdf, viewed 19 January 2014.

7 Glen Scott Allen, 'Master Mechanics & Evil Wizard: Science and the American Imagination from Frankenstein to Sputnik', *Massachusetts Review*, 33.4 (winter 1992), 548.

8 J. R. McNeill and David S. Painter, 'The Global Environmental Footprint of the US Military 1789–2003', in Charles E. Closman (ed.), *War and the Environment. Military Destruction in the Modern Age* (College Station: Texas A&M University Press, 2009), 21.

9 James A. Donovan, *Militarism USA* (New York: Charles Scribner's Sons, 1970), 29.

10 Department of Defense, 'Active Duty Military Personnel by Rank/Grade' (30 November 2013), at https://www.dmdc.osd.mil/

appj/dwp/reports.do?category=reports&subCat=milActDutReg, viewed 19 January 2014.

11 Renae Merle, 'Census Counts 100,000 Contractors in Iraq', *Washington Post* (5 December 2006). Also see P. W. Singer, *Corporate Warriors: The Rise of the Privatized Military Industry* (New York: Cornell University Press, 2008).

12 Kim Sengupta, 'Blood Money', *Independent* (29 March 2014).

13 This is a 2011 statistic. Thom Shanker, 'US Arms Sales Make Up Most of Global Market', *New York Times*, (26 August 2012).

14 Michael Hardt and Antonio Negri, *Multitude: War and Democracy in the Age of Empire* (London: Hamish Hamilton, 2004), 334.

15 ForcesWatch, *The Last Ambush? Aspects of Mental Health in the British Armed Forces* (London: ForcesWatch, 2013), 27–8, at http://www.forceswatch. net/sites/default/files/The_Last_Ambush_web.pdf, viewed 30 March 2014.

16 Leo Hickman, 'Why Do the British Armed Forces Still Allow 16-Year-Olds to Enlist?', *Guardian* (23 April 2013).

17 'Camouflage', at http://www.army.mod.uk/camouflage/default.aspx and http://army.mod.uk/camouflage/101.aspx, viewed 30 March 2013.

18 Chris Atkins, 'Young British Army Recruits at Higher Risk of PTSD and Suicide, Says Report', *Guardian* (18 October 2013).

19 ForcesWatch, *The Last Ambush?*, op. cit.

20 American Civil Liberties Union, *Soldiers of Misfortune. Abusive US Military Recruitment and Failure to Protect Child Soldiers* (New York: ACLU, 2008), 13.

21 United States Army Recruiting Command, 'School Recruiting Program Handbook' (1 September 2004), 3.

22 This refers to a survey of one thousand children in grades nine to twelve: American Civil Liberties Union, *Soldiers of Misfortune*, op. cit., 11.

23 Ibid., 20–1.

24 This was report on *News House with Jim Lehrer*, 'High School: Recruiting', PBS Television, broadcast 1 December 2004, in ibid., 20.

25 Henry Giroux, *The University in Chains: Confronting the Military–Industrial–Academic Complex* (Boulder, CO: Paradigm Publishers, 2007), 14–5.

26 Stuart W. Leslie, *The Cold War and American Science: the Military–Industrial–Academic Complex at MIT and Stanford* (New York: Columbia University Press, 1993), 14.

27 Major Anita J. Fitch, 'The Solomon Amendment: A War on Campus', *Army Law* (May 2006), 12. It was challenged in 2004 and upheld in 2006.

28 The US Secretary of Defense can deny federal funding to colleges and
   universities that prevent the armed forces from recruiting on their
   premises according to the Solomon Amendment of 1996. The Dean of
   Law was Anthony Kronman cited in Scott W. Johnson, 'JAGS Not
   Welcome', *Weekly Standard* (27 September 2005), at http://
   www.weeklystandard.com/Content/Public/Articles/000/000/006/
   132qedpc.asp, viewed 17 January 2014.
29 Tim Street with Martha Beale, 'Study War No More. Military
   Involvement in UK Universities' (October 2007), 14 and 20, at http://
   www.studywarnomore.org.uk/documents/studywarnomore.pdf.
30 Ibid.
31 Lisa W. Foderaro, 'New York Wants to Banish a Symbol of Love: Mute
   Swans', *New York Times* (29 January 2014).

CHAPTER ONE: IT'S ONLY WORDS

1 George Orwell, 'Politics and the English Language', 1st 1946
  (London: Penguin, 2013), at https://www.mtholyoke.edu/
  acad/intrel/orwell46.htm.
2 'Anzac', *On the Anzac Trail. Being Extracts from the Diary of a New Zealand
  Sapper* (London: William Heinemann, 1916), 121, entry for 28 April
  1915, and Henri de Man, *The Remaking of a Mind. A Soldier's Thoughts on
  War and Reconstruction* (London: Allen and Unwin, 1920), 199.
3 Letter by Second Lieutenant F. R. Darrow, *Letters from the Front. Being
  a Record of the Part Played by Officers of the Bank in the Great War
  1914–1919*, vol. 1 (Toronto: Canadian Bank of Commerce, 1920),
  241, and Captain Wilfred Thomas Colyer, 'Memoirs', no page numbers, part 5, chapter 18 (labelled Chapter 2 but located between
  chapters 17 and 19), Imperial War Museum, London (henceforth
  IWM), 76/51/1. Colyner was describing a comrade's feelings.
4 Ion Llewellyn Idriess, *The Desert Column. Leaves from the Diary of an
  Australian Trooper in Gallipoli, Sinai, and Palestine* (Sydney: Angus and
  Robertson, 1932), 171.
5 J. E. H. Neville, *The War Letters of a Light Infantryman* (London: Sifton
  Praed and Co., 1930), 54.
6 Alfred Duff Cooper, *Old Men Forget* (London: Rupert Hart-Davis,
  1953), 85.
7 Wesley D. Archer, *Death in the Air: The War Diary and Photographs of a
  Flying Corps Pilot* (London: Greenhill, 1985), 15.
8 Roderick Chrisholm, *Cover of Darkness* (London: Chatto and Windus,
  1953), 71. Also see a letter from the pilot 'John', no date but probably

January 1940, in Squadron Leader Hector Bolitho, 'Two in Twenty-Two Minutes', in *Slipstream. A Royal Air Force Anthology* (London: Eyre and Spottiswoode, 1946). Also see Hector Bolitho, *Combat Report. The Story of a Fighter Pilot* (London: B. T. Batsford, 1943), 54, quoting from a letter from pilot 'John', 10 April, probably 1940.

9 Kenneth Hemingway, *War over Burma* (London: Quality Press, 1944), 41–2 and 68–9. Also see Flight Lieutenant D. M. Crook, *Spitfire Pilot* (London: Faber and Faber, 1942), 28, 30–1 and 75.

10 See the interview of K. O. Moore and Alec Gibb in Bolitho, 'Two in Twenty-Two Minutes', op. cit., 10–11.

11 George MacDonald Fraser, *Quartered Safe Out Here. A Recollection of the War in Burma* (London: Harvill, 1992), 83.

12 William Nagle, 'Do You Remember When?', Australian War Memorial Archives PR89/148.

13 'Bob' interviewed in Wing-Commander Athol Forbes and Squadron-Leader Hubert Allen, *The Fighter Boys* (London: Collins, 1942), 84.

14 Cited in James J. Fisher, *The Immortal Deeds of Our Irish Regiments in Flanders and the Dardenelles* (Dublin: n.p., 1916), n.p. (no. 1).

15 An unnamed soldier in the *Waterford News*, cited in Tom Dooley, *Irishmen or English Soldiers* (Liverpool: Liverpool University Press, 1995), 135, and *With the First Canadian Contingent* (Toronto: Hodder and Stoughton, 1915), 76–77.

16 Major William Avery Bishop, *Winged Warfare. Hunting Huns in the Air* (London: Hodder and Stoughton, 1918), 9.

17 Flight Lieutenant Richard Charles Rivaz, *Tail Gunner* (London: Jarrards, 1943), 74.

18 Alexander Catto, *With The Scottish Troops in France* (Aberdeen: Aberdeen Daily Journal Office, 1918), 35; Coningsby Dawson, *The Glory of the Trenches* (London: John Lane, 1918), 12; H. Hesketh-Prichard, *Sniping in France* (London: Hutchinson and Co., 1920), 37; *Sniping, Scouting and Patrolling* (Aldershot: HMSO, no date), 1; A. Douglas Thorburn, *Amateur Gunner. The Adventures of an Amateur Soldier in France, Salonica and Palestine in The Royal Field Artillery* (Liverpool: William Potter, 1933), 155–7; Lieutenant-Colonel Neil Fraser Tyler, *Field Guns in France* (London: Hutchinson and Co., 1922), 90, letter on 17 July 1916; Major Gordon Casserly, *The Training of the Volunteers for War* (London: Hodder and Stoughton, 1915), 75; A. T. Walker, *Field Craft for the Home Guard* (Glasgow: John Menzies and Co. Ltd., 1940), 13; General Sir Archibald Wavell, 'Rules and Stratagems of War', in his *Speaking Generally. Broadcasts, Orders and Addresses in Time of War (1939–43)* (London: Macmillan and Co., 1946), 80, issued July 1942.

19 Herbert Wes McBride, *A Rifleman Went to War* (Plantersville: Small-Arms Technical Publishing Co., 1935), 106.

20 Harold Stainton, 'A Personal Narrative of the War', p. 12, IWM 78/11/1; John Beede, in Gavin Lyall (ed.), *The War in the Air, 1939–1945. An Anthology of Personal Experience* (London: Hutchinson, 1968), 278; Walter A. Briscoe, *The Boy Hero of the Air. From Schoolboy to VC* (London: Humphrey Milford, 1921), throughout; Crook, *Spitfire Pilot*, op. cit., 41–2. The Rev. E. J. Kennedy, *With the Immortal Seventh Division*, 2nd edition (London: Hodder and Stroughton, 1916), 114.

21 Sir Edward Hulse, letters, letter to 'Uncle Mi', 2 February 1915, p. 3, IWM 86/30/1 and Charles Gordon Templer, 'Autobiography of an Old Soldier', p. 25, IWM 86/30/1.

22 Philip Orr, *The Road to the Somme. Men of the Ulster Division Tell Their Story* (Belfast: Blackstaff Press, 1987), 155, quoting R. H. Stewart's reaction to killing during the Battle of the Somme.

23 Tytler, *Field Guns in France*, op. cit., 131–2. Letters dated 10 November 1916 and 8 May 1917.

24 Henry ('Jo') Gullett, *Not as a Duty Only. An Infantryman's War* (Melbourne: Melbourne University Press, 1976), 127.

25 R. Clapham, 'Sniping', *Arms and the Man* (14 June 1919), 232.

26 'Barbarous American Soldiery', *Arms and the Man*, lxiv.18 (21 July 1918), 348.

27 General Sir Thomas Blamey, quoted in George H. Johnston, *The Toughest Fight in the World* (New York: Duel, Sloan, and Pearce, 1944), 207.

28 'The Doings of the Peace Conference', *Daily Mail* (2 June 1899).

29 Fred. G. Engelbach, 'A Plea for the Dum-Dum', *Daily Mail* (12 June 1899). Also see Malvern Lumsden, 'New Military Technologies and the Erosion of International Law. The Case of the Dum-Dum Bullets Today', *Instant Research on Peace and Violence*, 4.1 (1974), 17.

30 Comment by the Surgeon-General Harvey (Director-General of the Indian Medical Service) in discussion after the lecture by William MacCormac, 'Some Remarks, By Way of Contrast, On War Surgery, Old and New', *British Medical Journal*, 2.2121 (24 August 1901), 462.

31 C. Ranger Gull, 'The Great Sport Revival', *Health and Efficiency* (July 1919), 146.

32 'Soldiers' Lingo', *Arms and the Man*, lix.25 (16 March 1916), 488.

33 Stephen Trask, 'The Gun That Halts the Hun', *Arms and the Man*, lxiv.14 (29 June 1918), n.p. (first page).

34 'The Sharpshooter's Rifle and the Telescopic Sight' (1917), *Arms and the Man*, lxi.21 (15 February 1917), 5.

35   'Noises that Bullets Make', *Arms and the Man*, Lvi.2 (1916), 30.

36   Brigadier-General the Right Honourable Lord Thomson, 'Aerial Warfare and Disarmament', *Survey* (1 February 1925), 504. Note that he wants western nations to disarm because this new weapon is too destructive.

37   Eric Prokosch, *The Simple Art of Murder. Antipersonnel Weapons and Their Developers* (Philadelphia: NARMIC, 1972), 13 and 19, and Michael Krepan, 'Weapons Potentially Inhumane: The Case of Cluster Bombs', *Foreign Affairs*, 52.3 (April 1974), 596.

38   Gordon Baxter, *13/13; Vietnam: Search and Destroy* (New York: The World Publishing Co., 1967), 72.

39   Major John Borgman, Commander of the Special Forces' Fifth Mobile Strike Force, cited in *San Francisco Chronicle* (31 March 1969), cited in J. B. Neilands, 'Vietnam: Progress of the Chemical War', *Asian Survey*, 10.3 (March 1970), 215.

40   Dr A. Behar, cited by Neilands, 'Vietnam', op. cit., 215.

41   Matt J. Martin with Charles W. Sasser, *Predator. The Remote-Control Air War Over Iraq and Afghanistan* (Minneapolis: Zenith Press, 2010), 37.

42   Bob Hersey, 'K Troop 11th Armored Cavalry Regiment' page, at http://www.ktroop.com/language.htm, viewed 6 February 2014.

43   'The Text-Book for Military Small Arms and Ammunition, 1894', *Quarterly Review* (July 1899), 153.

44   Andrew Exum, 'Armed for a Fight', *Wilson Quarterly*, 34.4 (autumn 2010), 91.

45   James Edminstan, *The Sterling Years. Small-Arms and the Men* (London: Leo Cooper, 1992), 3.

46   Winston Churchill, *The Story of the Malakand Field Force: An Episode of Frontier War* (London: Longmans, Green and Co., 1898) 287–8.

47   Henry J. Davis, 'Gunshot Injuries in the Late Greco-Turkish War with Remarks upon Modern Projectiles', *British Medical Journal* (19 December 1897), 1790.

48   Alex. Ogston, 'The Peace Conference and the Dum-Dum Bullet', *British Medical Journal* (29 July 1899), 279.

49   E. Newton Harvey, J. Howard McMillen, Elmer G. Butler, and William O. Puckett, 'Mechanism of Wounding', in Lieutenant-General Leonard D. Heaton (ed.), *Wound Ballistics* (Washington, DC: Office of the Surgeon General, Department of the US Army, 1962), 134 and 144.

50   R. I. H. Whitlock, 'Experience Gained from Treating Facial Injuries Due to Civil Unrest', *Annals of the Royal College of Surgeons of England*, 63 (1981), 37. Also see A. N. Black, B. Delisle Burns, and Solly

Zuckerman, 'An Experimental Study of the Wound Mechanism of High-Velocity Missiles', *British Medical Journal* (20 December 1941), 872.

51 Gary W. Dufresne, 'Wound Ballistics: Recognizing Wound Potential. Part I: Characteristics of Missiles and Weapons', *International Journal of Trauma Nursing*, 1.1 (January–March 1995), 5–6.

52 Ibid., 6–7.

53 David A. Volger, James P. Stannard, and Jorge E. Alonson, 'Ballistics: A Primer for the Surgeon', *Injury*, 36 (2005), 376.

54 Harvey, McMillen, Butler and Puckett, 'Mechanism of Wounding', op. cit., 146.

55 E. Newton Harvey, 'The Mechanism of Wounding by High Velocity Missiles', *Proceedings of the American Philosophical Society*, 92.4 (25 October 1948), 294.

56 Peter T. Kilborn, 'Threats and Responses: The Economy', *New York Times* (17 February 2003).

57 For instance, see Tim Hsia and Jared Sperli, 'How Cyberwarfare and Drones have Revolutionized Warfare', *New York Times* (17 June 2013).

58 Robert A. Bailey, 'Application of Operations-Research Techniques to Airborne Weapon System Planning', *Journal of the Operations Research Society of America*, 1.4 (August 1953), 188.

59 Cariol Cohen, 'Sex and Death in the Rational World of Defense Intellectuals', *Signs*, 12.4 (summer 1987), 691, and http://science.howstuffworks.com/nuclear-bomb6.htm, viewed 21 December 2013.

60 Cohen, 'Sex and Death', op. cit., 692.

61 'For Fighting at Close Quarters', *Daily Mail* (13 March 1900).

62 K. S. Dance, 'Diary', 6 March 1916, IWM 84/58/1; Norman Shaw, 'Papers', letter on 14 July 1916, IWM 84/9/1; Harold Stainton, 'A Personal Narrative of the War', 28, IWM 78/11/1.

63 Major Ralph W. French and Brigadier-General George R. Callender, 'Ballistic Characteristics of Wounding Agents', in Heaton (ed.), *Wound Ballistics*, op. cit., 111.

64 Major Ralph W. French and Brigadier-General George R. Callender, 'Physical Aspects of the Missile Casualty', in Heaton (ed.), *Wound Ballistics*, op. cit., 115.

65 Duncan MacPherson, *Bullet Penetration. Modeling the Dynamics and the Incapacitation Resulting from Wound Trauma* (El Segundo: Ballistic Publications, 1994), 52.

66 Eric Mottram, '"The Perverse Lips"': Men and Guns in America, the West', *Journal of American Studies*, 10.1 (April 1976), 63.

67 Surgeon-Major-General J. B. Hamilton, 'The Dum-Dum Bullet',

258 Notes

British Medical Journal (11 June 1898), 1559. The term was widely used: see 'The New Service Bullet', British Medical Journal, 2.1957 (2 July 1898), 39.

68 'The New Service Bullet', op. cit.

69 Lieutenant-Colonel W. C. Moffat, 'Influence of Missile Type and Velocity', Proceedings of the Royal Society of Medicine, 66 (March 1977), 291.

70 'Disruptive Wounds from High-Velocity Projectiles', British Medical Journal (20 December 1941), 881.

71 Frank E. Grubbs, 'Expected Target Damage for a Salvo of Rounds with Elliptical Normal Delivery and Damage Functions', Operations Research, 16.5 (September–October 1968), 1021.

72 Charles J. V. Murphy, 'The Airmen and the Invasion', Life, xvi (10 April 1944), 105.

73 Philip C. Winslow, Sowing the Dragon's Teeth. Land Mines and the Global Legacy of War (Boston: Beacon, 1997), 2.

74 Ibid.

75 Michael Krepan, 'Weapons Potentially Inhumane', op. cit., 598–9.

76 Ibid.

77 Martin with Sasser, Predator, op. cit., 18. He is quoting someone else.

78 A. A. Liebow, 'Encounter with Disaster – A Medical Diary of Hiroshima, 1945', Yale Journal of Biology and Medicine, 38.2 (1965), 235. Also see Wilfrid Edward Le Gros Clark, 'The Contribution of Anatomy to the War', British Medical Journal (12 January 1946), 40, and Charles N. Bressel, 'Expected Target Damage for Pattern Firing', Operations Research, 19.3 (May–June 1971), 655.

79 J. Wilson, 'Wound Ballistics', West Journal of Medicine, 127 (July 1977), 51.

80 Ibid.

81 Prokosch, The Simple Art of Murder, op. cit, 11.

82 Velma Maxson, cited in Kilborn, 'Threats and Responses', op. cit.

83 Seth Wiard, 'Ballistics as Applied to Police Science', American Journal of Police Science, 1.6 (November–December 1930), 538.

84 Bailey, 'Application of Operations-Research Techniques', op. cit., 192.

85 L. G. Fogg, 'No Abbey Service', Manchester Guardian (15 August 1945).

86 John Edwards, Superweapon. The Making of MX (New York: W. W. Norton, 1982), 78.

87 General Curtis Emerson LeMay with MacKinlay Kantor, Mission with LeMay. My Story (New York: Doubleday and Co., 1965), 496.

88 Richard Norton-Taylor, 'British Forces to be Equipped with Glock Pistols for Protection in Afghanistan', Guardian (11 January 2013).

Other weapons are called 'life-savers', for instance, see the website of 'Self-Defense: A Basic Human Right', 'P32 Pocket Pistol', at http://www.a-human-right.com/p32/performance.html, viewed 3 October 2013.

89 Edward C. McDonald, 'Social Adjustment to Militarism', *Sociology and Social Research*, 29 (July–August 1945), 445–50.

90 Robert Jay Lifton, *Home from the War. Vietnam Veterans: Neither Victims nor Executioners* (London: Wildwood House, 1974), 347.

91 Jacques Leslie, *The Mark. A War Correspondent's War Memoirs of Vietnam and Cambodia* (New York: Four Walls Eight Windows, 1995), 79–80.

92 Richard P. Feynman, 'Los Alamos from Below', in http://calteches.library.caltech.edu/34/3/FeynmanLosAlamos.htm, based on a talk he gave in 1975, viewed 21 December 2013, and Robert Jungk, *Brighter than a Thousand Suns: A Personal History of the Atomic Scientists*, trans. James Cleugh (New York: Harcourt, Brace, and Co., 1956), 197.

93 Richard Greening Hewlett and Oscar Edward Anderson, *The New World, 1939/46: A History of the United States Atomic Energy Commission*, vol. 1 (University Park: Pennsylvania State University Press, 1962), 386.

94 C. N. Hill, *Black Knight. Britain's First Ballistic Rocket* (n.p.: A BROHP Publication, 2007), 3.

95 Kathryn Moore, 'The Knife and Gun Club Just Adjourned: Managing Penetrating Injuries in the Emergency Department', *Journal of Emergency Nursing*, 38.1 (January 2012), 102.

96 Ibid.

97 Moffat, 'Influence of Missile Type and Velocity', op. cit., 291. My emphasis.

98 Captain Roy S. Tinney, 'The New Hun Target Developed at the National Proving Station', *Arms and the Man* (5 April 1919), 25.

99 Hiram Maxim interviewed in 'A Visit to a Famous Inventor', *Chums* (5 September 1894), 31.

100 Martin with Sasser, *Predator*, op. cit., 42.

CHAPTER TWO: THE CIRCULATION OF VIOLENCE

1 Vera Brittain, 'War Service in Perspective', in George Andrew Panichas (ed.), *Promise of Greatness: The War of 1914–1918* (New York: John Day, 1968), 373, and Vera Brittain, *Testament of Youth*, 1st pub. 1933 (New York: Penguin, 1989), 211, 339, 384, 410, 423, 469 and 655.

2 James E. Hopkins, 'Casualty-Survey – New Georgia and Burma Campaigns', in Lieutenant-General Leonard D. Heaton (ed.), *Wound*

Ballistics (Washington, DC: Office of the Surgeon-General, Department of the Army, 1962), 277.

3 For a description of these campaigns during the Second World War, see The National Archives WO32/11675.

4 Frank R. Dutra, 'Progress in Medico-Legal Investigation of Gunshot Wounds', *Journal of Criminal Law and Criminology*, 39.4 (November–December 1948), 524.

5 Ibid.

6 Stephen Graham, *The Challenge of the Dead* (London: Cassell and Co., 1921), 121.

7 Henri de Man, *The Remaking of a Mind: A Soldier's Thoughts on War and Reconstruction* (London: Allen and Unwin, 1920), 200.

8 Therese Benedek, *Insight and Personality Adjustment. A Study of the Psychological Effects of War* (New York: Ronald, 1946), 90. Also see Ray R. Grinker and John P. Spiegel, *Men Under Stress* (London: Blakiston, 1945), 308 and 362; Guy Cromwell Field, *Pacifism and Conscientious Objection* (Cambridge: Cambridge University Press, 1945), 23; William Ernest Hocking, *Morale and Its Enemies* (New Haven: Yale University Press, 1918), 113.

9 Jerome Johns, interviewed in Peter T. Chews, 'The Forgotten Soldiers, Black Veterans Say They're Ignored', *National Observer* (10 March 1973).

10 Mardi J. Horowitz and George F. Solomon, 'A Prediction of Delayed Stress Syndromes in Vietnam Veterans', *Journal of Social Issues*, 31.4 (1975), 73.

11 Dane Archer and Rosemary Gartner, *Violence and Crime in Cross-National Perspective* (New Haven: Yale University Press, 1984), 92, and their 'Violent Acts and Violent Times: A Comparative Approach to Postwar Homicide Rates', *American Sociological Review*, 41.6 (1976), 958.

12 Alfred Marks, 'Bullets – Expansive, Explosive, and Poisoned', *Westminster Review* (June 1902), 624.

13 For some of this evidence, see Audrey Kurth Cronin, 'Behind the Curve: Globalization and International Terrorism', *International Security*, 27 (2002–3), 30–58; Jenna Jordan, 'When Heads Roll. Assessing the Effectiveness of Leadership Decapitation', *Security Studies*, 18.4 (2009), 719–55; Aaron Manes, 'Testing the Snake Head Strategy: Does Killing or Capturing its Leaders Reduce a Terrorist Group's Activities?', *Journal of International Policy Solutions* (2009), 40–9.

14 John Markoff, 'War Machines: Recruiting Robots for Combat', *New York Times* (27 November 2010).

15 CBS, 'Al Qaeda's Anwar al-Awlaki Killed in Yemen', at
    http://www.cbsnews.com/news/al-qaedas-anwar-al-awlaki-killed-
    in-yemen/.
16 Philip Alston, cited in 'US Warned on Deadly Drone Attacks', at BBC,
    http://news.bbc.co.uk/2/hi/8329412.stm.
17 Eric Schlosser, 'Nuclear Weapons: An Accident Waiting to Happen',
    Guardian (14 September 2013).
18 Eric Schlosser, *Command and Control. Nuclear Weapons, the Damascus
    Accident, and the Illusion of Safety* (New York: Penguin, 2013).
19 Schlosser, 'Nuclear Weapons', op. cit. '
20 Eric Schlosser, 'In 1956, A Plane Crashed in Rural Suffolk, Nearly
    Detonating an Atomic Bomb', *Guardian* (14 September 2013).
21 Ed Lavandera, 'Drones Silently Patrol US Borders', CNN, uploaded 13
    March 2013, at http://www.cnn.com/2010/US/03/12/border.
    drones/index.html, viewed 1 October 2013.
22 United Press International, 'Spy Drones Will Monitor UK Citizens',
    uploaded 23 January 2010, in http://www.upi.com/Top_News/
    International/2010/01/23/Spy-drones-will-monitor-UK-citizens/
    UPI-31351264292495, viewed 1 October 2013
23 House of Representatives, 'FAA Modernization and Reform Act of
    2012', 112th Congress 2d Session, Report 112-381, at http://www.
    gpo.gov/fdsys/pkg/CRPT-112hrpt381/pdf/CRPT-112hrpt381.
    pdf.
24 Naomi Wolf, 'The Coming Drone Attack on America', *Guardian* (21
    December 2012).
25 The US Department of Justice, 'Justice Department and FBI
    Announce Formal Conclusion of Investigation into 2001 Anthrax
    Attacks', 19 February 2010, at http://www.justice.gov/opa/
    pr/2010/February/10-nsd-166.html, viewed 21 March 2014, and
    Sonia Ben Ouagrham-Gormley, 'Barriers to Bioweapons: Intangible
    Obstacles to Proliferation', *International Security*, 36.4 (spring 2012),
    83.
26 Monica J. Casper and Lisa Jean Moore, 'Dirty Work and Deadly
    Agents: A (Dis)Embodied Weapons Treaty and the Illusion of Safety',
    Women's Studies Quarterly, 39.1/2 (spring/summer 2011), 95–119.
27 Clare Dyer, 'Skin Sold for Chemical Warfare Research', *British Medical
    Journal* (17 February 2001), 384.
28 Harry Cullumbine, 'Chemical Warfare Experiment Using Human
    Subjects', *British Medical Journal*, 2.4476 (19 October 1946), 577.
29 George E. P. Box, *An Accidental Statistician. The Life and Memories of
    George E. P. Box* (Hoboken: John Wiley and Sons, 2013), 29.

30 Hugh Dudley, 'Tests on Volunteers at Porton Down', *British Medical Journal*, 309 (26 November 1949), 1443.

31 Peter J. Gray, 'CS Gas is not a Chemical Means of Restraining a Person', *British Medical Journal*, 314 (3 May 1997), 1353.

32 Kenneth Watkins, 'Chemical Agents and 'Expanding' Bullets: Limited Law Enforcement Exceptions or Unwarranted Handcuffs', *International Legal Studies. US Naval War College*, 82 (2006), 196–7, from *Hansard*, vol. 795, c. 17–18 written answers February 1970.

33 Steve Wright, 'New Police Technologies: An Exploration of the Social Implications of Some Recent Developments', *Journal of Peace Research*, 15.4 (1978), 307.

34 Ibid.

35 Churchill Papers, 16/16, 12 May 1919, cited in Derek Gregory, 'In Another Time-Zone, the Bombs Fall Unsafely . . . : Targets, Civilians, and Late Modern War', *Arab World Geographer*, 9.2 (2006), 91.

36 Nicholas Wade, 'Technology in Ulster: Rubber Bullets Hit Home, Brainwashing Backfires', *Science*, new series, 176.4039 (9 June 1972), 1102.

37 R. Miller, W. H. Rutherford, S. Johnston and V. J. Malpotia, 'Injuries Caused by Rubber Bullets', *British Journal of Surgery*, 49 (1975), 480–6, and Wright, 'New Police Technologies', op. cit., 310.

38 J. B. Neilands, 'Vietnam: Progress of the Chemical War', *Asia Study*, 10.3 (March 1970), 217.

39 Raymond McClean, 'Riot-Control Agents: Personal Experience', *British Medical Journal*, 3.5671 (13 September 1969), 652.

40 Major W. G. Johnston, 'A Review of Wound Ballistics Studies at CDE Porton', 15 September 1971, The National Archives WO188/2213.

41 Letter from Robert Scott (RAMC) to Professor T. K. Marshall of the Department of Forensic Pathology, Queen's University Belfast, 19 September 1974, in The National Archives WO188/2217.

42 Wade, 'Technology in Ulster', op. cit., 1102.

43 R. I. H. Whitlock, 'Experience Gained from Treating Facial Injuries Due to Civil Unrest', *Annals of the Royal College of Surgeons of England*, 63 (1981), 31; J. Shaw, 'Pulmonary Contusion in Children Due to Rubber Bullet Injuries', *British Medical Journal*, 4.5843 (30 December 1972), 764; Vincent J. M. DiMaio, *Gunshot Wounds: Practical Aspects of Firearms, Ballistics, and Forensic Techniques*, 2nd edn (Boca Raton: CRC Press, 1999), 305.

44 Whitlock, 'Experience Gained from Treating Facial Injuries Due to Civil Unrest', op. cit., 31.

45 Wright, 'New Police Technologies', op. cit., 303–7. '

46 DiMaio, *Gunshot Wounds*, op. cit., 305.

47 'A Short History of the Plastic Bullet', *Fortnight,* 182 (July–August 1981), 4.

48 Lawrence Rocke (Senior Registrar at the Royal Victoria Hospital), cited by Andrew Pollack, 'Plastic Bullets: Adding Up the Medical Evidence', *Fortnight*, 186 (May–June 1982), 4.

49 'A Short History of the Plastic Bullet', op. cit., 4.

50 Ibid. My emphasis.

51 Cited in Sid Perkins, 'Not-So-Deadly Force', *Science News*, 153.10 (7 March 1998), 157.

52 Miller, Rutherford, Johnston and Malpotia, 'Injuries Caused by Rubber Bullets', op. cit., 480–6.

53 Ibid.

54 Ibid.

55 Matthew J. Wargovitch, Donald O. Egner, William M. Busey, B. K. Thein, and E. B. Shank, 'Evaluation of the Physiological Effects of a Rubber Bullet, a Baseball and a Flying Baton', US Army Human Engineering Laboratory, Aberdeen Proving Grounds (1975), cited in Wright, 'New Police Technologies', op. cit., 309. '.

56 V. J. M. di Maio and W. V. Spitz, 'Variations in Wounding Due to Unusual Firearms and Recently Available Ammunition', *Journal of Forensic Science*, 17 (1972), 277 and 385.

57 S. O. Berg, 'Supersonic Gunshot Wounds', *Fingerprint and Identification Magazine*, 55.7 (January 1974), 7.

58 Jordan J. Paust, 'Dum-Dum Bullets, Law and 'Objective' Scientific Research: The Need for a Configurative Approach to Decisions', *Jurimetrics Journal*, 18 (1977–78), 273.

59 Cited in Dermot Purgavie, 'Outlawed – But the Cops are Using Dum-Dum', *Daily Mail* (27 September 1974).

60 Ibid.

61 James B. Brady, 'The Justifiability of Hollow-Point Bullets', *Criminal Justice and Ethics*, 9 (summer/fall 1983), 10–12.

62 Charles G. Wilber, *Ballistic Science for the Law Enforcement Officer* (Springfield, Ill.: Charles C. Thomas Pub., 1977), 170. Professor of Zoology and Director of the Forensic Science Laboratory, Colorado State University. He is quoting from Irvin K. Owen (20 years as a special agent for the FBI), 'What About Dum-dums?', *Law Enforcement Bulletin*, no date or page given.

63 Wilber, *Ballistic Science for the Law Enforcement Officer*, op. cit., 165.

64 Christopher Greenwood, cited in Alfons Vanheusden, W. Hays Parks and William H. Boothby, 'The Use of Expanding Bullets in Military

Operations: Examining the Kampala Consensus', *Military Law and the Law of War Review*, 50.3–4 (2011), 545.

65 Watkins, 'Chemical Agents and 'Expanding' Bullets', op. cit.

66 UK Ministry of Defence and Defence Infrastructure Organisation, 'Dartmoor Firing Times', (2014) at https://www.gov.uk/government/publications/dartmoor-firing-programme, viewed 14 January 2014.

67 Department of Defense, *Base Structure Report. Fiscal Year 2009 Baseline (A Summary of DoD's Real Property Inventory* (Washington, DC: Office of the Deputy Under Secretary of Defense (Installations and Environment), c.2009), 2 and 7.

68 John Robert McNeill and David S. Painter, 'The Global Environmental Footprint of the US Military 1789–2003', in Closman (ed.), *War and the Environment*, 21.

69 US Department of Energy, Nevada Operations Office, 'United States Nuclear Tests, July 1945 through September 1992' (December 1994), at www.nv.doe.gov/library/publications/historical/DOENV_209_REV15.pdf, viewed 21 March 2014; Richard L. Miller, *Under the Cloud: The Decades of Nuclear Testing* (London: Macmillan, 1986); Douglas Holstook and Frank Barnaby (eds), *The British Nuclear Weapons Programme, 1952–2002* (London: Frank Cass, 2003).

70 Vera Brittain, *Thrice a Stranger* (London: Gollancz, 1938), 345.

CHAPTER THREE: KIND-HEARTED GUNMEN

1 LeMay was dubbed the 'Caveman in a Jet Bomber' by I. F. Stone, 'Cave Man in a Jet Bomber', in Karl Weber (ed.), *The Best of I. F. Stone* (New York: Public Affairs, 206), 326–38. The other descriptions of him were in common use.

2 Warren Kozak, *LeMay. The Life and Wars of General Curtis LeMay* (Washington, DC: Regnery Publishing, 2009), ix.

3 Paul Lashmar, 'Killer on the Edge', *New Statesman and Society*, 8.370 (9 January 1995), 20.

4 General Curtis Emerson LeMay with MacKinlay Kantor, *Mission with LeMay. My Story* (New York: Doubleday and Co., 1965), 10.

5 Ibid., viii.

6 Ibid., 383–4.

7 Michael N. Schmitt, '*Bellum Americanum*: The US View of Twenty-First Century War and its Possible Implications for the Law of Armed Conflict', *Michigan Journal of International Law*, 19 (summer 1998), 1057–90.

8 The phrase is used by Ian Brownlie, 'Thoughts on Kind-Hearted

Gunmen', in Richard B. Lillich (ed.), *Humanitarian Intervention and the United Nations* (Charlottsville: University Press of Virginia, 1973), 139.

9   Chris af Jochnick and Roger Normand, 'The Legitimation of Violence: A Critical History of the Laws of War', *Harvard International Law Journal*, 35.1 (winter 1994), 50.

10 The best account is Michael Walzer's *Just and Unjust Wars: A Moral Argument with Historical Illustrations* (Harmondsworth: Penguin, 1980), but also see Alexander Gillespie's *A History of the Laws of War* (Oxford: Hart, 2011).

11 Richard Shelly Hartigan, *Lieber's Code and the Law of War* (Chicago: Precedent Publishing, 1983), 21.

12 Ibid., 123.

13 Andrew Dickson White, *The First Hague Conference* (Boston: The World Peace Foundation, 1912), 63. White was the head of the US delegation.

14 James Brown Scott, *The Proceedings of the Hague Peace Conferences. Translations of the Official Texts* (New York: Oxford University Press, 1920), 6–7.

15 Lord Ismay, *The Memoirs of General Lord Ismay* (London: Heinemann, 1960), 157.

16 Moe William Royse, *Aerial Bombardment and the International Regulation of Warfare* (New York: Harold Vidal, 1928), 1928), 131–2.

17 Thomas W. Smith, 'The New Law of War: Legitimizing Hi-Tech and Infrastructural Violence', *International Studies Quarterly*, 46.3 (September 2002), 362.

18 Frits Kalshoven, *Constraints on the Waging of War* (Geneva: The International Committee of the Red Cross, 1987), 81. In the 2001 edition, this is on pages 42–3.

19 'The Text-Book for Military Small Arms and Ammunition, 1894', *Quarterly Review*, 190 (July 1899), 153 and 173.

20 Charles G. Wilber, *Ballistic Science for the Law Enforcement Officer* (Springfield, Ill.: Charles C. Thomas Pub., 1977), 170. Professor of Zoology and Director of the Forensic Science Laboratory, Colorado State University. He is quoting from Irvin K. Owen, 'What About Dum-dums?', *Law Enforcement Bulletin*, no date or page given.

21 Ibid.

22 George MacDonald Fraser, *Quartered Safe Out Here. A Recollection of the War in Burma* (London: Harvill, 1992), 118.

23 LeMay with Kantor, *Mission with LeMay*, op. cit., 384.

24 Dan Balz and Edward Cody, 'US Raises Estimate of Iraqi Armor

Destroyed: Bodies Pulled from Rubble in Baghdad', *Washington Post* (15 February 1991).

25 'Defence Press Briefing. Wound Ballistics Tests – CDE Porton, April 1975' and 'Notes for Meeting on Wound Ballistics Facility', memo PTA/98/1/1420/75, 11 April 1975, both in The National Archives 188/2217.

26 af Jochnick and Normand, 'The Legitimation of Violence', op. cit., 76.

27 Surgeon-Major-General J. B. Hamilton, 'The Dum-Dum Bullet', *British Medical Journal* (11 June 1898), 1559.

28 Ibid.

29 For an extended discussion, see Surgeon-Colonel W. F. Stevenson, 'The Effects of the Dum-Dum Bullet from a Surgical Point of View', *British Medical Journal* (21 May 1898), 1324–5; 'The Peace Conference', *British Medical Journal* (10 June 1899), 1420; 'The Text-Book for Military Small Arms and Ammunition 1894', op. cit., 174–5.

30 'The Philistines Be Upon Thee, Samson! Some Enemies of Rifle Shooting, Their Sayings and Doings', *NRA Journal and Shooting News. The Official Organ of the National Rifle Association*, 9.1 (September 1922), 165.

31 'GIs Test the Killer Dart Gun', *Daily Mail* (12 December 1963).

32 LeMay with Kantor, *Mission with LeMay*, op. cit., 12, 380–1 and 388.

33 US War Department, 'Instructions for the Government of Armies of the United States in the Field. Prepared by Francis Lieber, Promulgated as General Order No. 100 by President Lincoln, 24 April 1863', in Dietrich Schindler and Jiri Toman (eds), *The Laws of Armed Conflicts* (Dordrecht: Martinus Nijhoff Publishers, 1988), 8.

34 Elbridge Colby, 'War Crimes', *Michigan Law Review*, 23.5 (March 1925), 509.

35 W. Hays Parks, 'Joint Service Combat Shotgun Program', *Army Law* (1997), 23.

36 James D. Fry, 'Contextualized Legal Reviews for the Methods and Means of Warfare: Cave Combat and International Humanitarian Law', *Columbia Journal of Transnational Law*, 44 (2006), 516.

37 Ibid. Also see David B. Kopel, 'Guns, Gangs, and Preschools: Moving Beyond Conventional Solutions to Confront Juvenile Violence', *Barry Law Review*, 1 (2000), 84.

38 Robin M. Coupland, 'Abhorrent Weapons and 'Superfluous Injury or Unnecessary Suffering': From Field Surgery to Law', *British Medical Journal*, 315 (29 November 1997), 1450–1.

39 Video interview of Robin M. Coupland, at http://www.medicalpeace working.org/fileadmin/user_upload/videos/Robin_Coupland.wmv, 2007, viewed 10 November 2013.

40 Coupland, 'Abhorrent Weapons and "Superfluous Injury or Unnecessary Suffering"', op. cit., 1451.

41 See Robin M. Coupland, 'The Red Cross Classification of War Wounds: The EXCFVM Scoring System', *World Journal of Surgery*, 16 (1992), 910–17, and Captain (Reserve) Andrew W. Kirkpatrick, Rosaleen Chun, Lcdr (Navy) David Ross Brown and Richard K. Simons, 'Optimism about Superfluous Injury and Unnecessary Suffering: A System of Measurement with Potential for Controls', *Journal of the American College of Surgeons*, 190.4 (April 2000), 483–90.

42 Coupland, 'The Red Cross Classification of War Wounds', op. cit., 912.

43 Ibid., 911.

44 Ibid., 912.

45 ICRS, *SIrUS Project: Towards a Determination of Which Weapons Cause 'Superfluous Injury or Unnecessary Suffering'*, ed. Robin M. Coupland (Geneva: ICRC, 1997), 112.

46 Ibid., 23.

47 Coupland, 'Abhorrent Weapons and 'Superfluous Injury or Unnecessary Suffering', op. cit., 1452.

48 Kirkpatrick, Chun, Brown and Simons, 'Optimism about Superfluous Injury and Unnecessary Suffering', op. cit., 483.

49 Brian Rappert, 'Prohibitions, Weapons and Controversy: Managing the Problem of Ordering', *Social Studies of Science*, 35.2 (April 2005), 217.

50 Fry, 'Contextualized Legal Reviews for the Methods and Means of Warfare', op. cit., 486.

51 For a discussion, see my *The Story of Pain: From Prayer to Painkillers* (Oxford: Oxford University Press, 2014).

52 Andrew Koch, 'Should War Be Hell?', *Jane's Defense Weekly* (10 May 2000), 4.

53 Major Donna Marie Verchio, 'The SIrUS Project: Well-Intentioned, but Unnecessary and Superfluous', *Air Force Law Review*, 51 (2001), 206–7.

54 Ibid., 211.

55 Video interview of Robin M. Coupland, op. cit.

56 Coupland, 'Abhorrent Weapons and "Superfluous Injury or Unnecessary Suffering"', op. cit., 1451–2.

57 Benjamin Valentino, Paul Huth and Sarah Croco, 'Covenants Without the Sword. International Law and the Protection of Civilians in Times of War', *World Politics*, 58 (April 2006), 339–40.

58 Oona A. Hathaway, 'Do Human Rights Treaties Make a Difference?', *Yale Law Journal*, 111.8 (June 2002), 1940.

59 Ibid., 2013–14, and Valentino, Huth and Croco, 'Covenants Without the Sword', op. cit., 374–5.

60 ICRC, Conference of Red Cross Experts on the Reaffirmation and Development of International Humanitarian Law Applicable to Armed Conflicts, The Hague, 1–6 March 1971, *Report of the Work of the Conference* (Geneva: ICRC, 1971), 29, and Michael Bothe, Karl Josef Partsch, and Waldemar A. Solf, *New Rules for Victims of Armed Conflicts* (The Netherlands: Martinus Nijhoff Publishers, 1982), 499–500.

61 Chairman, Joint Chiefs of Staff Instruction (CJCSI) 5810.10A, Implementation of the DoD Law of War Program', para. (6)(5) (27 August 1999), cited in Jack M. Beard, 'Law and War in the Virtual Era', *American Journal of International Law*, 103.3 (July 2009), 418.

62 Donald Rumsfeld, 'Manager's Journal: Rumsfeld's Rules', *Wall Street Journal* (29 January 2001).

63 W. Hays Parks, interviewed in Steven Keeva, 'Lawyers in the War Room', *ABA Journal*, 77.12 (December 1991), 55–6.

64 John Norton Moore, 'Law and National Security', *Foreign Affairs*, 15.2 (January 1973), 421.

65 Captain Matthew E. Winter, '"Finding the Law" – The Values, Identity and Function of the International Law Advisor', *Military Law Review*, 128 (spring 1990), 25, and Abraham D. Sofaer, 'Terrorism, the Law, and the National Defense', *Military Law Review*, 126 (1989), 90, he is legal adviser at the US Department of State.

66 Smith, 'The New Law of War', op. cit., 268.

67 Ibid. 368.

68 Keeva, 'Lawyers in the War Room', op. cit., 52.

69 US Department of Defense, *Conduct of the Persian Gulf Conflict: An Interim Report to Congress*, 2:7 (1991), cited in Normand and Jochnick, 'The Legitimation of Violence', op. cit., 395.

70 Winter, '"Finding the Law"', op. cit., 8.

71 Ibid.

72 Keeva, 'Lawyers in the War Room', op. cit., 55.

73 Ibid., 59.

74 'Memorandum of the Joint Chiefs of Staff, 59–63, Subject: Implementation of the DOD Law of War program', 1 June 1983, cited in Winter, '"Finding the Law"', op. cit., 30. My emphasis.

75 Keeva, 'Lawyers in the War Room', op. cit., 57.

76 Ibid.

77 Colonel G. I. A. D. Draper, 'Role of Legal Advisers in Armed Forces', *International Review of the Red Cross*, 18.202 (February 1978), 13.

78 Keeva, 'Lawyers in the War Room', op. cit., 56.

79 Winter, '"Finding the Law"', op. cit., 33.

80 Ibid., 25.

81 Ibid., 22.

82 Donald Knox, *The Korean War. An Oral History: Pusan to Chosin* (San Diego: Harcourt Brace Jovanovich, 1985), 552.

83 Michael Krepon, 'Weapons Potentially Inhumane: The Case of Cluster Bombs', *Foreign Affairs*, 52.3 (April 1974), 599–600.

84 John Borrie, *Unacceptable Harm: A History of How the Treaty to Ban Cluster Munitions was Won* (Herndon, VA: United Nations Publications, 2009)

85 Krepon, 'Weapons Potentially Inhumane', op. cit., 597–8.

86 Ibid., 604.

87 Cited in Ibid., 600.

88 Ibid.

89 Ibid., 601.

90 Ibid., 602.

91 Ibid., 604.

92 Ibid., 602.

93 Smith, 'The New Law of War', op. cit., 368.

94 Verchio, 'The SIrUS Project', op. cit., 224.

95 Ibid., 215–21.

96 LeMay with Kantor, *Mission with LeMay*, op. cit., viii.

97 'Two Kinds of Shooting', *Arms and the Man*, lvii.7 (12 November 1914), 134. Note that they reported that men ignored the prohibition.

98 William J. Fenrick, 'International Humanitarian Law and Combat Casualties', *European Journal of Population*, 21.2/3 (June 2005) 168.

99 Edward Hallett Carr, *The Twenty Years' Crisis, 1919–1939: An Introduction to the Study of International Relations* (London: Macmillan, 1946), 170.

100 Costas Douzinas, *Human Rights and Empire. The Political Philosophy of Cosmopolitanism* (London: Routledge-Cavendish, 2007), 225.

CHAPTER FOUR: WOUNDING THE INNOCENT

1 Alexander B. Downes, *Targeting Civilians in War* (Ithaca: Cornell University Press, 2008), 1.

2 *Safire's Political Dictionary*, 1st pub. 1972 (Oxford: Oxford University Press, 2008), 788.

3 Colin H. Kahl's website, at http://explore.georgetown.edu/people/chk34/, viewed 1 October 2013.

4 Colin H. Kahl, 'In the Crossfire of the Crosshairs? Norms, Civilian Casualties and US Conduct in Iraq', *International Security*, 32.1 (summer 2007), 8.

5 Ibid.

6 Carl von Clausewitz, *On War*, 1st pub. 1873, ed. and trans. Michael Howard and Peter Parel, preface by Joanna Bourke (London: Folio Society, 2011).

7 Kahl, 'In the Crossfire of the Crosshairs?', op. cit., 26–7.

8 Ibid.

9 Ibid., 36–7. My emphasis.

10 Edward Increase Bosworth, *The Christian Witness in War* (New York: YMCA, 1918), 8–10.

11 E. Griffith Jones, *The Challenge of Christianity to a World at War* (London: Duckworth and Co., 1915), 186.

12 An unnamed 'influential clergyman', quoted by Robert Coope, *Shall I Fight? An Essay on War, Peace, and the Individual* (London: Friends' Book Centre, 1935), 16, and Marshall Broomhall, *'Mine Own Vineyard'. Personal Religion and War* (London: Morgan and Scott, 1916), 45–6. For protests against sermons exhorting soldiers to love the German soldier while 'thrust[ing] his bayonet into his abdomen', see G. Stanley Hall, 'Morale in War and After', *Psychological Bulletin*, 15 (1918), 384, and Morris N. Kertzer, *With an H on my Dog Tag* (New York: Behrman House, 1947), 44.

13 William Temple to Ennis, 21 May 1943, Temple Papers, folio 129, cited in Andrew Chandler, 'The Church of England and the Obliteration Bombing of Germany in the Second World War', *English Historical Review*, 108.429 (October 1993), 934.

14 Father Grayson, quoted in Jon Oplinger, *Quang Tri Cadence. Memoir of a Rifle Platoon Leader in the Mountains of Vietnam* (Jefferson, NC: McFarland and Co., 1993), 91.

15 Kenneth Maddock, 'Going Over the Limit? – The Question of Australian Atrocities', in Maddock (ed.), *Memories of Vietnam* (Sydney: Random House, 1991), 163.

16 Major W. Hays Parks, 'Crimes in Hostilities. Pt. I', *Marine Corps Gazette* (August 1976), 21. Parks disagreed.

17 Drill Sergeant Kenneth Hodges, quoted in Michael Bilton and Kevin Sims, *Four Hours in My Lai. A War Crime and its Aftermath* (London: Penguin, 1992), 55.

18 Herbert C. Kelman and Lee H. Lawrence, 'Assignment of Responsibility in the Case of Lt. Calley: Preliminary Report on a National Survey', *Journal of Social Issues*, 28.1 (1972), 177–212. For civilian attitudes towards the conviction of Calley, also see Wayne Greenhaw, *The Making of a Hero. The Story of Lieut. William Calley, Jr.* (Louisville: Touchstone Publishing Co., 1971), 191; Robert D. Heinl,

'My Lai in Perspective: The Court-Martial of William L. Calley', *Armed Forces Journal*, 21 December 1970, 38–41; Tom Tiede, *Calley: Soldier or Killer?* (New York: Pinnacle, 1971), 16; Kenrick S. Thompson, Alfred C. Clarke and Simon Dinitz, 'Reactions to My-Lai: A Visual–Verbal Comparison', *Sociology and Social Research*, 58.2 (January 1974), 122–9.

19 For instance, see Rob Evans, Richard Norton-Taylor and David Leigh, 'WikiLeaks War Logs: British Forces Exposed Over Afghan Attacks', *Guardian,* 26 October 2010.

20 Below the line in Ian Drury, 'Marine Who Is Jailed for Life for Killing Wounded Taliban Insurgent is Cold Blood Fights Murder Conviction', *Daily Mail* (6 January 2014), at http://www.dailymail.co.uk/news/article-2534653/Royal-Marine-launches-murder-appeal-convicted-killing-injured-insurgent-fighting-Afghanistan.html, viewed 31 March 2014, and below the line in Natalie Evans, 'Royal Marine Jailed for Executing Taliban Insurgent Launches Appeal Against Murder Conviction and Life Sentence', *Daily Mirror* (6 January 2014), at http://www.mirror.co.uk/news/uk-news/royal-marine-alexander-blackman-jailed-2994835, viewed 31 March 2014.

21 'Marine A Petition Passes 10,000 Signatures Demanding Release of Alexander Blackman', *Huffington Post* (7 December 2013), and Steven Morris and Richard Norton-Taylor, 'Royal Marine Alexander Blackman Faces Life Sentence for Taliban Murder', *Guardian* (5 December 2013).

22 'Commanding Officer's Letter Defends Sergeant Alexander Blackman', BBC News (6 December 2013).

23 HM Government, e-petition, at http://epetitions.direct.gov.uk/petitions/56810, viewed 1 July 2014.

24 Patrick O'Brien, 'The Costs and Benefits of British Imperialism, 1846–1914', *Past and Present*, 120 (August 1988), 163.

25 Rashid Khalidi, *Resurrecting Empire. Western Footprints and America's Perilous Path in the Middle East* (London: I. B. Tauris, 2004), 27, and James Garner, 'Proposed Rules for the Regulation of Aerial Warfare', *American Journal of International Law*, 18 (1924), 56–81.

26 Alfred Marks, 'Bullets – Expansive, Explosive, and Poisoned', *Westminster Review* (June 1902), 633.

27 'A "Man-Killing" Bullet', *Daily Mail* (28 June 1898).

28 For the best discussion, see Priya Satia, 'The Defense of Inhumanity: Air Control and the British Idea of Arabia', *American Historical Review*, 111.1 (February 2006), 34.

29 Brigadier General The Right Honourable the Lord Thomson, 'Aerial Warfare and Disarmament', *Survey* (1 February 1925), 506.

30   F. H. Humphrey to Sir John Simon, 15 December 1932, in The National Archives AIR 8/94.

31   Sir John Bagot Glubb, *Arabian Adventures. Ten Years of Joyful Service* (London: Cassell, 1978), 148.

32   Cited in Charles Townshend, 'Civilization and "Frightfulness": Air Control in the Middle East Between the Wars', in Chris Wrigley (ed.), *Warfare, Diplomacy and Politics. Essays in Honour of A. J. P. Taylor* (London: Hamish Hamilton, 1986), 155.

33   Elbridge Colby, 'War Crimes', *Michigan Law Review*, 23.5 (March 1925), 483.

34   Quoting General Hull, 13 July 1812, from *Select British Documents of the Canadian War of 1812*, no. xiii (Toronto: n.p., 1920), vol. 1, 356–7, cited in Elbridge Colby, 'How to Fight Savage Tribes', *American Journal of International Law*, 21 (1927), 284.

35   Colby, 'How to Fight Savage Tribes', op. cit., 279–81, 284–5 and 287.

36   Professor Jesse S. Reeves at Williamstown in Massachusetts on 2 August 1923, cited in ibid., 280.

37   Colonel J. F. C. Fuller, *The Reformation of War* (London: Hutchinson and Co., 1923), 191.

38   War Office, *Manual of Military Law* (London: HMSO, 1914), 251.

39   Frederick Taylor, *Dresden: Tuesday, February 13, 1945* (London: Bloomsbury, 2004), 281.

40   Ibid., 8.

41   Frederick F. Clairmonte, 'Dresden: From Death to Resurrection', *Economic and Political Weekly*, 20.6 (9 February 1985), 232.

42   The lower estimate is from Landeshauptstadt Dresden, 'Erklärung der Dresdner Historikerkommission', 1 October 2008, 2. http//www.dresden.de/media/pdf/presseamt/Erklaerung_Historikerkommission.pdf, viewed 21 March 2014.

43   Margaret Freyer, 'The Bombing of Dresden, 14 February, 1945', in John Carey (ed.), *Eyewitness to History* (Cambridge, MA: Harvard University Press, 1987)

44   Stewart Halsey Ross, *Strategic Bombing by the United States in World War II. The Myths and Facts* (Jefferson, NC: McFarland and Co., 2003), 183.

45   Hans Rumpf, *The Bombing of Germany* (New York: Holty, Rinehart, and Winston, 1963), 160–1.

46   Canon E. J. Mahoney and Doctor Lawrence L. McReavy, 'Reprisals: A Second Opinion', *Clergy Review*, xx (February 1941), 138.

47   Gordon C. Zahn, *Chaplains in the RAF. A Study in Role Tension* (Manchester: Manchester University Press, 1969), 172.

48   Thomas Aquinas, *Summa Theologica*, in the Stanford Encyclopedia

of Philosophy, at http://plato.stanford.edu/entires/double-effect, viewed 21 March 2014.

49 *Church Times* (20 December 1940), 810.

50 Father George Zabalka, interviewed in Studs Terkel, *'The Good War'. An Oral History of World War Two* (London: Vintage, 1985), 531–6.

51 General Curtis Emerson LeMay with MacKinlay Kantor, *Mission with LeMay. My Story* (New York: Doubleday and Co., 1965), 352.

52 An unnamed radio operator who was killed on his next operational flight, quoted by Canon L. John Collins, *Faith Under Fire* (London: Leslie Frewin, 1965), 85–6.

53 John C. Ford, 'The Morality of Obliteration Bombing', *Theological Studies*, 5 (1 January 1944), 290–1.

54 Ibid., 299 and 302.

55 John Kenneth Ryan, *Modern War and Basic Ethics* (Milwaukee: Bruce Publishing Co., 1940), 106.

56 Michael Walzer, *Just and Unjust Wars. A Moral Argument with Historical Illustrations* (London: Basic Books, 1977), 155–6.

57 The Rev. John Herold in a letter to the *Church Times* (24 August 1945), 475. My emphasis.

58 *Hansard*, House of Commons, 14 September 1939, cited in A. C. Grayling, *Among the Dead Cities* (New York: Walker and Co., 2006), 149.

59 Winston Churchill, *Their Finest Hour. The Second World War*, vol. 2, 1st pub. 1949 (New York: Rosetta Books, 2013), 567.

60 Arthur Harris in a letter to Ira Eaker, cited in Wilbur H. Morrison, *Fortress Without a Roof: The Allied Bombing of the Third Reich* (London: W. H. Allen, 1982), 37.

61 LeMay with Kantor, *Mission with LeMay*, op. cit., 382.

62 Peter Kandela 'Iraq: Bomb Now, Die Later', *Lancet*, 337.8747 (20 April 1991), 967.

63 John E. Fagg, 'Autumn Assault on Germany', in Wesley Frank Craven and James Lea Cate, *The Army Air Forces in World War II, Volume 3. Europe: Argument to V-E Day, January 1944 to May 1945* (Washington, DC: Office of Air Force History, 1983), 667.

64 Roger Normand and Chris af Jochnick, 'The Legitimation of Violence: A Critical Analysis of the Gulf War', *Harvard International Law Journal*, 35.2 (spring 1994), 392.

65 Carl Conetta, 'Disappearing the Dead: Iraq, Afghanistan, and the Idea of a "New Warfare", PDA, Project on Defense Alternatives, Research Monograph #9 (Cambridge, MA: PDA, Commonwealth Institute, 2004), 24, at http://www.comw.org/pda/0402rm9.html, viewed 2 October 2013.

66 Human Rights Watch, *Off Target. The Conduct of the War and Civilian Casualties in Iraq* (New York: Human Rights Watch, 2003), 104.

67 Ibid., 16.

68 Jo Becker and Scott Shane, 'Secret "Kill List" Proves a Test of Obama's Principles and Will', *New York Times* (29 May 2012).

69 Human Rights Watch, *Off Target*, op. cit., 21–41.

70 Ibid., 24.

71 Ibid., 2.

72 Conetta, 'Disappearing the Dead', op. cit., 24.

73 Ibid.

74 Matt J. Martin with Charles W. Sasser, *Predator. The Remote-Control Air War Over Iraq and Afghanistan* (Minneapolis: Zenith Press, 2010), 310.

75 Ibid., 2–3, 11, 18, 46–7 211–13, 290 and 310.

76 LeMay with Kantor, *Mission with LeMay*, op. cit., 12, 380–1 and 388.

CHAPTER FIVE: THE DARK ART OF BALLISTICS

1 R. D. Eisler, A. K. Chatterjee, G. H. Burghart, and J. A. O'Keefe, 'Casualty Assessments of Penetrating Wounds from Ballistic Trauma. Final Report. February 1992 –May 1993', (Natick, MA: US Army Soldier and Biological Chemical Command, 2001), front page.

2 The Army Natick Soldier Systems Centre's front page: http://www.army.mil/info/organization/natick, viewed 10 October 2013.

3 William F. Whitmore, 'Military Operations Research – A Personal Retrospective', *Operations Research*, 9.2 (March–April 1961), 259. He was from Lockheed Missiles and Space Division, Sunnyvale, California.

4 Michael Pattison, 'Scientists, Inventors and the Military in Britain, 1915–19: The Munitions Invention Department', *Social Studies in Science*, 13.4 (November 1983), 522.

5 Solly Zuckerman, *From Apes to Warlords. The Autobiography (1904–1946) of Solly Zuckerman* (London: Hamish Hamilton, 1978), 334.

6 Alun Chalfort, 'Obituary: Lord Zuckerman', *Independent* (2 April 1993), and Steve King, 'From Boffin to Baron', *Spectator* (8 June 2001), 39.

7 Solly Zuckerman and A. N. Black, 'The Effect of Impacts on the Head and Backs of Monkeys', typescript, August 1940, Zuckerman Archive, University of East Anglia, SZ/OEMU/8/3/18, 1–2.

8 Zuckerman, *From Apes to Warlords*, op. cit., 117–18.

9 Letter from Henry Beecher to A. N. Richards, 16 October 1942, in

Folder 10, Papers of Walter B. Cannon, Countway Medical Library, Boston.

10 Lieutenant-Colonel Henry K. Beecher, 'Pain in Men Wounded in Battle', *Annals of Surgery*, 123.1 (January 1946), 98 and 104.

11 Gwilym G. Davis, 'The Effects of Small-Calibre Bullets as Used in Military Arms', *Annals of Surgery*, 25.1 (January 1897), 36.

12 Henry G. Beyer, 'Observations on the Effects Produced by the 6-mm Rifle and Projectile – Experimental Study', *Journal of the Boston Society of Medical Sciences*, 3.5 (January 1899), 126.

13 Davis, 'The Effects of Small-Calibre Bullets', op. cit., 36.

14 Ibid.

15 Colonel Louis Anatole LaGarde, *Gunshot Injuries. How They Are Inflicted, Their Complications, and Treatment* (New York: William Wood and Co., 1914), 41. Also see Dwight W. Rife, 'Recovery of Bullets from High Speed Ammunition', *Journal of Criminal Law and Criminology*, 30.3 (September–October 1939), 382.

16 Martin L. Fackler and Paul J. Dougherty, 'Theodor Kocher and the Scientific Foundation of Wound Ballistics', *Surgery, Gynecology and Obstetrics*, 172 (February 1991), 153–4. They are taking this from Kocher's 'Ueber die Sprengwirkung der modernen Kleingewehr-Geschosse' ('Concerning the Explosive Effects of the Modern Small Caliber Rifle Bullet'), 1975 and his book *Uebur Schusswunden. Experimentelle Untersuchungen ueber die Wirkungsweise der Modernen Klein-Gewehr-Gescosse* [*Concerning Gunshot Wounds, Experimental Investigations Concerning the Effects of the Modern Small Caliber Bullet*], 1880).

17 Victor Horsley, 'Remarks on Gunshot Wounds to the Head, Made on Opening a Discussion at the Medical Society of London on February 8th, 1915', *British Medical Journal*, 1.2825 (20 February 1915), 321.

18 R. I. H. Whitlock, 'Experience Gained from Treating Facial Injuries Due to Civil Unrest', *Annals of the Royal College of Surgeons of England*, 63 (1981), 37.

19 See Brue Lambert, 'Lord Zuckerman, 88, A Scientist of Scope who Guided Churchill', *New York Times* (2 April 1993), and Omond Solandt, 'Observation, Experiment, and Measurement in Operations Research', *Journal of the Operations Research Society of America*, 3.1 (February 1955), 8.

20 Major Ralph W. French and Brigadier-General George R. Callender, 'Physical Aspects of the Missile Casualty', in Lieutenant-Colonel Leonard D. Heaton (ed.), *Wound Ballistics* (Washington, DC: Office of the Surgeon General, Department of the US Army, 1962), 112.

21 Letter from J. D. Oliver, Australian Focus Officer, to F. P. Watkins, Ministry of Defence, Chemical Defence establishment, Porton Down, 16 January 1978, in The National Archives WO 188/2286.

22 Solandt, 'Observation, Experiment, and Measurement in Operations Research', op. cit., 3.

23 E. Newton Harvey, J. Howard McMullen, Elmer G. Butler and William O. Puckett, 'Mechanism of Wounding', in Heaton (ed.), *Wound Ballistics*, op. cit., 146.

24 Larry Owens, 'The Cat and the Bullet: A Ballistic Fable', *Massachusetts Review*, 45.1 (spring 2004), 179–80.

25 E. Newton Harvey, 'The Mechanism of Wounding by High-Velocity Missiles', *Proceedings of the American Philosophical Society*, 92.4 (25 October 1948), 295. Note; no lens is used.

26 Frank Thone, '"Explosions" in Wounds', *Science News-Letter*, 50.5 (3 August 1946), 74.

27 Harvey, McMullen, Butler and Puckett, 'Mechanism of Wounding', op. cit., 147.

28 Thone, '"Explosions" in Wounds', op. cit., 74–5.

29 Owens, 'The Cat and the Bullet', op. cit., 180.

30 Harvey, McMullen, Butler and Puckett, 'Mechanism of Wounding', op, cit., 134.

31 E. Newton Harvey, 'Studies on Wound Ballistics', in E. C. Andrus (ed.), *Advances in Military Medicine Made by American Investigators*, vol. I (Boston: Little, Brown, and Co., 1948), 191.

32 Letter from J. D. Oliver, Australian Focus Officer, to F. P. Watkins, Ministry of Defence, Chemical Defence Establishment, Porton Down, 16 January 1978, in The National Archives WO 188/2286.

33 V. Clare, W. Ashman, P. Broome, J. Jameson, J. Lewis, J. Merkler, A. Mickiewicz, W. Sacco and L. Sturdivan, 'Computer Man Simulation of Incapacitation: An Automated Approach to Wound Ballistics and Associated Medical Care Assessments', *Proceedings of the Annual Symposium on Computer Application in Medical Care*, 4 (November 1981), 1009–13.

34 R. P. Craig, 'Gunshot Wounds Then and Now: How Did John Hunter Get Away With It?', *Annals of the Royal College of Surgeons of England* (1995), 16–18.

35 Ibid., 19.

36 Ibid., 16 (fig. 5.3) and 17 (fig. 5.4)

37 French and Callender, 'Physical Aspects of the Missile Casualty', op. cit., 92.

38 Harvey, 'The Mechanism of Wounding by High-Velocity Missiles', op. cit., 294.

39 French and Callender, 'Physical Aspects of the Missile Casualty', op. cit., 133–4, and J. Wilson, 'Wound Ballistics', *West Journal of Medicine*, 127 (July 1977), 53.

40 Wilson, 'Wound Ballistics', op. cit., 51.

41 Ibid.

42 Ibid.

43 Ibid.

44 Eric Prokosch, *The Simple Art of Murder. Antipersonnel Weapons and Their Developers* (Philadelphia: NARMIC, 1972), 8.

45 David Smith, 'Oscar Pistorius Vomits as Reeva Steenkamp's Wounds Described in Court', *Guardian* (10 March 2014).

46 'Wound Ballistics at C. D. E. E.', initialled by 'G. D. H.', 22 September 1970, 2, in The National Archives WO 188/2213.

47 Wilson, 'Wound Ballistics', op. cit., 51.

48 Ibid.

49 Harry Cullumbine, 'Chemical Warfare Experiment Using Human Subjects', *British Medical Journal*, 2.4476 (19 October 1946), 578.

50 Brian Rappert, 'Prohibitions, Weapons and Controversy: Managing the Problem of Ordering', *Social Studies of Science*, 35.2 (April 2005), 225–6.

51 Larry Miller, 'Letter from London: Germ Lab will Open to Public', *Science News*, 94.5 (3 August 1968), 122.

52 Ibid.

53 D. S. Greenberg, 'CBW: Britain Holds Open House at its Biological Weapons Center', *Science*, new series, 162.3855 (15 November 1968), 782.

54 Zuckerman, *From Apes to Warlords*, op. cit., 137 and 246.

55 Deborah Shapley, 'Defense Research: The Names are Changed to Protect the Innocent', *Science*, 175.4024 (25 February 1972), 866; Joel Primack and Frank von Hippel, 'Advice and Dissent. Scientists in the Political Arena' (1974), at http://dynamics.org/SWOPS/ADVICE_AND_DISSENT/, viewed 20 December 2013, (this was chapter 14 from their book of the same name).

56 'Wound Ballistics at C.D.E.E.', initialled G.D.H, 22 September 1970, in The National Archives WO188/2213 and labelled 'Confidential'.

57 Letter from W. S. S. Ladell, Assistant Director (Medical) of the Medical Division, 'Wound Ballistics', memo MED.A./Co.1301/3312/66, on 29 December 1966, in The National Archives WO188/2213.

58 French and Callender, 'Physical Aspects of the Missile Casualty', op. cit., 93.

59   Herbert K. Weiss, 'Combat Models and Historical Data: The US Civil War', *Operations Research*, 14.5 (September–October 1966), 760.

60   Michael N. Schmitt and Jeffrey S. Thurnher, '"Out of the Loop": Autonomous Weapon Systems and the law of Armed Conflict', *Harvard National Security Journal*, 4 (2012–13), 232.

61   http://www.darpa.mil/NewsEvents/Releases/3013, viewed 2 January 2014.

62   Jonathan Beard, 'DARPA's Bio-revolution', on the DARPA's website http://websearch.darpa.mil/search, viewed 2 January 2014.

63   Michael O'Hanlon, 'Can High Technology Bring US Troops Home?', *Foreign Policy*, 113 (winter 1998–9), 72.

64   US Department of Defense, *FY2009-2034 Unmanned Systems Integrated Roadmap* (Washington, DC: U.S. Department of Defense, 2009), xiii, at http://www.dtic.mil/docs/citations/ADA522247, viewed 6 January 2014.

65   US Government Accountability Office, 'Unmanned Aircraft Systems: Comprehensive Planning and a results-Orientated Training Strategy Are Needed to Support Growing Inventories' (Washington, DC: U.S. Government Accountability Office, 2010), at http://www.gao.gov/new.items/d10331.pdf, viewed 6 January 2014.

66   US Department of Defense, *Quadrennial Defense Review Report* (Washington, DC: U.S. Department of Defense, 2006), 55, at www.defense.gov/qdr/report/report20060203.pdf, viewed on 14 January 2014.

67   Hannah Arendt, *The Origins of Totalitarianism*, 1st pub 1951, new edition (New York: Harcourt Brace Jovanovich, 1973), 279–80.

68   P. W. Singer, *Wired for War: The Robotics Revolution and Conflict in the Twenty-First Century* (New York: Penguin, 2009), 60.

69   Vik Kanwar, 'Post-Human Humanitarian Law: The Law of War in the Age of Robotic Weapons', *Harvard National Security Journal* (2011), 628.

70   Frank Main, 'Guard pilot Blames Drug with Fatal Bombing', *Chicago Sunday Times* (3 January 2003), 7, and Bruce Rolfsen, 'Sliding Home: A B-1B Arrives with Landing Gear Up', *Air Force Times* (2 October 2006).

71   Erik Baard, 'The Guilt-Free Soldier', *Village Voice* (21 January 2003).

72   Ibid.

73   B. von Suttner, *Memoiren* (Deutsche Verlags Anstalt, 1909), 134 and 271, cited in R. W. Reid, *Tongues of Conscience. Weapons Research and the Scientists' Dilemma* (New York: Walker and Co., 1969), 1.

74   Quoting Richard Gatling in Anthony Smith, *Machine Gun. The Story of*

the Men and the Weapon that Changed the Face of War (London: Piatkus, 2002).

75 Matt J. Martin with Charles W. Sasser, *Predator. The Remote-Control Air War over Iraq and Afghanistan* (Minneapolis: Zenith Press, 2010), 219 and 308.

76 Reid, *Tongues of Conscience*, op. cit., 20.

77 Quoting Richard Gatling in Smith, *Machine Gun*, op. cit., 108.

78 Zuckerman, *From Apes to Warlords*, op. cit., 334.

CHAPTER SIX: PLAYING WAR

1 William D. Ehrhart, 'Why I Did It', *Virginia Quarterly Review*, 56.1 (winter 1980), 19–31.

2 Rikke Schubart, Fabian Virchow, Debra White-Stanley and Tanja Thomas (eds), *War Isn't Hell, It's Entertainment. Essays on Visual Media and the Representation of Conflict* (Jefferson, NC: McFarland and Co.: 2009).

3 Robert Louis Stevenson, 'The Land of Counterpane', in his *A Child's Garden of Verses*, illustrated by Jessie Wilcox Smith (New York: Charles Schribner's Sons, 1905), 18.

4 Roy Selwyn-Smith in the foreword to Henry I. Kurtz and Burtt R. Ehrlich, *The Art of the Toy Soldier. Two Centuries of Metal Toy Soldiers 1770–1970* (London: New Cavendish Books, 1987), 6.

5 Andrew Rose, *The Collector's Guide to Toy Soldiers. A Record of the World's Miniature Armies from 1850 to the Present Day* (London: Salamander Books Ltd.: 1997), 8.

6 Jan Susina, 'Toy Wars: The Epic Struggle Between G.I. Joe, Barbie, and the Companies that Make Them', *Lion and the Unicorn*, 23.2 (1999), 301.

7 Ibid.

8 'Tin Soldiers', *The Times* (10 December 1935).

9 Jean Nicollier, *Collecting Toy Soldiers* (Tokyo: Charles E. Tuttle Co., 1967), 5–6.

10 Ian McKenzie, *Collecting Old Toy Soldiers* (London: B. T. Batsford, 1975), 15.

11 Nicollier, *Collecting Toy Soldiers*, op. cit., 6. My emphasis.

12 M. Leicester Hewitt, 'Toy Soldiers', *The Times* (21 November 1939). Also see M. E. Jerrey, 'Military Toys', *The Times* (14 November 1939).

13 A. D. Olmsted, 'Morally Controversial Leisure: The Social World of Gun Collectors', *Symbolic Interaction*, 11.2 (fall 1988), 279.

14 McKenzie, *Collecting Old Toy Soldiers*, op. cit, 15. Also see 'Tin Soldiers', op. cit. .

15 Hewitt, 'Toy Soldiers', op. cit.

16 'Star Wars Jawa Figure Auctioned for £10,200', at http://www.bbc.co.uk/news/uk-england-tees-24660920, 24 October 2013, viewed 25 October 2013.

17 Stanley Breslow, cited in D. Blank, Gordon Cotler, and Brendan Gill, 'Why?', *New Yorker* (11 March 1950).

18 Angela F. Keaton, 'Backyard Desperadoes: American Attitudes Concerning Toy Guns in the Early Cold War Era', *Journal of American Culture*, 33.3 (2010), 186.

19 Dorothy Barclay, 'Behind all the Bang-Bang', *New York Times Magazine* (22 July 1962).

20 Patrick M. Regan, 'War Toys, War Movies, and the Militarization of the United States', *Journal of Peace Research*, 31.1 (February 1994), 54.

21 Paul L. Adams and Jan Arrow, 'Children in Violence', *Journal of the American Academy of Psychoanalysis and Dynamic Psychiatry*, 24 (1996), 179.

22 Donald Duncan, *The New Legions* (London: Victor Gollancz, 1967), 199.

23 '12 Nuclear Toys from the Dawn of the Atomic Age', at http://www.gizmodo.com.au/2011/10/12-nuclear-toys-from-the-dawn-of-the-atomic-age/, 15 October 2011, viewed 23 December 2013.

24 Ibid.

25 See http://www.tellyads.com/show_movie_vintage.php?filename=VA0884, viewed 21 December 2013.

26 'Bomb Game Protest by IRA Victim's Son', *The Times* (20 November 1981).

27 Roger Stahl, 'Have You Played the War on Terror?', *Critical Studies in Media Communication*, 23.2 (2006), 31.

28 Karen J. Hall, 'War Games and Imperial Postures: Spectacles of Combat in United States Popular Culture, 1942–2001', PhD thesis, Syracuse University, 2003), xi.

29 Nick Midgley, 'Anna Freud: The Hampstead War Nurseries and the Role of Direct Observation of Children for Psychoanalysis', *International Journal of Psychoanalysis*, 88 (2007), 946.

30 For example, see Emma Harrison, 'Clue to Reds in Parent Hatred', *New York Times* (6 December 1958).

31 See Fritz Redl, 'Give Your Child a Chance to Let Off Steam', *Parent's Magazine* (December 1952), 122.

32 'Warlike Children. Frightfulness in the Nursery', *The Times* (21 December 1915).

33 'Toy Soldiers for Christmas', *The Times* (8 November 1939).

34 Norbert Bromberg, 'Hitler: Hitler's Character and its Development: Further Observations', *American Imago*, 28 (1971), 292; Norbert Bromberg, 'Hitler's Childhood', *International Review of Psycho-Analysis*, 1 (1974), 235; Erich Fromm, *The Anatomy of Human Destructiveness* (Harmondsworth: Penguin, 1981), 493–522.

35 Moira Keenan, 'The Toy Shop Explosion', *The Times* (1 October 1969).

36 Jennifer Klinesmith, Tim Kasser and Francis T. McAndrew, 'Guns, Testosterone, and Aggression: An Experimental Test of a Mediational Hypothesis', *Psychological Science*, 17.7 (July 2006), 568–71.

37 For example, see Gary Cross, *Kid's Stuff: Toys and the Changing Worlds of American Childhood* (Cambridge, MA: Harvard University Press, 1998).

38 Penny Holland, *We Don't Play with Guns Here. War, Weapon, and Superhero Play in the Early Years* (Maidenhead: Open University Press, 2003).

39 Gillian Brown, 'Child's Play', *differences: A Journal of Feminist Cultural Studies*, 11.3 (fall 1999), 77.

40 C. Grocock, R. McCarthy and D. J. Williams, 'Ball Bearing (BB) Guns, Ease of Purchase, and Potential for Significant Injury', *Annals of the Royal College of Surgeons of England*, 88 (2006), 402.

41 Ibid.

42 Ibid., 402–4.

43 Bruce Barak Koffler, 'Zip Guns and Crude Conversions. Identifying Characteristics and Problems', *Journal of Criminal Law, Criminology, and Police Science*, 60.4 (December 1969), 520-31, and Bruce Barak Koffler, 'Zip Guns and Crude Conversions. Identifying Characteristics and Problems', *Journal of Criminal Law, Criminology, and Police Science*, 61.1 (March 1970), 115–25.

44 Koffler, 'Zip Guns and Crude Conversions' (1969), op. cit., 520.

45 'Firearms Crime on the Rise', *Guardian* (5 January 2003), and Grocock, McCarthy and Williams, 'Ball Bearing (BB) Guns', op. cit., 402.

46 Jason Burke, Tony Thompson, Martin Bright, Gaby Hinsliff, Antony Barnett and David Rowan, 'Where the Gun Rules and the Innocent Go in Fear', *Guardian* (5 January 2003).

47 Grocock, McCarthy and Williams, 'Ball Bearing (BB) Guns', op. cit., 402.

48 Pamela D Kelso, Raymond G. Miltenberger, Marit A. Waters, Kristin Egemo-Helm and Angela G. Bagne, 'Teaching Skills of Second and Third Grade Children to Prevent Gun Play: A Comparison of Procedures', *Education and Treatment of Children*, 30.3 (August 2007), 30.

49 Ibid., 29.

50 Adams and Arrow, 'Children in Violence', op. cit., 179.

51 NRA website at http://home.nra.org/history, viewed 5 December 2013.

52 'Children with Toy Guns Potentially Dangerous', *Science News-Letter*, 85.2 (11 January 1964), 24.

53 'L. B.', 'War Games for Children', *The Times* (7 January 1902).

54 Jacob Middleton, 'The Cock of the School: A Cultural History of Playground Violence in Britain 1880–1940', *Journal of British Studies*, 52 (October 2013), 1–21.

55 R. Blake Brown, '"Every Boy Ought to Learn to Shoot and to Obey Orders": Guns, Boys, and the Law in English Canada from the Late Nineteenth Century to the Great War', *Canadian Historical Review*, 93.2 (June 2012), 199.

56 Ibid., 199 and 201.

57 Ibid., 207.

58 Robert Baden-Powell, *Scouting for Boys*, 1st pub. 1908 (Oxford: Oxford University Press, 2005), 11.

59 A. G. Fulton. 'Notes in Rifle Shooting', *Arms and the Man* (18 December 1913), 232; 'Some Anxious Boys Seek a Range', *Arms and the Man* (1919), 128.

60 'Let *Your* Boy Try for the Famous Winchester Medals', *Arms and the Man*, 64.15 (6 July 1918), 282.

61 Ibid.

62 Lisa Looper video 'New Energy', at http://home.nra.org/history/video/new-energy-lisa-looper, viewed on 5 December 2013.

63 'Savile Lumley', at http://www.spartacus.schoolnet.co.uk/ARTlumley.htm, viewed 23 December 2013. The son's name is Paul Gunn.

64 'US Weapons Put on Show by Museum', *Chicago Tribune* (15 March 1968), and 'New War Game in America: Shoot the Grass Shacks', *Los Angeles Times* (17 March 1968).

65 Kylie Kontour, 'War, Masculinity, and Gaming in the Military Entertainment Complex: A Case Study of *Call of Duty 4: Modern Warfare*', PhD thesis, University of Colorado (2011), 30.

66 Lieutenant Commander Howard P. Rome, 'Motion Pictures as a Medium of Education', *Mental Hygiene*, 30 (January 1946), 9–20. For more on the use of films in training, see 'The Work of Army Psychiatrists in Relation to Morale', January 1944, 3, The National Archives CAB 21/914.

67 For a description, see Claudia Springer, 'Military Propaganda: Defense Department Films from World War II and Vietnam', *Cultural Critique*, 3 (spring 1986), 164.

68 Nick Turse, *The Complex. How the Military Invades our Everyday Lives* (London: Faber and Faber, 2009), 106–7.

69 Video on the front page of the website of the Air Force Entertainment Liaison Office, at http://www.airforcehollywood.af.mil/shared/media/document/AFD-120613-066.wmv, viewed 7 December 2013. Also see 'Andrew', 'Transformers Movie Promotes the Military. Propaganda, Some Say', *Future Weapon Technology*, 20 April 2007, at www.futurefirepower.com/transforers-movie-promotes-the-military-propaganda-dome-say and D. Axe, 'Pentagon, Hollywood Pair Up for *Transformers* Sequel', *Wired* (28 December 2008).

70 At http://www.defense.gov/News/NewsArticle.aspx?ID=33023, viewed 11 November 2013.

71 Website of the US Air Force Entertainment Liaison Office, at http://www.airforcehollywood.af.mil/, viewed 3 December 2013.

72 Video on the front page of the website of the Air Force Entertainment Liaison Office, op. cit.

73 Ibid.

74 Jonathan Turley, Foreword, in David L. Robb, *Operation Hollywood. How the Pentagon Shapes and Censors the Movies* (New York: Prometheus Books, 2004), 18.

75 Stephen Stockwell and Adam Muir, 'The Military–Entertainment Complex: A New Facet of Information Warfare', *Fibreculture Journal* (5 November 2003), at http://one.fibreculturejournal.org/fcj-004-the-military-entertainment-complex-a-new-facet-of-information-warfare, viewed 26 September 2013.

76 Philip Coorey and Leo Schlink, 'Howard Joins Attack on Paris', *Free Republic* (15 March 2003), at www.freerepublic.com/focus/f-news/864694/posts, viewed 16 January 2014.

77 J. L. Yeck, 'An Interview with Lew Ayres', *Magills Cinema Annual 1986* (Pasadena: Salem, 1986), 13, cited in Andrew Kelly, *'All Quiet on the Western Front': The Story of a Film* (London: I. B. Tauris, 2002), 160.

78 C. Laemmle in *Exhibitors' World Herald* (13 December 1930), cited in Kelly, *'All Quiet on the Western Front'*, op. cit., 160.

79 Guy Westall, *War Cinema. Hollywood on the Front Line* (London: Wallflower, 2006), 24.

80 Philip Caputo, *A Rumor of War* (London: Henry Holt and Co., 1977), 14.

81 Anthony Swofford, *Jarhead: A Marine's Chronicle of the Gulf War* (London: Simon and Schuster, 2003), 6–7.

82 Quoted by Rev. Edward John Hardy, *The British Soldier. His Courage and Humour* (London: T. Fisher Unwin, 1915), 37.

83 Unnamed Canadian informant, in Barry Broadfoot, *Six War Years*

1939–1945. Memories of Canadians at Home and Abroad (Toronto: Doubleday, 1974), 89.

84 Frank Elkins's diary for 1 July 1966, in Indochina Curriculum Group, *Front Lines. Soldiers' Writings from Vietnam* (Cambridge, MA,: Indochina Curriculum Group, 1975), 101.

85 Jacques Leslie, *The Mark. A War Correspondent's War Memoirs of Vietnam and Cambodia* (New York: Four Walls Eight Windows, 1995), 77.

86 Ibid., 65.

87 Mark Baker, *Nam. The Vietnam War in the Words of Men and Women Who Fought There* (New York: Morrow, 1982), 58.

88 Philip Caputo, *A Rumor of War* (London: Pimlico, 1977), 290 and 305–6.

89 Matt J. Martin with Charles W. Sasser, *Predator. The Remote-Control Air War Over Iraq and Afghanistan* (Minneapolis: Zenith Press, 2010), 11.

90 Michael Herr, *Dispatches* (New York: Knopf, 1977), 169. Also see Hans Halberstadt, *Green Berets. Unconventional Warriors* (London: Arms and Armour, 1988), 133.

91 William Broyles, 'Why Men Love War', *Esquire* (November 1984), 56.

92 Patrick M. Regan, 'War Toys, War Movies, and the Militarization of the United States', *Journal of Peace Research*, 31.1 (February 1994), 54.

93 Josh Cruze, interviewed in Kim Willenson, *The Bad War. An Oral History of the Vietnam War* (New York: New American Library, 1987), 61. Also see Dale Barnes and 'Nelson' interviewed by Shirley Dicks, *From Vietnam to Hell. Interviews with Victims of Post-Traumatic Stress Disorder* (Jefferson, NC: McFarland, 1990), 5 and 19.

94 Ehrhart, 'Why I Did It', op. cit., 31.

CHAPTER SEVEN: VIOLENT GAMING

1 Dan Nosowitz, 'My Three Hours with the Most Violent Videogame I've Ever Seen', *Popular Science*, 5 October 2012, at http://www.popsci.com/technology/article/2012-04/sniper-elite-v2, viewed 2 October 2013.

2 Ibid.

3 For a fascinating account, see Kylie Kontour, 'War, Masculinity, and Gaming in the Military Entertainment Complex: A Case Study of *Call of Duty 4: Modern Warfare*', PhD Thesis, University of Colorado, 2011, 154–5.

4 Nosowitz, 'My Three Hours with the Most Violent Videogame I've Ever Seen', op. cit.

5 Quoting Chris Chambers, *America's Army*'s deputy director, in 2005 in

Seth Schiesel, 'On Maneuvers With the Army's Game Squad', at http://www.nytimes.com/2005/02/17/technology/circuits/17army.html?_r=0, uploaded 17 February 2005, viewed 20 September 2013.

6 *Battlefield Vietnam. Prima's Official Strategy Guide* (Roseville: Prima Games, 2004).

7 From Steven Williamson, 'Retrospective. Unforgettable Gaming Moments – #1: Killing Hitler', in http://www.psu.com/a010900/Retrospective – Unforgettable-Gaming-Moments – 1 – Killing-Hitler-?page=0, post on 7 March 2011, seen 20 September 2013.

8 Nosowitz, 'My Three Hours with the Most Violent Videogame I've Ever Seen', op. cit.

9 Ibid.

10 Schiesel, 'On Maneuvers With the Army's Game Squad', op. cit.

11 Margaret Davis, Russell Shilling, Alex Mayberry, Phillip Bossant, Jesse McCree, Scott Dossett, Christian Buhl, Christopher Chang, Evan Champlin, Travis Wiglesworth and Michael Zyda, 'Making *America's Army*. The Wizardry Behind the US Army's Hit PC Game', The MOVES Institute: Naval Postgraduate School, at http://gamepipe.usc.edu/~zyda/pubs/BrendaLaurelPaper2004.pdf, 6, viewed 27 August 2013.

12 Ibid.

13 Schiesel, 'On Maneuvers With the Army's Game Squad', op. cit.

14 Andrew Williams, 'The Reaffirmation of National Myths in World War II Digital Games', PhD thesis, University of Wisconsin-Madison, 2011, 67.

15 *Battlefield Vietnam. Prima's Official Strategy Guide*, op. cit., 2.

16 This story is told in Ed Halter, *From Sun Tzu to Xbox: War and Video Games* (New York: Thunder's Mouth Press, 2006), 131.

17 See http://www.dadgum.com/halcyon/BOOK/ROTBERG.HTM, viewed 17 July 2014.

18 Colonel Anthony Krogh was also the director of the National Simulation Center, cited in Lance M. Bacon, 'New Software Comes to Army Gaming Site', at http://www.armytimes.com/article/2010 1211/NEWS/12110310/New-software-comes-to-Army-gaming-site, uploaded 11 December 2010, viewed 20 September 2013.

19 T. Lenoir, 'All But War is Simulation: The Military–Entertainment Complex', *Configurations*, 8 (2000), 328.

20 'USC Institute for Creative Technologies Receives $135 Million Contract Extension from US Army', in http://ict.usc.edu/news/usc-institute-for-creative-technologies-receives-135-million-contract-

extension-from-u-s-army, posted 1 September 2011, viewed 20 September 2013.

21 Ibid.

22 Louis Caldera cited in ibid.

23 http://ict.usc.edu/?s=emotions&site_section=site-search, viewed 27 August 2013.

24 Michael R. Macedonia, 'Entertainment Technology and Virtual Environments for Military Training and Education', *Forum Futures* (2001), 35–8.

25 'Full Spectrum Video Games', in http://ict.usc.edu/prototypes/full-spectrum, dated 2003-2005, viewed on 20 September 2013.

26 Statement by Geoff Keighley, Associate Chairmen, Games Critics Awards Contributing Writer, in 'Full Spectrum Video Games', in http://ict.usc.edu/prototypes/full-spectrum, dated 2003–2005, viewed on 20 September 2013.

27 'ICT's New Army Training Aid Wins Best Original Game and Best Simulation Game @ E3', at http://ict.usc.edu/news/icts-new-army-training-aid-wins-best-original-game-and-best-simulation-game-e3, post on 9 June 2003, viewed 20 September 2013.

28 Sandra I. Erwin, 'Video Games Gaining Clout as Military Training Tools', at http://www.nationaldefensemagazine.org/archive/2000/November/Pages/Video_Games7199.aspx?PF=1, posted November 2000, viewed 20 September 2013.

29 Joshua Lewis, 'A Common Component-Based Software Architecture for Military and Commercial PC-Based Virtual Simulation', PhD thesis, University of Central Florida, 2006, 16.

30 'Military Fears Over PlayStation2', BBC (17 April 2000), at http://news.bbc.co.uk/2/hi/asia-pacific/716237.stm, viewed 27 August 2013.

31 Karin A. Orvis, Kara L. Orvis, James Belonich and Laura N. Mullin, *The Influence of Trainee Gaming Experience and Computer Self-Efficacy on Learner Outcomes of Video Game-Based Learning Environments*, US Army Research Institute for the Social and Behavioural Sciences, No. 1164 (Arlington: Army Research Institute, 2005), available at http://www.dtic.mil/cgi-bin/GetTRDoc?AD=ADA437016, viewed 27 August 2013.

32 Rob Riddell, 'Doom Goes to War', at http://www.wired.com/wired/archive/5.04/ff_doom_pr.html, uploaded 19 March 2004, viewed 30 July 2013.

33 Michael R. Macedonia, 'Games Soldiers Play', *IEEE Spectrum*, 39.3 (March 2002), 32-7 and eSim Games, 'Steel Beasts Professional – Review', 2004 and eSim Games Outlook to 2005, (press release), 6 January 2005.

34 Orvis, Orvis, Belonich and Mullin, *The Influence of Trainee Gaming Experience and Computer Self-Efficacy or Learner Outcomes of Videogame Based Learning Environments*, op. cit., 1 and 17.

35 http://www.sourcewatch.org/index.php/America%27s_Army, viewed 27 August 2013.

36 Robert J. Stadt, 'War Games: Citizenship and Play in Post-Industrial Militarism', PhD thesis, The Pennsylvania State University, 2004, 155.

37 Dan Tochen, 'America's Army Game Gets New Firepower', GameSpot, at http://www.gamespot.com//news/americas-army-game-gets-new-firepower-6137060, uploaded 3 November 205, viewed 27 August 2013.

38 Bill Shein, 'End 'America's Army' Funding', at http://www.reasongonemad.com/columns/2010/2/19/end-americas-army-funding.html, uploaded 19 February 2010, viewed 20 September 2013.

39 Davis, Shilling, Mayberry, et al., 'Making *America's Army*', op. cit.

40 Nina B. Huntemann, 'Interview with Colonel Casey Wardynski', in Huntemann and Matthew Thomas Payne (eds), *Joystick Soldiers. The Politics of Play in Military Video Games* (New York: Routledge, 2010), 179.

41 Ibid.

42 *America's Army* website, at http://www.americasarmy.com, viewed 20 September 2013.

43 Casey Wardynski, David S. Lyle, and Michael J. Colarusso, 'Accessing Talent: The Foundation of a U.S. Army Officer Corps Strategy', part of the 'Officer Corps Strategy Series (February 2010), at http://www.StrategyStudiesInstitute.army.mil/pdffiles/PUB972.pdf, viewed 20 September 2013.

44 Davis, Shilling, Mayberry, et al., 'Making *America's Army*', op. cit.

45 Ibid.

46 Michael Zyda, Alex Mayberry, Casey Wardynski, Russell Shilling and Margaret Davis, 'The MOVES Institute's *America's Army* Operations Game', in http://www.movesinstitute.org/~zyda/pubs/I3D-Demo-Paper-2003.pdf, viewed 27 August 2013.

47 Amanda Lenhart, Joseph Kahne, Ellen Middaugh, Alexandra Rankin McGill, Chris Evans and Jessica Vitak, 'Teens, Violent Games and Civics. Teens' Gaming Experiences are Diverse and Include Significant Social Interaction and Civic Engagement' (Washington, DC: Pew Internet and American Life Project, 2008), 9, at http://www.pewinternet.org/~/media//Files/Reports/2008/PIP_Teens_Games_and_Civics_Report_FINAL.pdf.pdf, viewed 27 August 2013.

48 Ibid.

49 Tom Curtis, 'Seven Years of *World of Warcraft*', in http://www.
gamasutra.com/view/news/128323/Seven_Years_Of_World_Of_
Warcraft.php, viewed 29 August 2013.

50 Lenhart, Kahne, Middaugh, McGill, Evans and Vitak, 'Teens, Violent
Games and Civics', op. cit., 1.

51 Marc Saltzman, 'Army Gives New Meaning to War Games – On a
PC', *USA Today* (22 May 2002).

52 Nick Dyer-Witheford and Greig de Peuter, *Games of Empire. Global
Capitalism and Video Games* (Minneapolis: University of Minnesota
Press, 2009), xiii.

53 Bill Shein, 'End "America's Army" Funding', (19 February 2010), at
http://counter-recruitment.blogspot.co.uk/2010/02/end-americas-
army-funding.html, viewed 27 August 2013.

54 American Civil Liberties Union, *Soldiers of Misfortune. Abusive US
Military Recruitment and Failure to Protect Child Soldiers* (New York:
ACLU, 2008), 167.

55 'Army Achieves FY 2003 Recruitment Goals', 6 October 2003, at
http://usmilitary.about.com/cs/armyjoin/a/recruitinggoal.htm,
viewed 27 August 2013.

56 Sgt 1st Class Bo Scott cited by Josh White, 'It's a Video Game, and an
Army Recruiter', *Washington Post* (27 May 2005).

57 Bacon, 'New Software Comes to Army Gaming Site', op. cit.

58 'USC Institute for Creative Technologies Receives $135 Million Contract
Extension from US Army', in http://ict.usc.edu/news/usc-institute-
for-creative-technologies-receives-135-million-contract-extension-from-
u-s-army, posted 1 September 2011, viewed 20 September 2013.

59 Citing General L. Jones (Marine Corps Commandant) in Sandra I.
Erwin, 'Video Games Gaining Clout as Military Training Tools', at
http://www.nationaldefensemagazine.org/archive/2000/November/
Pages/Video_Games7199.aspx?PF=1, posted November 2000,
viewed 20 September 2013.

60 Lieutenant Scott Barnett cited in Riddell, 'Doom Goes to War', op. cit.

61 Citing General L. Jones (Marine Corps Commandant) in Erwin,
'Video Games Gaining Clout as Military Training Tools', op. cit.

62 Citing Warren Katz, chief executive officer of Mäk Technologies Inc.,
in ibid.

63 J. F. Morie, 'Re-Entry: Online Virtual Worlds as a Healing Space for
Veterans' at http://ict.usc.edu/events/jacki-morie-re-entry-online-
virtual-worlds-as-a-healing-space-for-veterans/viewed 28 August
2013 and 'USC Institute for Creative Technologies Receives $135

Million Contract Extension from U.S. Army', op. cit.; http://ict.usc.edu/news/us-army-chief-of-staff-visits-ict/, posted 15 June 2013, viewed 20 September 2013; 'Army Hopeful About Virtual Reality for Treating Post Traumatic Stress', at http://ict.usc.edu/news/army-hopeful-about-virtual-reality-for-treating-post-traumatic-stress, posted 6 May 2010, viewed 20 September 2013.

64 Bob Brewin, 'Army Studying Use of Virtual Reality to Treat Post-Traumatic Stress', at http://www.nextgov.com/heath/2010/02/army-studying-use-of-virtual-reality-to-treat-post-traumatic-stress/46012, posted 22 February 2010, viewed 20 September 2013.

65 'Army Studies Virtual Iraq – ICT's Virtual Reality System for Treating PTSD' at http://ict.usc.edu/news/army-studies-virtual-iraq-icts-virtual-reality-system-for-treating-ptsd, posted 19 April 2010, viewed 20 September 2013.

66 Robertson Allen, 'The Army Rolls through Indianapolis: Fieldwork of the Virtual Army Experience', *Paxis*, 2 (2009), n.p.

67 Frequently asked questions, http://www.americasarmy.com/aa/support/faqs.php?t=9.

68 Quoting Chris Chambers, *America's Army*'s deputy director in 2005, in Schiesel, 'On Maneuvers With the Army's Game Squad', op. cit.

69 'US Army Chief of Staff Visits ICT', at http://ict.usc.edu/news/us-army-chief-of-staff-visits-ict/, posted 15 June 2012, viewed 20 September 2013.

70 Lenhart, Kahne, Middaugh, McGill, Evans and Vitak, 'Teens, Violent Games and Civics', op. cit., 18.

71 Anthony King, *The Combat Soldier. Infantry Tactics and Cohesion in the Twentieth and Twenty-First Centuries* (Oxford: Oxford University Press, 2014).

72 Specialist Alfred Trevino interviewed in Jose Antonio Vargas, 'Virtual Reality Prepares Soldiers for Real War; Young Warriors Say Video Shooter Games Help Hone Their Skills', *Washington Post* (14 February 2006).

73 Ibid.

74 Lieutenant-Colonel Scott Sutton interviewed in ibid.

75 Matt J. Martin with Charles W. Sasser, *Predator. The Remote-Control Air War Over Iraq and Afghanistan* (Minneapolis: Zenith Press, 2010), 30.

76 J. Der Derian, *Virtuous War: Mapping the Military–Industrial–Media–Entertainment–Network* (Boulder: Westview Press, 2001).

77 Retired Marine Colonel Gary W. Anderson interviewed in Vargas, 'Virtual Reality Prepares Soldiers for Real War', op. cit.

78 Martin with Sasser, *Predator*, 46–7.

79 Ibid.
80 Ibid., 219 and 3.
81 Sergeant Sinque Swales interviewed in Vargas, 'Virtual Reality Prepares Soldiers for Real War', op. cit.
82 David Bartlett interviewed in ibid.

CHAPTER EIGHT: PROTEST

1 For example, see Theodor Meron, 'The Humanization of Humanitarian Law', *American Journal of International Law*, 94.2 (April 2000), 240.
2 Costas Douzinas, 'What is Resistance?', unpublished paper (2013).
3 Gene Sharp, *The Politics of Nonviolent Action*, 3 vols. (Boston: Porter Sargent, 1973).
4 Andrew Loewen, 'Slavoj Zizek at Occupy Wall Street' (9 October 2011), second clip, at http://www.thepaltrysapien.com/2011/10/slavoj-zizek-at-occupy-wall-street/, viewed 16 February 2014.
5 For a trenchant critique of first-person shooters, see Lieutenant-Colonel Dave Grossman, *On Killing: The Psychological Costs of Learning to Kill in War and Society* (New York: Back Bay, 1996).
6 Friedrich Ernst, *Krieg dem Krieg* (Berlin: Internationales Kriegsmuseum, 1930), 233. For a discussion, see Dora Apel, '"Heroes" and "Whores": The Politics of Gender in Weimar Antiwar Imagery', *Art Bulletin*, 79.3 (September 1997), 376.
7 Charles Stewart Alexander, letter to his cousin from France, 3 November 1917, Auckland Institute and Museum Library MSS 92/70.
8 Cecil H. Cox, 'A Few Experiences of the First World War', 2, IWM 88/11/1.
9 '"The War is Not a Game": Gold Star Families Speak Out Expresses [*sic*] Outrage at Video Game Based on Deadly Battle in Iraq', 8 April 2009, at https://www.commondreams.org/newswire/2009/04/08-16, viewed 18 November 2013.
10 Mathias Jansson, 'Interview: Joseph Delappe, Pioneer of Online Game Performance Art', www.gamescenes.org/2010/05/interview-with-joseph-delappe-a-pioneer-of-on-line-performancewhen-did-you-start-to-use-on-line-gaming-for-your-performances.html, posted 2010, viewed 30 July 2013. See http://www.unr.edu/art/delappe/gaming/MOH%20online/MOH%20screen%20shots%20JPEGS.html, viewed 30 July 2013.
11 Joseph Delappe, 'dead-in-iraq: Performance/Memorial/Protest', *TDR: The Drama Review*, 522.1 (spring 2008), 2.

12 'Interview: Joseph DeLappe, Pioneer of Online Game Performance Art', *Gamescene. Ary in the Age of Videogames*, at www.gamescenes.org/ 2010/05/interview-with-joseph-delappe-a-pioneer-of-on-line-performancewhen-did-you-start-to-use-on-line-gaming-for-your-performances.html (May 2010), viewed 30 July 2013.

13 Delappe, 'dead-in-iraq', op. cit., 2.

14 'iraqimemorial.org. Commemorating Civilian Deaths', at http:// www.iraqimemorial.org/, viewed 30 July 2013.

15 Hannah Draysen, 'Players Unleashed! Modding *The Sims* and the Culture of Gaming by Tanja Sihvonen', *Leonardo*, 45.5 (2012), 491.

16 Zvi Rosen, 'Mod, Man, and Law: A Reexamination of the Law of Computer Game Modifications', *Journal of Intellectual Property*, 4 (2004–5), 197.

17 Anne-Marie Schleiner's web profile, http://profile.nus.edu.sg/ fass/cnmams/, viewed 30 July 2013.

18 'Velvet-Strike: Counter-Military Graffiti for CS', posted 3 February 2002, at www.opensorcery.net/velvet-strike/about.html, viewed 1 September 2013.

19 Wellcome Library, London.

20 Trevor Griffiths, *The Gulf Between Us or The Truth and Other Fictions* (London: Faber and Faber, 1992), 49.

21 Interview of Trevor Griffiths in ibid., vii.

22 To view the entire clip, see http://www.thedailyshow.com/watch/ thu-december-19-2002/war-widow-barbie, viewed 30 July 2013.

23 Code Pink, 'We Call to You', at www.codepink4peace.org/ article.php?list=type&type=3, viewed 19 November 2013.

24 See 'Raging Grannies International', at http://raginggrannies.org/, viewed 19 November 2013. These organisations are discussed in Rachel V. Kutz-Flamenbaum, 'Code Pink, Raging Grannies, and the Missile Dick Chicks: Feminist Performance Activism in the Contemporary Anti-War Movement', *NWSA Journal*, 19.1 (spring 2007), 89.

25 Missile Dick Chicks, 'Welcome' (2005) in www.missiledickchicks.net, viewed 14 February 2014.

26 Oliver Stone, cited in David L. Robb, *Operation Hollywood. How the Pentagon Shapes and Censors the Movies* (New York: Prometheus Books, 2004), 25.

27 Adrienne Rich, 'Legislators of the World', *Guardian* (18 November 2006).

28 Antiwar.com's website, at http://antiwar.com/who.php, viewed 1 February 2014.

29 European Commission of Human Rights, 'Pat Arrowsmith against the
    United Kingdom: report of the Commission on 12 October 1978'
    (Strasbourg: European Commission of Human Rights, 1978).

30 Dr A. Maude Royden, 'Reminder to Youth', *New World* (November
    1931), 7.

31 Pat Arrowsmith (ed.), *To Asia in Peace: Story of a Non-Violent Action
    Mission to Indo-China* (London: Sidgwick and Jackson, 1972), 4. There
    were similar plans drawn up by the Gulf Peace Team.

32 Tod Ensign, 'The New Face of the Antiwar Movement', *New Labor
    Forum*, 15.2 (summer 2006), 96.

33 Website of Vietnam Veterans Against the War, at http://www.
    vvawai.org/archive/sw/sw31/pgs_35-44/operation_raw.html,
    viewed 3 February 2014.

34 Paige Sarlin, 'New Left-Wing Melancholy: Mark Tribe's "The Post
    Heron Project" and the Politics of Reenactment', *Framework: The Journal
    of Cinema and Media*, 1 and 2 (spring and fall 2009), 151–2. The videos
    can be found at http://ivaw.org and http://thisiswherewetakeourstand.
    com/. Also see Aaron Glantz, *Winter Soldier: Iraq and Afghanistan:
    Eyewitness Accounts of the Occupation* (Chicago: Haymarket Books, 2008).

35 Lisa Leitz, 'Oppositional Identities: The Military Peace Movement's
    Challenge to Pro-Iraq War Frames', *Social Problems*, 58.2 (May 2011),
    235.

36 David Goodman, 'Breaking Ranks: An Interview with Mike Hoffman',
    Mother Jones (11 October 2004), at http://www.motherjones.com/
    politics/2004/10/breaking-ranks-interview-mike-hoffman, viewed 3
    February 2014.

37 Leitz, 'Oppositional Identities', op. cit., 251.

38 Garett Reppenhagen, cited in Matthew Gutmann and Catherine Lutz,
    'Becoming Monsters in Iraq', *Anthropology Now*, 1.1 (April 2009), 15.

39 John Desmond Bernal, *The Social Function of Science* (London: G.
    Routledge and Sons, 1939).

40 John Desmond Bernal, *World Without War* (London: Routledge and K.
    Paul, 1958).

41 'A Society for Social Responsibility in Science', *Science*, 110 (1949),
    460.

42 Quoting from a letter by Albert Einstein, in William F. Hewitt, 'Social
    Responsibility in Science', *Science*, 112 (1950), 760–1.

43 Henry A. Giroux, 'The Militarization of US Higher Education After
    9/11', in Kostas Gouliamos and Christos Kassimeri (eds), *The
    Marketing of War in the Age of Neo-Militarism* (London: Routledge, 2012),
    252.

44 Ellen Lamar Thomas, 'Shall We Go On Making Little Soldiers?', *The Clearing House. A Journal for Modern Junior and Senior High Schools*, 11.7 (March 1937), 390.

45 Sharon Anne Cook, 'Give Peace a Chance: The Diminution of Peace in Global Education in the United States, United Kingdom, and Canada', *Canadian Journal of Education*, 31.4 (2008), 889–93.

46 John Lennon, 'Imagine' (1971). © Lenono Music.

47 Costas Douzinas, *Philosophy and Resistance in the Crisis: Greece and the Future of Europe* (Cambridge: Polity, 2013), 9.

48 Sasha Roseneil, 'The Global Common: The Global, Local, and Personal Dynamics of the Women's Peace Movement in the 1980s', in Alan Scott (ed.), *The Limits of Globalization. Cases and Arguments* (London: Routledge, 1997), 67.

49 Margaret L. Laware, 'Circling the Missiles and Staining Them Red: Feminist Rhetorical Invention and Strategies of Resistance at the Women's Peace Camp at Greenham Common', *NWSA Journal*, 16.3 (autumn 2004), 19.

50 Hugh Gusterson, *Nuclear Rites: A Weapon's Laboratory at the End of the Cold War* (Berkeley: University of California Press, 1998), 198.

51 Unnamed demonstrator, cited in Susan Leigh Foster, 'Choreographies of Protest', *Theatre Journal*, 55.3 (October 2003), 410.

52 Ibid.

53 Ibid.

54 Maurice Merleau-Ponty, cited in R. W. G. Gibbs, *Embodiment and Cognitive Science* (New York: Cambridge University Press, 2006), 14

55 Joanna Bourke, *Fear: A Cultural History* (London: Virago; New York: Shoemaker and Hoard, 2005).

56 Slavoj Zizek, *Welcome to the Desert of the Real! Five Essays on September 11 and Related Dates* (London: Verso, 2002), 49.

BIBLIOGRAPHY

LIBRARIES AND ARCHIVES CONSULTED

American Philosophical Society (Philadelphia)
Australian War Memorial Archives (Canberra)
Countway Medical Library (Boston)
Imperial War Museum (London)
Library of Congress (Washington, DC)
The National Archives (London)
National Archives at College Park, Maryland
National Army Museum (London)
Zuckerman Archive, University of East Anglia

SELECTED RECOMMENDED READING

American Civil Liberties Union, *Soldiers of Misfortune. Abusive US Military Recruitment and Failure to Protect Child Soldiers* (New York: ACLU, 2008)

Arendt, Hannah, *The Origins of Totalitarianism*, 1st pub. 1951, new edition (New York: Harcourt Brace Jovanovich, 1973)

Bourke, Joanna, *Fear: A Cultural History*, (London: Virago and New York: Shoemaker & Hoard, 2005)

——, *An Intimate History of Killing: Face-to-Face Killing in Twentieth Century Warfare* (London: Granta and New York: Basic, 1999)

——, *Dismembering the Male: Men's Bodies, Britain and the Great War* (London: Reaktion Press and Chicago: University of Chicago Press, 1996)

——, *What It Means to Be Human: Reflections from 1791 to the Present* (London: Virago and New York: Shoemaker & Hoard, 2011)

——, *The Story of Pain: From Prayer to Painkillers* (Oxford and New York: Oxford University Press, 2014)

Brittain, Vera, *Testament of Youth*, 1st pub. 1933 (New York: Penguin, 1989)

——, *Thrice a Stranger* (London: Gollancz, 1938)

Brown, R. Blake, "'Every Boy Ought to Learn to Shoot and to Obey

Orders": Guns, Boys, and the Law in English Canada from the Late
  Nineteenth Century to the Great War', *Canadian Historical Review*,
  93.2 (June 2012)

Casper, Monica J. and Lisa Jean Moore, 'Dirty Work and Deadly Agents:
  A (Dis)Embodied Weapons Treaty and the Illusion of Safety', *Women's
  Studies Quarterly*, 39.1/2 (spring/summer 2011)

Closman, Charles E. (ed.), *War and the Environment. Military Destruction in
  the Modern Age* (College Station: Texas A&M University Press, 2009)

Cohen, Cariol, 'Sex and Death in the Rational World of Defense
  Intellectuals', *Signs*, 12.4 (summer 1987)

Conetta, Carl, 'Disappearing the Dead: Iraq, Afghanistan, and the Idea of
  a 'New Warfare', PDA, Project on Defense Alternatives, Research
  Monograph #9 (Cambridge, MA: PDA, Commonwealth Institute,
  2004), at http://www.comw.org/pda/0402rm9.html

Der Derian, J., *Virtuous War: Mapping the Military–Industrial–Media–
  Entertainment–Network* (Boulder: Westview Press, 2001)

Douzinas, Costas, *Human Rights and Empire. The Political Philosophy of
  Cosmopolitanism* (London: Routledge-Cavendish, 2007)

——, *Philosophy and Resistance in the Crisis: Greece and the Future of Europe*
  (Cambridge: Polity, 2013)

Downes, Alexander B., *Targeting Civilians in War* (Ithaca: Cornell
  University Press, 2008)

Dyer-Witheford, Nick and Greig de Peuter, *Games of Empire. Global
  Capitalism and Video Games* (Minneapolis: University of Minnesota
  Press, 2009)

Foster, Susan Leigh, 'Choreographies of Protest', *Theatre Journal*, 55.3
  (October 2003)

Fry, James D., 'Contextualized Legal Reviews for the Methods and Means
  of Warfare: Cave Combat and International Humanitarian Law',
  Columbia Journal of Transnational Law, 44 (2006)

Gillespie, Alexander, *A History of the Laws of War* (Oxford: Hart, 2011)

Giroux, Henry, *The University in Chains: Confronting the Military–Industrial–
  Academic Complex* (Boulder, CO: Paradigm Publishers, 2007)

Gouliamos, Kostas and Christos Kassimeri (eds), *The Marketing of War in
  the Age of Neo-Militarism* (London: Routledge, 2012)

Gregory, Derek, 'In Another Time-Zone, the Bombs Fall Unsafely . . . :
  Targets, Civilians, and Late Modern War', *Arab World Geographer*, 9.2
  (2006)

Grossman, Dave, *On Killing: The Psychological Costs of Learning to Kill in War
  and Society* (New York: Back Bay, 1996)

Gusterson, Hugh, *Nuclear Rites: A Weapon's Laboratory at the End of the Cold
  War* (Berkeley: University of California Press, 1998)

Gutmann, Matthew and Catherine Lutz, 'Becoming Monsters in Iraq', *Anthropology Now*, 1.1 (April 2009)

Halter, Ed, *From Sun Tzu to Xbox: War and Video Games* (New York: Thunder's Mouth Press, 2006)

Hardt, Michael and Antonio Negri, *Multitude: War and Democracy in the Age of Empire* (London: Hamish Hamilton, 2004)

Hathaway, Oona A., 'Do Human Rights Treaties Make a Difference?', *Yale Law Journal*, 111.8 (June 2002)

Human Rights Watch, *Off Target. The Conduct of the War and Civilian Casualties in Iraq* (New York: Human Rights Watch, 2003)

Huntemann, Nina B. and Matthew Thomas Payne (eds), *Joystick Soldiers. The Politics of Play in Military Video Games* (New York: Routledge, 2010)

Jochnick, Chris af and Roger Normand, 'The Legitimation of Violence: A Critical History of the Laws of War', *Harvard International Law Journal*, 35.1 (winter 1994)

Kanwar, Vik, 'Post-Human Humanitarian Law: The Law of War in the Age of Robotic Weapons', *Harvard National Security Journal* (2011)

Keaton, Angela F., 'Backyard Desperadoes: American Attitudes Concerning Toy Guns in the Early Cold War Era', *Journal of American Culture*, 33.3 (2010)

Laware, Margaret L., 'Circling the Missiles and Staining Them Red: Feminist Rhetorical Invention and Strategies of Resistance at the Women's Peace Camp at Greenham Common', *NWSA Journal*, 16.3 (autumn 2004)

Leitz, Lisa, 'Oppositional Identities: The Military Peace Movement's Challenge to Pro-Iraq War Frames', *Social Problems*, 58.2 (May 2011)

Lenoir, T., 'All But War is Simulation: The Military-Entertainment Complex', *Configurations*, 8 (2000)

Macedonia, Michael R., 'Entertainment Technology and Virtual Environments for Military Training and Education', *Forum Futures* (2001)

Meron, Theodor, 'The Humanization of Humanitarian Law', *American Journal of International Law*, 94.2 (April 2000)

Normand, Roger and Chris af Jochnick, 'The Legitimation of Violence: A Critical Analysis of the Gulf War', *Harvard International Law Journal*, 35.2 (spring 1994)

Ouagrham-Gormley, Sonia Ben, 'Barriers to Bioweapons: Intangible Obstacles to Proliferation', *International Security*, 36.4 (spring 2012)

Owens, Larry, 'The Cat and the Bullet: A Ballistic Fable', *Massachusetts Review*, 45.1 (spring 2004)

Rappert, Brian, 'Prohibitions, Weapons and Controversy: Managing the Problem of Ordering', *Social Studies of Science*, 35.2 (April 2005)

Robb, David L., *Operation Hollywood. How the Pentagon Shapes and Censors the Movies* (New York: Prometheus Books, 2004)

Roseneil, Sasha, 'The Global Common: The Global, Local, and Personal Dynamics of the Women's Peace Movement in the 1980s', in Alan Scott (ed.), *The Limits of Globalization. Cases and Arguments* (London: Routledge, 1997)

Schlosser, Eric, *Command and Control. Nuclear Weapons, the Damascus Accident, and the Illusion of Safety* (New York: Penguin, 2013)

Schmitt, Michael N., '*Bellum Americanum*: The US View of Twenty-First-Century War and its Possible Implications for the Law of Armed Conflict', *Michigan Journal of International Law*, 19 (summer 1998)

Schmitt, Michael N. and Jeffrey S. Thurnher, '"Out of the Loop": Autonomous Weapon Systems and the Law of Armed Conflict', *Harvard National Security Journal*, 4 (2012–13)

Schubart, Rikke, Fabian Virchow, Debra White-Stanley, and Tanja Thomas (eds), *War Isn't Hell, It's Entertainment. Essays on Visual Media and the Representation of Conflict* (Jefferson, North Carolina: McFarland and Co.: 2009)

Sharp, Gene, *The Politics of Nonviolent Action*, 3 vols (Boston: Porter Sargent, 1973).

Singer, P. W., *Wired for War: The Robotics Revolution and Conflict in the Twenty-First Century* (New York: Penguin, 2009)

Smith, Thomas W., 'The New Law of War: Legitimizing Hi-Tech and Infrastructural Violence', *International Studies Quarterly*, 46.3 (September 2002)

Stahl, Roger, 'Have You Played the War on Terror?', *Critical Studies in Media Communication*, 23.2 (2006)

Turse, Nick, *The Complex. How the Military Invades our Everyday Lives* (London: Faber and Faber, 2009)

Valentino, Benjamin, Paul Huth, and Sarah Croco, 'Covenants Without the Sword. International Law and the Protection of Civilians in Times of War', *World Politics*, 58 (April 2006)

Von Clausewitz, Carl, *On War*, 1st pub. 1873, ed. and trans. Michael Howard and Peter Parel, preface by Joanna Bourke (London: Folio Society, 2011)

Walzer, Michael, *Just and Unjust Wars: A Moral Argument with Historical Illustrations* (Harmondsworth: Penguin, 1980)

Wright, Steve, 'New Police Technologies: An Exploration of the Social Implications of Some Recent Developments', *Journal of Peace Research*, 15.4 (1978)

Zizek, Slavoj, *Welcome to the Desert of the Real! Five Essays on September 11 and Related Dates* (London: Verso, 2002)

Acknowledgements

As always, this book is dedicated to the person who inspires me in all spheres of life, Costas Douzinas. He brings hope to my world.

I am grateful to all those people whose friendship and practical help have enabled me to write this book. The enthusiasm and erudition of my students and colleagues at Birkbeck (University of London) is inspiring; administrators in the Department, School and College have created an environment that is conducive to teaching, thinking and writing; Zoe Dinga is a miracle-worker. My agent Andrew Wylie and James Pullen always give me good advice. At Virago, thanks must go to Zoe Gullen, Zoe Hood and Linda Silverman. My gratitude to my editor Lennie Goodings is enormous: she is an astute critic and adviser.

My family and friends take turns criticizing and then reassuring me. I am particularly grateful to my brothers and sisters, their spouses and my nieces, nephews and great-niece. Micah Fleming taught me some war-gaming tricks while Jonas Fleming stood by asking difficult questions. Special thanks must go to my two colleagues in the Birkbeck Pain Project – Dr Louise Hide and Dr Carmen Mangion – without whom this work would have taken much longer and been less fun. Thanks also to Julie Anderson, Efi Avdela, Alexandra Bakalaki, Rika Benveniste, Sean Brady, Rosi Braidotti, Ana Carden-Coyne, Phaedra Douzina-Balalaki, Nikos Douzinas, Julia Eisner, Marianne Elliott, Richard Evans, Vanessa Harding, Kostas Hatzykyriakos, Yanna Kandilorou, Maria Komninos, Christos Lyrintzis, Fiona Macmillan, Akis Papataxiarchis, Annick Paternot, Dorothy Porter and Samis Taboh.

Index

Engelbach, Frederick George 21–2
entertainment, war-orientated: adult
    'collecting' of toys and action figures
    163–5; Bombshell (Waddington's game)
    168–9, 172; conversion of replica guns
    174; effects on children of 170–3;
    enticing nature of 5, 160–6; feminist
    voices 172; First World War and 170;
    games used in military training 173,
    201–2, 203–5, 210; gender and 161;
    G.I. Joe toy 163; historical connections
    with lethal-shooting 175–6; history of
    toy soldiers 161–6; injuries caused by
    173–4; links between arms
    manufacturers and toy companies 169;
    marketing of at male sex 161; Mighty
    Morphin Power Rangers 163; military
    recruitment and 178–80; military
    toys as lucrative business 166–7;
    military–industrial–entertainment
    complex 11–12, 180–4, 190, 216–17,
    226–7, 232; miniature model kits 160;
    opposition to 171–5; paintballing 4,
    173; pervasiveness of 3, 6, 160; poison
    gas incorporated into games 170;
    psychologists' use of 169–70; Second
    World War and 170–1; social-scientific
    research on 172–3; *Star Wars* figures
    163, 166; toys and games based on
    nuclear war 167–8, 168*fig*; war-themed
    toys 4, 160, 161–5, 166–70, 172,
    173–5, 189; *see also* cinema and film;
    computer games
environmental damage 60–1, 238
e-petitions 246
Ernst, Friedrich, *Krieg dem Krieg* (*War
    against War*, 1924) 226*fig*

'failed states' 59–60
Fairbanks, Jr, Douglas 161
Faslane peace camp 246
Federal Theatre Project (1930s) 234
Fellowship of Reconciliation 238
feminism 4, 172, 225, 232, 235–6, 238,
    245
Fenrick, William J., 'International
    Humanitarian Law and Combat
    Casualties' (2006) 99
Finnish Combat School 205
First World War: Vera Brittain's
    experience of 39–41, 61–2; centenary
    commemorations 4, 104–5, 227, 228;

children's play and 170; combatants'
    elated descriptions of killing 18;
    combatants who refused to kill 228–9;
    confusion of fiction for reality 189–90;
    film and fictive imagery used by
    combatants 187–8; 'lawful' killing and
    99; poetry and 19, 105, 230, 233;
    recruitment posters 5, 178–9;
    scientists and 131–2; US heroes of
    160; use of poison gas in 170, 233; use
    of sporting analogies 19–20, 23
fitness boot camps 12
Ford, John C., 'The Morality of
    Obliteration Bombing' (1944) 119
Fort Benning 181, 195, 203
Fort Detrick 146
Foster, Susan Leigh 248
freedom and liberty, concepts of 130, 181,
    199–200, 231, 238, 249
French, Ralph W. 138, 149
Freud, Anna 169
Freyer, Margaret 115
Fulbright, J. William 10
Full Spectrum Warrior (computer game,
    2004) 126, 203–4, 211
Fuller, J. F. C., *The Reformation of War*
    (1923) 113
Fulton, John 132, 139
fusion bombs 30

games and toys, war-themed *see* computer
    games; entertainment, war-orientated
GameSpot Review 191
Gandhi, Mahatma 239
Gartner, Rosemary 43
Gatling, Richard J. 31, 155
gender: attitudes to war 4–5, 232, 234*fig*,
    235–6, 245; computer games and 5,
    211, 212, 214–15, 225, 232;
    domestic violence on military bases
    238; feminism 4, 172, 225, 232,
    235–6, 238, 245; gun collectors and
    165–6; training of children in use of
    firearms 176–7; war play and 161,
    170, 172, 173, 175–7, 189; women as
    absent in virtual gaming environments
    211, 212
Geneva Protocol 51
G.I. Joe toy 163
Giroux, Henry 244
global positioning systems 12, 124–5
global warming 238

shrapnel 23, 38, 138
Simon, Sir John 110–11
Singer, P. W., *Wired for War: The Robotics
Revolution and Conflict in the Twenty-First
Century* (2009) 152
Six Days in Fallujah (computer game)
229–30
Smith, Thomas W., 'The New Law of
War' (2002) 90
Sniper Elite V2 (computer game) 191–3,
195, 196
Society for Social Responsibility in Science
243
Soldier Systems Center, Natick,
Massachusetts 130, 154
Solomon, George F. 43
Sony PlayStation 2 console 204, 205
Southampton University 11
Spain 246; Civil War (1936–9) 233–4
Spearhead II (computer game, 2003) 204
'Special K' missiles 38
Spielberg, Steven 197, 199
Stanford Workshops on Political and Social
Issues 147–8
Star Wars figures 163
Steel Beasts II (computer game) 205
Steenkamp, Reeva 145
steroids 153
Stevens, Cat, 'Peace Train' 237
Stevenson, Robert Louis 161
Stewart, Jon, *The Daily Show* 235
Stewortby, near Bedford 133–4
Stimson, Henry 36
Stockwell, Stephen 184
Stone, Oliver 236
Stop the War Coalition 229–30
Strategic Air Command, US 34
Strub, Philip 183
stun guns 56
Suttner, Bertha von 154, 155
Sutton, Scott 216
SUVs 12
Swales, Sinque 216, 219
Swedish Combat School 205
Swofford, Anthony, *Jarhead: A Marine's
Chronicle of the Gulf War and Other Battles*
(2003) 186–7
syndicalist movements 238
Syria 44

Taliban 5
taxation 5, 7, 8–9, 11, 249

Temple, William 105–6
terrorist organisations: drone technology
and 45; 'post-human warfighter' and
152, 153
'The Text-Book for Military Small Arms
and Ammunition' (1899) 73
Thatcher, Margaret 237
Thirteen Days (film, 2000) 183
Thomas, Ellen Lamar 244
Thomas, Richard 185
Thomson, Lord 24–5, 110
THQ (game publisher) 203
Thuraya Telecommunications Company
124
Thurlow, Geoffrey 40
The Times 170–1
Top Gun (film, 1986) 182, 183
toys and games, war-themed *see* computer
games; entertainment, war-orientated
tranquillisers 56
Transformers (film series) 9, 182
Trenchard, Lord 111
Trevino, Alfred 215–16
Tunisia 246
Twitter 247

United Nations 72; Optional Protocol on
the Involvement of Children in Armed
Conflicts 9
United States: 1970s and 1980s crime
anxieties 57–8; 9/11 terrorist attacks
231, 233, 249–50; annual firearm
fatalities 6, 174–5; atomic and nuclear
testing 61; domestic use of drone
technology 47–8; international law and
88, 89–93, 96–9; military expenditure
8; military–industrial–entertainment
complex in 11–12, 180–4, 190,
216–17, 226–7, 232; as a nation of
guns 6, 13, 174–5, 176; nuclear
weapon accidents 46; popularity of
computer games in 208–9; use of
extra-judiciary assassinations 45; war
toy sales in 167
United States military 3, 5; civilian victims
of in Iraq 102, 103–4, 123, 124, 125;
civilian victims of in Vietnam 89,
93–6, 102–3, 107–8, 114, 239;
civilian victims of in WW2 34, 65–6,
70, 75, 78, 98, 114, 118, 121–3,
128–9, 183; cooperation with
computer game industry 196–9,